In *Yet Will I Praise Him*, Terry and Shirley Law present the vivid, intertwining stories of both their lives:

> *Terry's rebellious youth; his fear that God had no real purpose for his life; the self-doubt that assailed him even when he led successful Christian musical groups into Africa and behind the Iron Curtain; the dangers he encountered ministering in the Soviet Union.*

> *And Shirley's chronicle of the abuse and emotional neglect she suffered as a young girl; the faith that strengthened her through turmoil and heartaches in her first marriage.*

> *Then the heartbreak of the tragic deaths of both their spouses; and God's divine appointment for bringing Shirley and Terry together.*

Through their unforgettable story, you will learn spiritual lessons on faith, prayer, and believing God. Those who are doubtful of God's love and sovereignty in times of trial or tragedy will find their faith revived. *Yet Will I Praise Him* gives you profound insights into the sufficiency of God's grace.

Yet Will I PRAISE HIM

Terry & Shirley Law
with David Hazard

Chosen Books

A Division of Baker Book House
Grand Rapids, Michigan 49506

Library of Congress Cataloging-in-Publication Data

Law, Terry.
    Yet will I praise him.

    "A Chosen Book"
    1. Law, Terry. 2. Law, Shirley. 3. Evangelists—
United States—Biography. I. Law, Shirley. II. Title.
BV3780.L33 1987   269′.2′0922 [B]   87-9836
ISBN 0-8007-9106-1

A Chosen Book
Copyright © 1987 by Terry Law
Chosen Books are published by Fleming H. Revell
a division of Baker Book House Company
P.O. Box 6287, Grand Rapids, Michigan 49516-6287

ISBN: 0-8007-9106-1

Sixth printing, October 1992

Printed in the United States of America

To Shirley,

I have found a virtuous woman and her price is far above rubies. Strength and honor are her clothing and she shall rejoice in the time to come. She opens her mouth with wisdom and in her tongue is the law of kindness. Her children arise up and call her blessed. Her husband also praises her.

Terry

To Terry,

I dedicate all the love and truths that my Lord Jesus Christ taught me in past difficulties to my husband and his ministry . . . to be a help, to support, to honor as husband and minister, and to cherish.

Shirley

Contents

PROLOGUE
The Journey Begins   9

TERRY
1 Night Vision   15
2 Collision Course   24

SHIRLEY
3 "Dad's Not Well"   38
4 Behind the Mask   46

TERRY
5 Mountains of Difficulty   58
6 Surprise Visit   70

SHIRLEY
7 Meeting of the Hearts   84
8 Obstacles   97

TERRY
9 Living Sound   108
10 Disaster   118

SHIRLEY
11 The Walls Come Down   133
12 This Thing Called Faith   147

TERRY
13 A Party in Poland   163

14   Higher Mountains   179

SHIRLEY

15   The Enemy   195
16   Crossing Over   210

TERRY

17   Where Angels Tread   228
18   A Deeper Love   244

EPILOGUE

A New Path   261

Prologue:
The Journey Begins

TERRY:

I couldn't believe I'd blown it again.

Looking out through the church's rain-streaked window, I watched dismally as a group of young guys muscled each other good-naturedly around the parking lot. They were long-haired, like most young people in 1969. Through the half-opened door of the prayer room, where I'd come to be alone, a loud murmur rose from the sanctuary.

On this drizzly June evening in Portland, Oregon, most of the church had turned out to hear our group, Living Sound. The sixteen-member contemporary gospel music team was my idea. Now Jan, my bride of only six months, and I were leading the team across the U.S. and Canada, performing the new "Jesus" music and raising money for a missionary trip to Africa. Everywhere we went, crowds of young and not-so-young came to hear us—from small children to grandmas and grandpas.

The guys in the parking lot quit horsing around and

walked toward the church. For me, the thought of all those smiling Christians filling the pews out in the sanctuary gave me a sinking feeling. I glanced at my watch. In twenty minutes I would pick up my bass guitar and lead the group out before this crowd to sing. During the concert I'd give a message about the love of Jesus.

And I had just made a cutting, uncalled-for remark to Jan over something petty. Shock and hurt had mingled in her pretty, dark eyes.

Right now, I thought miserably, *she's probably in the ladies' room retouching her mascara.* I knew she was too loyal to mention the tiff to any of the other girls in the group—but that did nothing to make me feel better.

Still staring out the window, I came up with a million excuses. We'd been traveling for weeks, pinching pennies to save for the Africa trip. I was responsible for this group of college students on leave from Oral Roberts University, most of whom were in their late teens or, like Jan and me, their twenties. It meant tight schedules, meals on-the-road, heavy equipment, a different bed each night. Though this appealed to some sort of wanderlust in me it was wearying for Jan.

Try as I might to justify myself, the hard truth was that Jan had made an innocent comment, and I had hurt her. Even coming to this prayer room and confessing my wrongdoing didn't help; I felt terrible. Maybe I'd never be good enough to deserve Jan's love . . . to deserve God's love. And now it was almost time to pick up my guitar, slap on a smile, and lead the group out onto the platform to sing and tell others about what it meant to follow Jesus.

At that moment Larry Dalton, the musical director of Living Sound, peered into the room. "Terry, we're on in a half hour," he said calmly. "We should have the group together for prayer."

Seeing him only increased my self-doubting. Though I was the team's spiritual leader I didn't feel like one just then. Now Larry, on the other hand, always seemed so easygoing. He was taller than I, with long hair and a broad, ready smile. Compared to him, I looked and acted like a tensely coiled spring. I was shorter, my hair a wiry copper-blond that I had to keep close-cropped or risk having it go wild. And I had a fireplug build made tough by years of farm work when I was younger.

Maybe someone less intense should lead this group, I thought—then caught myself. Why did I have such negative, condemning thoughts?

I nodded. "Call 'em in."

When he disappeared the inner voice continued with a cutting edge. *You're going to pray now? After what you did to Jan? Who do you think you're fooling? You're still the same old Terry Law—no better than when you were a wild kid.*

In a moment Jan walked in. She took my hand. I leaned my head against hers and whispered, "I'm sorry."

"That's okay, hon," she said, giving my hand a squeeze.

That was Jan's gentle manner. But it wasn't okay—not when I was too busy being nice to others to love my own wife, but I couldn't pursue the point just then because the others had come in. We joined hands in a circle to pray.

When we walked out onto the platform we were greeted by hundreds of smiling faces. The sanctuary grew quiet, and I poised my fingers on the strings of the bass guitar.

In the moment before we hit the opening bars a thought caught me off-guard: *Someday I'm going to learn how to be a good Christian. Maybe one day I'll be able to walk on stage and not feel like a hypocrite.*

Then our drummer hit the downbeat and I was caught up in the music.

11

There was no way I could have even guessed the terrible fire through which I'd pass before that prayer was answered. Nor could I have imagined the unusual way God would team me with someone who was watching me from the audience at that very moment. . . .

SHIRLEY:

A s the music began I smoothed my skirt and settled back in the pew. The group, Living Sound, had a lively, contemporary style with a slight country twang, which I liked. Ron, whom I'd been dating for a couple of years, was at my side. His feet were already tapping to the easy drumbeat.

Gently, he laid his hand on mine.

I stiffened involuntarily and kept staring at the performers. Though we were surrounded by friends from our young adult group I felt strangely isolated. I tried to slip my hand from his unnoticed.

Ron glanced at me sidelong with a wounded look. With my now-free hand I pretended to smooth my hair, and riveted my eyes on the singers. Poor Ron.

He was a nice guy—and good-looking. He embarrassed me sometimes by telling our friends how attracted he was to slender blondes with green eyes. Sometimes, though, he was possessive, demanding my attention, and that bothered me. I was only eighteen and not ready to marry.

I looked at Ron now. Our eyes locked and I could read his pleading look: *Why can't I get close to you? Can't you tell me?*

I had to turn away. What could I tell him? That his touch set off a chain reaction of emotions and a sense of being trapped? That his touch was strong and overpowering— like that of my father?

My fingers went cold at the thought. In my mind's eye I saw myself as a younger girl sitting in this very church. Dad had been head usher here, respected.

Then the scene shifted. Dad was standing at the door of my room, smiling with a frightened smile. I begged him to leave. He shut the door and reached for me. . . .

Living Sound finished a song and I focused on the front of the church again.

The bass guitar player took the mike and introduced himself as Terry Law, the group's founder. He seemed to have a magnetic confidence about him, especially when he announced that he was leading the group to Africa in the fall. I'd always been attracted to men with strong beliefs. That was part of the problem with Ron.

Before I stopped to think what I was saying—let alone how Ron would feel—I leaned over and whispered, "See that man up there?"

He nodded.

"Someday I'm going to marry a man in the ministry. Someone who loves God the way that man does."

Ron looked at me blankly.

As I listened to Terry Law speak, on that rainy Sunday evening in the summer of 1969, those words were like a prophecy. But I had little confidence that my life could ever be happy or fulfilled. How could I ever overcome the wounds of the past—the horrible things my own father said and did to me?

It seemed that life was nothing but a struggle to survive from day to day. Even my very earliest memories were shadowed. . . .

Yet Will I PRAISE HIM

1

TERRY:
Night Vision

The incident that remapped my life occurred the summer I was fourteen.

Mom and Dad had packed our car for the short trip from the parsonage in Vernon to the coastal wilderness of British Columbia. It was 1957, and as a pastor in provincial Canada my father did not make enough money to take us on fancy vacations. So every summer in July the family packed off for a week at Bible camp. My sister, Lois, who was almost twelve, thought it was fortunate that the camp we were going to this year was located within earshot of the Pacific breakers. The trip began happily enough with only a hint of the confrontation ahead.

As we bumped along the dirt road leading to the camp I hung my head out one of the back windows, breathing the scent of Douglas firs and salt air. Lois had occupied the seat by the other back window, and Clayton, our young brother, was still grumbling at being stuck in the middle. He gave my ribs a poke. I poked him back even harder.

I'd already determined this was going to be a week of fun, and maybe a little mischief.

Dad had been watching in the rearview mirror. He was no clairvoyant, but he read the look on my face. "Terry," he said sternly, negotiating a tight curve, "there will be no fooling around this week. Is that clear?"

Looking up, I could see Dad's broad shoulders and wavy hair. And then I saw his burning brown eyes reflected in the rearview mirror. They flashed a warning from under knitted brows. Whenever he looked at me that way I felt as if I was under final judgment. Why did he always equate *me* with *trouble?*

Mother glanced over her shoulder and, as always, spoke more gently. "Remember. Behave yourself, Terry."

Settling back on the seat, I let Clayton climb over me and assume the window. In a moment, Dad pulled in at the registration office and went in to get the key to our lodging.

As we waited, I nursed my bruised feelings. Yet I knew my folks had good reason to be concerned about my behavior. Being at Bible camp was like being on display. Pastors and their families from all over the province would be here. They all knew Bert and Ann Law and respected their hard work, pioneering churches for our denomination in some of the wild regions of Canada. We had braved life in remote cabins, where the harsh winter wind would cut through chinks in the logs, blowing the Indian blankets Mom had hung as insulation. Besides preaching, Dad chopped poplars and red willows with a broadaxe to support us. He could fell a moose or an elk with one shot. Dad knew the Word of God and proclaimed it fearlessly. And back home if a farmer in our church needed help, Dad could drive a combine as easily as he played the guitar or preached. He was a man's man. Even though there would be many leaders at this camp, Dad was incomparable in my eyes.

On the other hand, if my dad hadn't excelled at everything he did—if he hadn't been such a good man—my life might have been easier. I knew deep down that I could never be as good as he was.

The same energy that propelled Dad drove me, too. For one thing we shared a love for knowledge. Many mornings as a small boy I'd shuffle into the kitchen, bleary-eyed, rummaging for a box of cereal, when Dad appeared from his study, yawning and stretching. He'd have been up all night ferreting out some thought from Scripture. With his encouragement I was an avid reader, devouring whole series—the Hardy Boys, Zane Grey, and especially the classics. I barely had to study to get good grades in school.

Many folks said I was just like Dad—except that he always did *good* things. I had a bad habit of falling in with the wildest kids around and usually became the ringleader. We'd moved a lot and in the three towns where Dad had pastored since I was born—two in the province of Saskatchewan and now in Vernon—people said, "Watch out for that preacher's kid. He's the worst of the bunch!"

When Dad emerged from the camp office with the key, I'd finished sulking. We drove to our cabin and unpacked the car. Lois, Clayton, and I then charged off to comb the beach for driftwood and shells with a warning from Dad to be on time for the evening meeting at the tabernacle.

Our minor run-in that morning was just a prelude.

That evening I missed the bell that called us to meeting. When I realized it I sprinted up the pine-shaded path, skidding into the tabernacle out of breath and panting.

Fortunately the song service had begun. Quietly, I eased onto one of the wooden benches at the back and glanced around for my family. The tabernacle was really a lofted, hip-roofed barn, with a few hornets droning around the exposed beams overhead. The walls were wooden panels hinged at the top so they could be swung up to let in the summer air. Wood shavings covered the floor. On the platform up front a woman with meaty arms, her hair tied up in a bun, was making the upright piano bounce to the tune of "I'll Fly Away." Seated on a bench near the front were Mother, Lois, and Clayton—and Dad, who was watching me with an angry look.

My shoulders slumped; he'd witnessed my late arrival. *I never do anything right*, I chastised myself.

The late sun was angling inside the tabernacle when the singing ended. Our speaker for the week was an American named Dwight McLaughlin. He had a strong jawline and graying hair. Though he was probably only in his early fifties he seemed to me like Moses as he stood and laid his thick black Bible on the pulpit.

I'd sat through this sort of meeting a thousand times. As I understood it, our church taught that God forgave our sins because Jesus shed his blood on the cross for us. Every time you sinned, however, you made a mockery of His precious blood and cut yourself off from God. Pastor McLaughlin began more softly than my dad might have, but before long he was revved up. Why was it, he asked, that people so readily turned to sin?

As he spoke, a thin slice of pain beat within my chest. I knew that person he was describing, the one who turned away from God.

When his sermon ended with the usual call to rededicate our lives to Christ, many got up from their seats and scuffed through the wood shavings to kneel at the altar rail. Pastors were gathering around to pray with them. This scene suddenly seemed like a portrait of my whole life, fenced in as it was by church meetings and church rules.

And there was always one flaw in the picture: me.

Much as my heart ached, I could not make my legs move to respond. Not one more time. For all the impassioned sermons I'd heard on turning from wrong I'd probably knelt in repentance just as many times. But it never worked. Something in me was just plain bad. And every time I heard one of these sermons lately, I felt a growing uneasiness that I could never stop being bad. God could not possibly love someone like me.

That night, long after Clayton had fallen asleep in the bunk above me, I lay awake. Outside, the waves beat rhythmically on the moonlit shore. In the darkness I stared at the sagging springs above me, rethinking all the times I'd *meant* to do right but failed.

Immediately my mind drifted back eight years to the kitchen of our parsonage in Parkside, Saskatchewan, on a spring morning when I was just six. . . .

The hardwood chair was cool against my legs where they stuck out of my short pants. My feet dangled listlessly, inches from the floor. Mother had sat me there, like a criminal awaiting interrogation, and gone to get my dad.

I could still hear her voice: "You're going to tell him *exactly* what you did."

In a moment Dad loomed before me. "Go on, son," he prompted. His eyes cut into my soul.

My lips trembling, I confessed: A half hour before I'd wandered into a shop just down the street. The proprietor was busy with another customer. His back was turned. I surveyed the candy shelf. My hand shot out. The chocolate bar slipped so easily into my pocket.

When I'd wandered into Mom's kitchen licking chocolate from my fingers she wanted to know where I'd gotten it. I told her someone had bought it for me—which was not farfetched, since people who knew I was the preach er's kid sometimes gave me treats when we met on the street. But she had seen through the lie.

Even worse, now Dad knew.

He looked so disappointed as he fished in his pocket. Pulling out a nickel, he dropped the coin into my small hand. "You've got to go back and pay for what you've done."

Clayton shifted in his sleep, bringing me back to the dark room. Dad's words were fresh in my thoughts. I *hadn't* paid for what I'd done. I'd gone up to the shop door but couldn't face the owner, shaming my father publicly. Later I told my parents the man had accepted the money. That coin burned in my pocket as I lied.

Restlessly, I punched my pillow and tried to stop my mind from racing. Somewhere in heaven that stolen chocolate bar was still unpaid for on the record of my sins. And stealing candy was by far the least of the things I'd done in breaking the rules of our church.

In the rural Canadian towns we'd lived in there was little for kids to do. I remembered smoking Players cigarettes on the way to school with my friend Dennis Bjorgan at age eight. A little later I'd learned to swig liquor with a group of farm boys. At nine, when we had settled in Prince Albert, Saskatchewan, I'd gotten my first job selling newspapers on the streets. It was then I began to slip into the hardware store and listen to Elvis Presley and other forbidden "rock 'n rollers" on the radio. I even learned how to sneak into the local theater. Hiding behind a curtain, I was mesmerized by the cowboy and Indian chases up front on the huge, glowing screen.

In short, by the age of ten, I'd done almost everything that our church declared evil. And on Sunday nights when Dad finished describing the black anguish of an eternity without Christ, I'd run to the altar rail, weeping, begging God to forgive me.

By Monday afternoon, however, a friend would offer me a cigarette. And I'd fail again. Before I turned fourteen, I'd decided that there was just too much bad in me.

A breeze ruffled the curtain at the cabin window. I rolled over in my bunk one more time. The covers were twisted beyond straightening. Drowsiness came over me—and another memory: A friend and I were sitting in a pew in Dad's church, flipping pages in what we called "The Devil Book." Grotesque, laughing demons with bat wings thrust pitchforks at the men and women who writhed beneath them in flames, their faces distorted with screaming.

I fell asleep and dreamed: The face of one figure chained in that fiery prison was mine.

For the rest of the week, Dwight McLaughlin's call to repentance haunted me. But I could not answer his invitation to "come forward and get right with God"—not for the hundredth time.

Friday night I sat through another sermon, unaware that this was to be the most startling night of my young life.

When the service ended I could not move from the rough bench, not even after the last penitent had dried his eyes and gone up the dark path to the cabins. Mother and Dad allowed me to remain. I found a bench in the back. When a man came to turn off the lights he didn't even notice me.

For some time I stared out of my dark corner as the moon cast faint shadows inside the tabernacle. An ocean breeze blew through the firs, stirring the smell of shavings at my feet. In this place there had been music, praising, hearts made right with God; but I felt lost. Surely God had turned His face from me. I sat on that hard bench for an hour or more, listening to the intermittent cry of an owl in the forest.

After a long time—past midnight, I guessed—I heard

footsteps outside. Quietly a man walked in at the front of the tabernacle. Moonlight traced his strong features: It was Dwight McLaughlin. I sat stock still. He rummaged for something on the pulpit. Then, as if startled, he looked up.

"Someone's here," he called gently. "Where are you?"

He couldn't see me, not hidden here in the shadows. I stilled my breath.

"I can help," he called again.

Still I hesitated, feeling awkward. Finally I said, "I'm here—in the back corner."

Groping along the benches he made his way to my side and sat down.

I told him who I was. "You know," he said thoughtfully, "the Lord must have sent me to you. Just a few minutes ago, I was asleep in bed. I woke from a sound sleep with a voice reminding me I'd left my Bible on the pulpit. I was going to wait till morning to get it. But—well, now I'm here and I can pray for you," he finished. "Would you mind?"

I fidgeted. I'd already gotten cynical enough to notice the way pastors spiritualized everything.

He asked again, "May I pray for you?"

I shrugged. "Okay."

When he laid his hand on my shoulder, a strange thing happened. Warmth slowly radiated into me. He started to pray, then caught his breath, as if in awe. "Lord! The vastness of Your plan for this boy!"

As he prayed his words painted a vivid picture in my head—like nothing I'd ever imagined.

He described a broad field and a flood of faces—hundreds of thousands of faces! In my hand was an open Bible. Somehow—though these people could not speak English and I had no idea what language they spoke—my words were going straight to their hearts.

When Dwight McLaughlin took his hand off my shoulder a few minutes later, both of us were quiet.

Then, because it was late, he urged me to go to my cabin and get some sleep. As we parted on the path I was amazed: How could it be that this wonderful man of God saw such promise in a weak, sinful fourteen-year-old?

As I quietly closed the cabin door I realized that, for the first time in a week, I felt *good*. God might not be disgusted with me after all.

The next morning, Saturday, during the early service Dwight McLaughlin embarrassed me by calling me up before the crowded tabernacle. Pointing to me he announced, "I want you all to have a good look at this young man. He is called of God to a worldwide mission."

I looked at Dad sitting near the front. His eyes were shining. Mom's were filled with tears. From the crowded benches there were amens and even some applause.

But standing in front of these good church people, both excited and nervous, I felt questions hammering inside me. I had been through emotional commitments before. I could imagine one of my friends at home holding out a liquor bottle. I whetted my lips.

How was I going to stay "clean"? How could I overcome that longing to be accepted by my buddies, in order to feel accepted by God?

As the service ended and I helped Dad load the car for the trip home to Vernon, I knew I had a struggle ahead of me.

And all the way home I kept stealing glances at Dad's eyes, reflected in the rearview mirror. In my heart I made a vow: *Someday you're going to be proud of me, Dad. You'll see.*

23

2

TERRY:
Collision Course

Once we got home from Bible camp, 'the thought that God had a special "plan" for me brought with it a buoyant feeling. It was as if Dwight McLaughlin's reassuring hand still rested on my shoulder. Sure I was just a teenager, but *someone* believed I was headed for higher things.

To my parents' delight, I stayed out of trouble the rest of that year.

The following spring, in 1958, Dad accepted a new pastorate and we moved to Regina, Saskatchewan, a farming community tucked among the flat russet grainfields in central Canada. On the day we carried our meager furniture into the two-story parsonage about a mile from the church some men and boys came to help. One lady brought warm homemade bread and an apple pie.

At lunchtime I saw two of the teenaged boys sneaking out behind the house. I ran down the hall and peered out the bathroom window which overlooked the backyard.

24

One pulled a pouch out of his overalls and took a pinch of chewing tobacco, then offered it to the other one.

I stayed away from them the rest of the afternoon.

The bad thing about the move was that I'd left all my old friends behind. Clayton had just turned nine and at fifteen I wasn't interested in hanging around with him—and certainly not with my sister.

So our first week in Regina I scuffed along the sidewalks alone trying to get a sense of "home" in this place. It was lonely. Whenever I'd pass a group of kids, I'd feel their eyes on my back. Inside I'd squirm. What were they thinking?

One afternoon Mom sent me out to the store for a gallon of milk. Out the back screen door I banged, plunged down the steps and out to the street. At the end of the block I rounded a corner and stopped dead.

There, leaning against a brick wall, were three guys about my age. All three were in jeans and tee shirts, each wearing a baseball cap over close-cropped hair. One had a wad of something in his mouth that distorted his cheek as if he were chewing a golfball.

I was about to pass when the kid slurred around his wad, "Hey, you're the preacher's kid, ain't ya?"

I squared my shoulders. "Yeah. I am."

A sluice of brown tobacco juice hit the sidewalk at my feet. The kid with the wad wiped his lip and glanced at his buddies. They were smirking. From the pocket of his jeans he pulled out a squashy looking pack of Players cigarettes. He stuck them out at me in a friendly manner. "You want a smoke?"

I hesitated. Their eyes were probing me. Being a new kid, and a preacher's kid at that, was a tough and lonely position in that moment.

I reached out and accepted the pack. Cocking a cigarette casually in my lips, I said, "Thanks. Who's got a match?"

And with that small rite I was welcomed into their circle. I hoped God wasn't looking.

But on Sunday morning I had to face Him again.

Mom was up on the platform playing the piano before Dad preached. All around me were men in white shirts and suits and women in their finest Sunday dresses. In my blue Sunday suit, my curly hair slicked down neatly, I looked as angelic as Clayton or Lois, who sat beside me, Bibles in hand. As Dad launched into his message, however, I could feel my face reddening.

"Some people come to church on Sunday morning and ask for God's blessing and guidance. And that's fine," he said. He paced behind the pulpit, the energy inside him like a mounting storm. His voice rose: "But on Monday morning you go about your business, falling headlong into every trap the world sets without giving the Lord a second thought."

His voice billowed through the small sanctuary now. Anxiety burned and tingled along my skin. "If you live that way," he thundered, "the Bible says you are double-minded—lukewarm. God will spit you out of His mouth."

Whatever he said after that was lost on me. Worms of fear bore into my stomach. My soul felt like a rotted rag.

On the way home from church Clayton and Lois skipped on ahead of me. I slunk along. I was one of those double-minded people Dad talked about. I didn't have the guts to pass up the first cigarette that was offered. How could I possibly have believed that God had a worldwide mission for me? That was like glimpsing a far-off mountain peak with raging rivers and dense jungles in between. There was no way someone like me, so short on commitment, could reach so high a goal.

Turning in at our walk I knew one thing for sure: I couldn't make any more "repentances." If there were a quota, I'd surely used up mine. But I had also failed in my vow to make Dad proud of me. It was too wrenching to think of making another commitment only to fail again. I could no longer stand the guilt. Suddenly my mind was made up.

After that I sought out more kids to befriend—and not the goody-goody types either. Most of the guys I hung around with came to our church—not because they wanted to, but because their folks made them. Most of them smoked. One kid, who was in my Sunday school class, told the dirtiest jokes I'd ever heard.

I also met two guys at school, Murray and Neil. We were in some of the same classes. When I learned that they liked to tinker with chemicals—setting off small explosions—we hit it off right away.

Every day that fall when I walked in the door from school I hoped Mom couldn't smell the cigarette smoke on my clothes. Even if I couldn't be a Christian, the acceptance of my friends, especially Murray and Neil, deadened the guilt.

Mom and Dad did not miss the change in my attitude. When we were smaller, Mom had taught Lois and me to harmonize. We got so good that Dad let us sing on a weekly children's radio broadcast he hosted at the time. Mom even taught me to play the accordion until I protested that it was a "woman's instrument."

But now, at fifteen, Christian songs seemed hokey to me. Mom looked crestfallen every time I refused to sing with Lois at church. But I couldn't get up and sing like an angel when most of the kids sitting in the pews knew I was a devil just like them. To my relief, neither Mom nor Dad ever pressed me on such matters.

Once again I took on the roll of ringleader. Okay, so I couldn't cut it with God. But when I was with my friends I felt like a big man. If someone had a crazy, wild prank in mind, I'd be the one to pull it. Something in me loved the lure of the dangerous.

There was another side to me, though, a more positive side. Like Dad, I was a hard worker. Even though I was underage, I lied on a job application and landed an after-school position stocking shelves in a Dominion grocery store a couple of blocks from home. Before long I was making good money—more than Dad was making in the ministry—and feeling good about myself.

But this financial success just drove me even further from my folks.

One late spring evening in 1959, after I'd turned sixteen, I drove home in a gleaming robin's-egg blue Pontiac with a two-tone, blue-and-white top. I had paid cash for it. Granted it was vintage 1952, but it was in top shape. I imagined the admiration in the eyes of Lois and Clayton when they saw me in the driver's seat. And I imagined the look of pride in my accomplishment that I would see in Dad's eyes.

Pulling into our driveway I tooted the horn. In a moment, Clayton and Lois came bounding out the front door and across the lawn. They didn't disappoint me.

Clayton whistled, "Man, Terry—can I have a ride?" Lois ran her hand along the shiny finish. "Me, too, Terry?"

Mom and Dad had joined them on the sidewalk. I flashed a triumphant grin at Dad. "What do you think? She's a real beauty, huh?"

Dad nodded, only the hint of a smile on his face. "You'll have to take good care of this car, son. I don't want to hear about your hot-rodding around in it with your buddies."

Not: "You've worked hard, Terry. You deserve this."

Not: "I'm proud of you, son."

As I drove off with Clayton and Lois, leaving Mom and Dad waving from the curb, the victorious homecoming I'd cooked up seemed not as full. Why couldn't Dad's eyes have bugged, even a little? The simple fact was that Dad was not impressed with flashy cars. He was so sold out to preaching the Kingdom of God that material possessions just didn't excite him.

Lois and Clayton "oohed" and waved to friends as we drove through town. Silently, I berated myself. Here I was trying to prove I was good for something—hoping for a word of encouragement—and I wasn't even competing on the right playing field.

That summer I seemed to crave the attention and admiration of my friends more than ever. *They* were impressed by the Pontiac. I gave in to any wild impulse that struck. We drank, smoked, went drag racing. Sometimes, late at night, a group of my buddies would come with a ladder and help me sneak out my upstairs bedroom window. We'd meet girls, or just drink ourselves drunk.

Late one summer night my buddies stealthily propped the ladder outside my window. When I climbed down to them we decided to pull a raid on the local "lovers' lane."

Only the *chirring* of crickets disturbed the silence as we crept up behind the lone car. I peeked in the rear window. Sure enough, there were a young man and woman, locked in each other's arms.

One of the guys had swiped a garden hose and I quietly tied one end to the rear bumper while another guy tied the other end to a tree. The rest crouched nearby awaiting the signal.

Someone "whooped" and we attacked, shouting, banging on the car with sticks, dancing around like demons. Startled, the girl screamed, while her boyfriend fumbled with the keys. The engine roared, the car shot into gear, tires spitting gravel. In an instant the hose snapped taut and the bumper flew off, hitting the road with a metallic *clang*.

We took off across the fields for town, careful to stay off the roads in case the guy came looking for us.

Crossing the Dominion store parking lot, just when we thought we were safe, someone spotted a black-and-white police cruiser. Like buckshot, we scattered, tearing through flower gardens and over fences. Dogs started barking all over town.

When I hit our backyard I groped my way up the ladder, my heart pumping with the rush of adrenalin. How I loved that feeling! The curtains brushed my face as I crawled in my bedroom window. I was halfway inside when, from the darkness of my room, a terrified voice stopped me. "Don't move, or I'll call the police!"

My heart fell. It was Mother. The ruckus outside must have wakened her. "It's Terry, Mom," I whispered, trying to calm her.

"No, it's not!" she came back, her voice nearly breaking with fear. In that moment she hit the light switch and the flood of brightness hurt my eyes. There stood Mom in a nightgown and curlers, squinting in the light—and there I was, my flank still hanging out the window. If Mom had not been so white with fear I might have laughed.

The next day, however, when I had to face Dad, it was no laughing matter.

Lois and Clayton sat white-knuckled at the table. Mother kept clearing her throat nervously. Dad had called them in to listen as he read me the "riot act."

Pacing, he said angrily, "Terry, what you're doing challenges everything I stand for.

"As a pastor I have to rule my own house. That means I have to rule you," he said, pointing a finger in my face.

I stood there, silent, sizing him up. I was about his height now, though he was thick-chested, and his arms were definitely more muscled and more powerful than mine. So what? I was ready for a showdown. If I wasn't good enough that was his tough luck. Facing me, toe-to-toe, Dad growled, "Do you hear me?"

Defiantly, I thrust out my chin, silently daring him with my eyes.

Like a bull seeing red, Dad threw back his arm and slammed the heel of his hand into my jaw.

The blow sent me sprawling backward with a crash onto the kitchen table. Mother drew a sharp breath and Lois and Clayton began to cry.

Leaping up I thrust my chin at him again. Without hesitating he slammed that powerful hand into my jaw again, knocking me back onto the table.

Before I could move he towered over me. "Make your choice, Terry," he shouted. "Either you live here and tow the mark or you hit the streets. It's up to you."

The confrontation broke up in an angry silence.

In the end I decided to stay, mostly because I had nowhere else to go. Under the surface the showdown was really only a stalemate. I would just conceal my rebellion more carefully—play it "straight" in front of my folks.

I continued going to church every Sunday for my two remaining years of high school—and even felt a twinge of conviction whenever I recalled the event at Bible camp—but mostly my heart was a million miles away.

One Halloween night in my senior year, Murray, Neil, and I decided to have some fun. In our chemistry class that year we had discovered formulas for creating more high-powered explosives. Down in Murray's basement workshop we'd built pipe bombs. While most kids were out in costume, looking for treats, we thought we would play tricks with some of the outdoor toilets that graced a few farmyards just outside of town.

Stealing along a farmer's fence that pitch-dark October night, Murray and Neil chickened out. "Give me the pipe," I whispered in a cocky way. "I'll do it."

As they retreated I crept up to the outhouse. The hinges creaked as I opened the door and propped the pipe against the seat inside. Unscrewing the lid of the acid bottle, I dumped the contents onto the wadded-up toilet paper in the pipe. Like a jackrabbit, I took off, clearing the fence with a leap. I knew I had only seconds before the acid soaked through the paper and ignited the explosive in the bottom half of the pipe.

I was halfway down the darkened path when I heard the roar. The trees and fields around me lit up like the Fourth of July. Glancing over my shoulder I saw brilliant flames and shreds of wood blown high into the air.

Murray, Neil, and I laughed secretly about that for the next three weeks while the police hunted for the mystery bombers.

A month later, on a Friday evening, Neil invited me over to his house to play pool. When we were alone in the game room I leaned over to rack up the balls. Neil whispered to me.

"Murray called. He wants us to come over later. He found a book with the formula for picric acid."

I straightened and looked at Neil with an excited grin. Picric acid, I knew from chemistry class, was the yellow powder used in plastic explosives. It was the explosive commandos used in blowing up bridges. We could have a ball with that stuff.

For some reason we never did get to Murray's house that evening. The next morning, when the phone rang just after breakfast, I expected to hear Murray's voice, complaining that he'd waited for us.

Instead, it was Neil. "Terry," he began, then choked up.

"What is it?" I prompted.

"Did you hear the news?"

"No."

"Murray was killed last night."

Suddenly Neil's voice seemed far-off. He said, from what the police could tell, Murray had been mixing chemicals in his basement and triggered an explosion. The blast killed him instantly.

The words were bullets. I don't remember hanging up the phone.

The next few days seared images into my brain: Murray's hands, still, folded, and pale in the coffin at the funeral home, the heavy-hung scent of flowers, the anguished sobs of his mother. And then the solid weight of that coffin was on my shoulder, and the coldness of the polished metal as six of us, Murray's "buddies," bore it to the freshly dug grave.

As we lowered the coffin, one thought pulsed with each heartbeat: *You never told Murray about Jesus. Where is his soul now?*

In the months after, the tormenting thought dimmed just a little—but never fully eased.

Even the following June, as I marched up to receive my diploma with the graduating class of 1960, Murray's face was before me.

I looked around at the auditorium full of friends. For the three years I'd been in Regina, I'd tried to prove I was more than a week-kneed preacher's kid. What had I won for it? Murray's blood was on my hands. If I'd been caught blowing up an outhouse or ripping a bumper off a car, I could have worked to pay for the damage. But this? There was no way I could buy back Murray's life. No way I could pay for the sin of hiding my Christian faith—nominal as it was—and allowing my friend's soul to be flung into a Christless eternity. I thought, *Murray should be here—alive. I'm the one who should be dead.*

It was an unbearable load for a seventeen-year-old. That night after graduation I drank until I vomited.

All that summer, my drinking and partying got worse. I had decided to go to a nearby university to study law, which meant I could save money by living at home. And in September, when weekend beer parties capped off a tough week of classes, even my earlier resolve to stay "straight" in front of my parents was shot.

My first few weeks at university were great, and I was excited about being there. My immediate goal was to graduate with a degree in criminal law and then go into politics. Characteristically, I wanted to make a name for myself, and maybe someday even run for prime minister of Canada.

My dreams may have been lofty, but many Friday nights, friends would leave me off on my folks' doorstep, staggering drunk. I would weave inside, barely able to totter up the stairs to bed. On a couple of occasions, the light was still burning in my parents' room and I'd focus on Mom's form as she knelt beside their bed, praying. I had no doubt she was begging God to change me. Didn't she know I was hopeless?

It was at this point, when I thought I'd become just about as ungodly as you could get, that an extraordinary thing happened.

I had gone out with a couple of friends on a Sunday afternoon in October with only one thing in mind—to sit around a pub and get roaring drunk. Both of these guys had grown up in Dad's church and, like me, had kicked over the traces of this "holiness garbage."

By early evening, when everything we said seemed hilarious, one of the guys thought it would be funny if the folks at church could see us. I bit the bait. Dad was having a special guest speaker at the service that evening. Wouldn't it be a riot to show up drunk and knock around a few ushers when they tried to kick us out?

When we slumped into a rear pew, right in the middle

of the opening hymn, we were primed for trouble. Fueled by our drinking, we joined right in, singing and laughing boisterously. I could see Dad up front, but he did not look back at me. Everyone else was ignoring us, sloppy and loud as we were.

After a few songs the guest speaker stood up. One of the guys kept trying to belch out loud. I was nearly sick from laughing. Where were the ushers? We managed to settle down a little as the man at the pulpit set his Bible aside.

Curiously, something he said caught me off-guard.

"Tonight I want to talk to you about a man who loved His friends so much He willingly gave His life for them—though they did nothing to earn that love. They gave themselves over to sin, and yet Jesus Christ took that blood-guilt upon Himself."

One of the guys elbowed my ribs, but I only smiled lamely. What was it about this preacher's message? Something was different.

I listened, riveted, as he painted a vibrant word picture of Jesus' death and resurrection: the red whip-scores inflicted on Jesus' body, the merciless crown of thorns piercing his scalp. My hands and feet got sweaty as he described the huge iron nails, the drops of blood blown by the storm winds spattering the ground red.

I'd heard sermons like this before. Usually they ended with the same note: Because Jesus had died for me, I had to live right. Otherwise, I was trampling the blood of Christ into the dirt. And I had surely trampled.

But something in this man's words was different. Or was it a different look on his face—a brightness? His voice was firm, but even from the back pew I could see that his face was full of compassion.

"Jesus is holding out His hands to you at this moment. Those hands are nail-scarred, but they are not pointing at you in judgment. You can only bring judgment on yourself if you refuse to come to Him to have your sins forgiven. He is beckoning to you in love.

"No matter who you are, no matter how far you've run from God, you can come to Him tonight. You don't have to make any promises to Him that you may break tomorrow. Just take the first step toward Him, and He will take care of tomorrow.

"There is no sin—no matter how great or small—that His blood cannot wash away. His plan for your life is good. His amazing love is new every morning."

No sin . . . . Inwardly I saw Murray's hands, folded and cold—felt the weight of his coffin.

He has a plan . . . . Something was happening to me. The weight was lifting.

His love is new . . . . I wanted to leap. What was this new face of God? Not a stern face, condemning my every failure. I saw the face of a Father who knew how weak His children could be and wanted to draw them to His loving arms—not because *they* were good, but because *He* was good.

And then I made a discovery: The dizziness was gone from my head. One of my buddies had slumped over, boozy and nearly asleep, and the other one slouched red-eyed. But I was suddenly stone-cold sober.

When the altar call came, a thousand protesting voices resounded in my head. *These people know you're a hypocrite. Your friends are going to roll in the aisles laughing at you.*

How many times had I responded to invitations to give my heart to Christ? I hardly knew. But the pull of that forgiving love . . . !

I was on my feet and moving down the aisle, drawn by the inner hunger to be embraced by this love. Dad met me at the front. Hope, uncertainty, relief were mixed in his eyes. As I knelt with him, I looked back. The pew where

I'd left my friends was empty. But I didn't care. I bowed my head and wept. I'd never felt like this before: *clean*.

And later that night, as I walked out of church into the fall night, I felt for the first time in years like a true son coming home to my father's house. If God had laid His hand gently on my shoulder three years before at Bible camp, I felt His embracing arms now.

It was then the merest flick of memory came back to me—the distant mountaintop call that Dwight McLaughlin had glimpsed. I took in a draught of cool air. Did God have some special path for me? Maybe. But I had made only the first small step on it.

Without doubt it was a good thing I couldn't see ahead, as I walked home that night, to the times when I would not be able to go on were it not for those uplifting arms.

I might have lost the courage to do what I felt I had to do now—to make a drastic break with my past and follow the upward call.

3

SHIRLEY:
"Dad's Not Well"

In the vague way that small children sense things, I felt from my earliest impressions that there was something wounded about our family.

Memories are vivid. Some were wonderful: the green fields of Grandpa Paintner's farm in North Dakota where Dad worked with his father; the small house where we lived; the cool blue summer sky overhead as I played, at age four, picking dandelions with my little brother, David; the radio playing country music, which was about all that Midwest stations offered in the early 1950s.

Other images were not so luminous.

Most Saturday evenings Dad took us into town. David and I went to the grocery store with my mother. Dad would disappear into a local bar with red neon signs in the window and the noise of a jukebox pulsing into the street every time the door opened.

David and I played as Mom put the brown paper grocery bags in the car. Then she took us down to the corner where a man sold fresh, hot popcorn from a sidewalk machine. People came in from the farms on Saturday evenings. Pretty soon Mom would be talking to an aunt or a friend while David and I played on the sidewalk with a cousin or two.

But as the sun set, my eyes always strayed down the street to where the bar's red neon sign was casting a red glow on the darkening sidewalk. I wanted my dad.

About the time David was ready to fall asleep on Mom's shoulder, Dad would saunter up. His eyes looked sad, glassy, and his breath smelled like beer.

Later, after Mom drove us home, my father didn't even look at David or me. I felt confused. Sometimes I wished he'd scoop me in his big arms, which were sunburned up to the sleeves of his tee shirt. Mostly, I stayed away from him. He'd veer down the hall into his room and slam the door.

Then Mom would say, with a warning look, "You kids be quiet. Daddy's not feeling good tonight." That was how she explained to us that he was drunk, which I somehow knew anyway.

There was another vagueness in our home. It had to do with God.

The problem seemed to be this: I'd heard Mother say that she was German Lutheran and that Dad's family was strict Catholic—whatever that meant. At first we rarely went to church at all.

Grandpa confronted my mother about this one day. She was peeling potatoes at the kitchen sink. David was playing with a ball on the floor. Grandpa, always firm and commanding, was seated at the table. He said simply, "Iola, it's time you and Francis took the children to church."

Maybe Grandpa's word was law—or maybe it was because we lived on his farm—but after that Mom saw to it that David and I rarely missed a Sunday trip to church. She chose not a Catholic *or* a Lutheran church, but another. Maybe she considered it neutral. Occasionally my father came, but grudgingly.

Grandma and Grandpa gave me a small pink Bible that swished against my pretty dress as we got out of the car at the white clapboard church that seemed to be lost among the wheatfields. Inside, the singing was lively and the minister could make his voice boom over the out-of-tune piano. He had a Bible, too, a large black one that he waved as he preached. Sometimes perspiration beaded on his forehead.

I'd lay my own small Bible open on my lap, smoothing the pages with my fingers. The preacher said God's Word was full of life-changing power. One message was hammered home Sunday after Sunday: God was a loving heavenly Father—but He was hidden from us because of sin. He had given His own Son, Jesus, to pay for those sins. We could ask Jesus to live in our hearts, to be a Savior and friend.

I must have understood something of what this meant. At what age, I can't recall, but I prayed along with the pastor one Sunday and asked God to come and live in my heart. Later, I would make a more mature commitment, but for now I believed in Jesus and His loving Father in heaven.

The preacher loved to read the Scriptures: "I am the way and the truth and the life. No man cometh unto the Father but by Me" and "You shall know the truth, and the truth shall make you free."

Free? I wondered. *Free from what?*

One day I would find out.

What also mystified me was this: At home we never once talked about God.

So I tried to hold in my head conflicting images: A loving Father in heaven whom I could always talk to in my heart, and a father on earth who seemed a million miles away. When I was tired or I'd skinned my knee I wouldn't think of crawling onto his lap. Something in me just couldn't. I'd sometimes awaken at night and hear him shouting at Mom, and David would cry in his crib.

These are hazy, background impressions, like wallpaper in the rooms of my childhood. But I remember one incident with special, terrifying clarity.

One night I awoke to a loud noise. I slipped from my bed. The floor was cold on my bare feet. Halfway to the door a shout made me freeze. Now I heard Mom's voice in the kitchen—and Dad's.

Tiptoeing down the hall, I stood at the kitchen door squinting in the light. Mom, whose stomach was big with another baby, was leaning away from Dad—cowering. Suddenly, he grabbed her by the arm and began shouting again.

"Francis, don't!" my mother screamed.

He shook her and pushed her. She fell and hit the floor hard.

David was screaming in his room. I didn't know whether to run and protect him or try to help Mom. My legs would not move.

Mom lay there, moaning, clutching her stomach. Then she looked at her hand and gave a small shriek.

"I'm bleeding! Oh, my baby, *my baby*. Francis, look what you've done—get away from me!"

From where I stood, I saw a small dab of red on her hand. My stomach went weak.

My father's angry look crumpled into one of remorse. He lifted Mother off the floor as she kept sobbing, "Leave me alone. Call someone to help me."

I don't know how my mother got to the hospital that night, or who took care of David and me. I only recall going into my room and crawling between the cold sheets. For a long time I prayed for the baby in Mother's stomach, even after I heard my parents return from the hospital very late at night.

Shortly, in May of 1956, my mother delivered a healthy baby boy whom they named Roger. She relied on me to look after David, and I did everything to keep him out of my dad's way. Sometimes, when I held one of Roger's cream-colored hands, I felt a fierce protectiveness for him, too.

My parents hardly spoke to each other for a long time. Dad would come home at the end of the day and scrub the tractor grease from his hands, leaving gray streaks in the bathroom sink. Even in those rare times when he tried to pull me to him for a kiss, I held onto his thumbs, as if I couldn't trust myself to those hands.

And then, the winter before I turned six, another incident occurred—like a steady hand reaching to me in the darkness.

My family was on one of those Saturday evening trips to town. Coat flapping about my legs, I followed Mom through the grocery store, pulling David at my side while Roger rode in the cart. Dad had gone to meet his friends at the bar. While Mom stood at the checkout, I saw that huge snowflakes had begun falling outside driven by a gusting wind. With her arms full of groceries, Mom made her way out to the car.

David, Roger, and I were in the back seat hoping the heater would warm up soon, when Dad slumped in the passenger side up front. Wind and cold and the smell of alcohol came in with him, and his eyes looked sad again.

Windshield wipers beating against the snow, Mom began to clutch the wheel as she drove slowly along the icy roads, our headlights cutting the winter night on the country lanes.

Dad's head was leaning against the side window, and I thought he was asleep. Suddenly, he heaved a sigh, and began to talk.

"I'm no good for you, Iola."

"Stop talking like that, Francis."

"It's true," he said, his voice thick with emotion. "I'm no good for anyone. No good at all."

Suddenly he reached for the handle and pushed the door open. Before Mom could react, he heaved himself out of the car.

Screaming, Mom braked. "Francis! Oh, my God!" She slammed the gearshift into park and jumped out. Frightened, I held David's hand. The baby began to cry. In that moment my family seemed to be coming apart.

I heard their voices outside the car. In a couple of minutes Mom helped Dad into his seat again. He was covered with snow but was apparently unhurt. She got in and, after calming herself, put the car in gear and continued navigating the wintry roads.

It was then, as I sat huddled in the dark backseat of our car, that the most unusual warmth came over me. Somehow, it was as if I were seeing two worlds at the same time.

There was the unhappy world all around me. And then, above and apart from all the hurts and disappointments of this life, there was God. In my mind's eye, I saw Him. Just for that moment He was more real, more solid and sure, than Mom or Dad or the boys or even me. As if a small drop of rare extract had touched my tongue, I think I tasted the eternal in an instant. And I heard the words that were in my small Bible: *You shall know the truth, and the truth shall set you free.*

Long after everyone was in bed that night I lay awake in my room thinking of what I had felt in the car on the way home. Had God revealed Himself to me? I never questioned it. I fell asleep at last, clinging to the sense that God was the only sure thing in my life, that if I held onto Him I would always be able to survive, no matter what happened to me.

It was exactly the thread of hope I would need.

Months later, after summer, Grandpa Paintner told Dad to take some time off between planting and haying. Mom's family often visited in Portland, Oregon, and she always wished we could go there. She talked about Portland as if it were the one place on earth where everything would be fine. Dad apparently saw this as a chance to do something especially kind and announced he was taking her there.

And so we packed off to Portland, where it seemed to rain every day. It was here that my family found its one bright moment.

Mom's brother Art, and his wife, Lillian, had come on the trip with us. Every night at supper Dad and Uncle Art talked about local companies that were hiring.

One day Dad went out on his own. When he returned, he was beaming. "Nabisco's hiring—and they took me on today," he announced at supper. "The pay is great. They want me to start as soon as possible."

Mom hesitated. "We're moving—just like that? What about the farm? What about our furniture?"

Daddy went to her side, slipped his arm around her waist, and drew her in tight. "We're not just moving. We're starting over." She relaxed a little in his arms.

Shortly, Mom returned to North Dakota by train to get Roger, whom they'd left at home with friends, and to pack some clothes and a few toys for shipment to Oregon. So our vacation became a turning point for my family—in many ways.

Right after Mom returned with Roger, my aunt was helping her lay shelf paper in the kitchen of the small home we'd rented. The boys were napping. I was arranging and rearranging cans on a lower shelf when I picked up my aunt's words.

"He hasn't had a drink since you left."

Mother brushed aside a wisp of hair. "Oh?" she said, sounding unconcerned.

"He's trying," my aunt persisted.

"I know," said Mom with a sigh. "It was the best thing to get him away from those old friends of his. Maybe being out here on his own with a wife and three kids will sober him up fast." She relaxed a little and chuckled.

"And you know," my aunt continued, "there's a wonderful church I think you'd like. Why don't you come with me this Sunday?" She paused and smiled. "Francis will like it, too."

That Sunday Dad was up early, shaved, and dressed in a suit. Whereas before he had gone to church to please Mom, from then on he was the one who eagerly hurried us into the car.

It was that first Sunday I remember most. Daddy had opened the church door for Mom, who had David by one hand and Roger in her other arm. I heard music inside. An usher greeted Dad with a handshake and a smile. "Nice looking family," the man offered.

Dad grinned. "Thanks. I think so, too."

As we walked inside, a few heads turned, taking note of us, the new family. Sitting at the far end of the pew from Dad, I wondered if my prayers had been answered. I still felt uneasy around him. But he was changing. I was beginning to think I could trust him.

$$=========\ 4\ =========$$

SHIRLEY:
Behind the Mask

As we adjusted to life in Portland, my father changed
startlingly. At least on the surface.

Leaving North Dakota *had* sobered him up, as Mom had
guessed. Suddenly, he was everybody's friend. If our new
pastor needed someone to drive a Sunday school bus, Dad
volunteered. When a snowstorm held us and our neigh-
bors housebound, Dad braved the drifts in his jeep to
bring them groceries.

Much as I liked this "new" Dad better, something did
not feel quite right. Though he spent a lot of time helping
other people, he rarely had a moment to toss a baseball
with David, or bounce Roger on his knee. Between Dad
and me, there was some great distance.

In the next couple of years I got to know other girls in
grade school and through our church. I always wondered
if their fathers acted like mine—if they were one way in
public and different at home. In church I watched other
fathers with their children. They seemed attentive, kind,

46

patient. When I started to daydream about growing up and getting married, I imagined myself with a loving husband who also loved God. Maybe even a minister.

But around Dad, Roger, David, and I felt increasingly uneasy. We never knew what might set him off. Like the Sunday morning after church when I tried to get his attention on a simple matter.

All through the sermon, Carol Maier, my best friend, was trying to mouth a silent message to me from across the church. We were both about eleven. She had become like a sister to me. Her friendship and the way her mother and father welcomed me into their home made me feel I belonged.

At the moment, though, I couldn't understand what she was trying to tell me.

Once more, in an exaggerated way that distorted her nose and mouth, Carol made her lips form the silent words: *Can you come to my house after church?*

I giggled. David and Roger stopped swinging their legs and looked at me. Dad had become an usher and, standing at the back of the church, he didn't notice the antics—but Mom was sitting next to me and she did. She squeezed my arm and gave me a severe look. Excited, I whispered Carol's request to her and got the standard response, "We'll have to ask your father."

Unfortunately, the moment our pastor said a final amen, Dad slipped out into the church foyer. All I could do was trail after him through the knots of people who lingered while the pianist continued to play.

By the time I reached him, he was already in conversation with two other ushers. I knew better than to interrupt him—but this was important.

I tugged at his coat sleeve. "Dad?"

"Not now, Shirley."

"Dad, please," I begged.

47

The other men were still talking. Dad pivoted suddenly and leaned down toward me, a flush of anger coloring his face. Between clenched teeth he growled in a low voice, "Leave me *alone*."

I stepped back, frightened. One of the other men must have seen the look on my face. "What's the matter, Shirley?" he asked.

Dad straightened up and smiled. His expression changed so quickly it was as if he had put on a mask. "It's always something with these kids," he laughed. "Now what did you want, Shirley?"

My lips trembled. But I did not want to cry in front of these men. Mother came up just then, with the boys in tow. She took up my case about going home with the Maiers. Breezily, Dad said it was fine.

During lunch at Carol's house, I was still hurting from my dad's harshness. Carl Maier, Carol's dad, apparently saw that I was picking at my lunch. He set his fork down and smiled at me. "Is something wrong?"

He had the kindest eyes I'd ever seen, and a cheerfulness that made the whole house seem warm. The food nearly stuck in my throat and again I fought the tears. "I'm okay."

He nodded and lunch went on—but I wasn't sure he was convinced. Carl Maier was sensitive and had a way of being on my level without being silly or childish. He made me feel like a young lady and not a kid. I dabbed my mouth with a napkin, wishing that my dad were like Carol's.

This gave me a twinge of guilt. Still, as Carol and I went off to her room to play, I could not help continuing to compare her dad with mine. Her father talked about God in a happy, casual way all the time. I was convinced that he must love God a lot. My dad had us in church almost every time the doors opened, but we never talked about

God at home or prayed or read the Bible, like Carol's family.

Carl Maier was gentle, too. He would often drape his arm on Carol's shoulder, like a friend. It was then I felt a longing. I thought, *Maybe that's what a family should be like.* Dad acted stiff and uncomfortable around me most of the time.

When Carol's father took me home later that afternoon, I had the strange feeling that I was returning to a house that was rotting around us—that the floor was going to give way beneath my feet at any moment.

As the months passed, Dad's mood swings got wider and more frequent, keeping us more and more off balance. He had left his job at Nabisco and become quite a successful hardware salesman, which often kept him away from home on business trips. In 1963, when I turned twelve, I noticed the change. Sometimes, when Dad came home from work in the evening, I smelled the familiar, sickening sweetness of liquor on his breath.

When he was in that condition, his fieriness was aimed at the boys. Mostly he continued to ignore me. Mom did, too, for that matter. It seemed to me as if she were building protective walls around herself. So, like me, the boys learned to stay out of Dad's way as they grew up. Hard as they tried, they didn't always succeed.

One Sunday afternoon that summer Mom and Dad had invited some friends from the church over for a barbecue. It was hot and all the adults were inside, except Dad who was grilling burgers over the charcoal fire. Roger and David were playing quietly at one end of the backyard when I came out with a plate for the meat. The boys began tussling over something, but I paid no attention.

"Are any of the hamburgers done?" I asked, holding out the plate.

Dad flipped one over with a spatula. "Not yet," he said absently. "I'll give 'em another minute."

David ran up just then, his arms wrapped around a toy. "I had it first," he announced loudly. Roger was hot on his heels. "Did not," he countered.

David tightened his grip. *"Did too."*

I opened my mouth to intervene when Dad's arm lashed out, catching David with a backhand slap that sent him sprawling on the grass. Roger stepped back, but not before a second backhand caught him on the ear.

Trembling, I dropped to my knees beside David. He held one hand to the red welt that was already rising on his cheek. Tears stood in his eyes and he glared at Dad. Roger was crying and holding his ear.

Then the back door opened and one of the men from church stepped out. "Anything I can do . . .?" He hesitated, surveying the situation.

Dad looked down at David and Roger, a sudden look of surprise on his face. "Now what are you boys up to?" He shook his head. I stood up and stared at him, disbelieving. How could he change so quickly?

He smiled at the man. "Thanks for the offer. Everything's under control out here—except these boys. Always roughhousing. You know how kids are."

Then he turned to the grill again. "Oh, gosh, Shirley. Hold that plate up here. Looks like these burgers are done."

Later, after we had eaten and the adults were conversing over coffee in the living room, I noticed that the man who had happened upon our scene in the backyard was watching me. There was a kindness about him that made my heart ache. Suddenly, I wanted to talk to him—to anyone. I wanted to say, "Can you see what's happening here? Can you help us?" A lump grew painfully tight in my throat and I turned my head so he would not see the tears. How I wanted this man to notice me—to feel sorry for me. When I looked back he had turned away. Apparently, he had not noticed me at all.

Shortly thereafter, the tension at home mysteriously eased. I had just turned thirteen and, suddenly, Dad began talking to me all the time. He seemed interested in talking to me about the boys from school and church and wanted to know what kind of attention they paid to me. I couldn't understand the abrupt change.

On a Saturday afternoon, I had slid potatoes in the oven to bake and reached for a cookbook to plan a stew for supper. Dad was somewhere in the house and Mom was out for the day. Because Dad was openly critical of Mom's housekeeping I'd begun to clean and organize things when she was not around, just to keep peace. Dad was a perfectionist and I thought that, if I could get the house just the way he wanted it, I might save Mom from his cutting remarks.

The radio was on that afternoon playing songs by a new group called the Beatles who, in 1964, were taking America by storm. I paid little attention. I took more notice when the announcer said it was three-thirty. The boys were supposed to be home. Mother hadn't asked where they were when she left, but I'd told them to be home by three o'clock. Where were they?

I was reaching for a skillet to brown the meat when I started: Dad was watching me from the kitchen doorway. He had come up so quietly.

He leaned against the door frame, his arms folded across his chest. His face was relaxed and he appeared to be in an unusually good mood. "You sure have turned into quite a young lady. It amazes me how much you look like your mother."

I smiled at the compliment. There was an indescribable

look in his eyes. I unwrapped the meat and threw the butcher paper in the garbage.

He sat down in a kitchen chair. "You know, I've been meaning to tell you something," he said. "Come on over here for a minute."

Curious, I wiped my hands on a towel and went to him. "What is it?" He continued to look at me, a half-smile on his face, and said nothing. "Dad?" I prompted again. "What is it?"

Nonchalantly, he took my arm and pulled me onto his lap. I smelled liquor and resisted. Suddenly his voice was peculiar. "You're not too big to sit on your daddy's lap, are you?"

"I've got to get supper—"

"Forget supper," he said, forcefully wrapping his arms around me. "Nobody's going to be home for a while—" His hands were moving all over me.

"*No,*" I cried.

I couldn't believe what was happening. I tried to wrestle away from him. He clenched my wrists tightly. It hurt and I screamed. Then he stood and half-carried me out of the kitchen and down the hall. When we reached my room, he pushed me inside, came in, and slammed the door.

A few minutes later the sudden noise of my brothers banging through the kitchen door saved me from more humiliation. Dad quickly rolled off the bed. I sat there crying, clutching at my shirt. He had torn two buttons off it. Moving to the bedroom door he stood still, listening. I heard Roger calling my name.

My father stared at me. He looked almost as shaken and upset as I. "Don't you ever tell anybody about this. Do you hear me?"

How I found the words, I don't know. My voice shook. "Don't *you* ever touch me like that again," I shot back.

The mask changed again. He bombarded me with

names—ugly, stupid, worthless. He said I was dirt. Then he opened the door and backed out, never taking his eyes off me. They were empty, lifeless, terrifying.

I glared at him. As if reading the challenge in my eyes he said, "And if you're thinking about telling someone—like your mother—don't bother. Who do you think she'd believe?"

Rage welled up in me, like nausea. I felt so trapped, so helpless.

"And if you don't think so, try it," he snickered. "You'll wind up in the street—like the trash you are." Then he quietly shut the door.

When he had gone my whole body trembled. I could not stand, but sat hugging my knees. My shoulders began to heave and I felt as though I were crumbling inside. Then I cried and cried.

In the weeks to come I was scared. Dad continued to force himself on me. Though he never forced me to have intercourse, the terror, the rough feel of his hands never left me day or night. He became more brutal with me. I knew he was sick. I became convinced that I must be sick, too. Otherwise, why would my own father be doing such a thing to me? I must be trash, just as he said.

For more than two years, he forced this horrible double life on me. Mentally, I began to suffer. I'd always been an A student. My grades dropped. At first, my mother questioned me about it. But she was obviously suffering emotionally, too, from Dad's up-and-down personality.

There was a boy in our church youth group who liked me—Ron. We sang in the choir together, and I began to like him, too. But when he tried to hold my hand or be affectionate I felt horrible and cheap.

How I longed for someone to talk to in those lonely years. But who? Carol was my best friend. But her family was so good, clean, and wholesome. How could I tell her about such a sick thing? All I longed to do was escape from it—to escape from myself.

As if the mounting pressure at home were not bad enough, during that time it seemed the whole West Coast began to come unglued. From southern California, the hippie movement spread up to the Northwest. Even in Portland barefooted, long-haired "flower children" were all over the streets and sleeping in parks. They brought with them little plastic bags of marijuana cigarettes and "tabs" of L.S.D.

I was shocked when I learned that even some Christian kids I knew were going to pot parties. One or two girls began to talk about sleeping with their boyfriends.

With all this peer pressure I wondered why I was struggling so hard to keep "straight," which was suddenly a derogatory term for anyone who *didn't* use dope or sleep around. A couple of boys besides Ron were asking me to go out with them. They were good-looking and popular. I'd turned them down because of their reputation. But my own father had already made me feel like a tramp. Why not just go all the way and become one?

I began to feel I was being pushed to the edge. I felt hated and useless—and desperately wanted to feel loved and worthwhile in someone's eyes.

One afternoon in September, when I was fifteen, I got home from school before Roger and David. Mother was not there. Just fifteen minutes later, to my horror, Dad walked in.

He had a wild look on his face. He forced me down the hall and into my room. When I fought him off he doubled his fists. I shielded my face. He pushed me on the bed, but instead of coming after me, he went out and I heard him go to his room. I wanted to run but was terrified he would catch me in the hallway.

When he came back into my room again, he was holding a pistol. Then he raised it, aiming at my head. Slowly, a step at a time, he walked toward me. "I'm going to kill you."

"Stop it," I begged him, crawling backward on the bed. *"Please!"*

"All of this is your fault—isn't it, Shirley?"

"Don't—"

"You wanted me to do this to you. Didn't you?"

"You're sick," I shouted.

He grinned. "Oh yeah? Well, you're going to turn out just like me."

"I'm not!"

Then, suddenly, the hardness in his face drained. The pistol wavered. My breathing was shallow and I thought I was going to vomit.

All at once, he raised the pistol to his own head. "I'm so terrible. Shirley—please forgive me. I'm so lousy." On and on he went, pathetically.

I felt confused—even sorry for him. But I just wanted him to go away.

Finally his shoulders sagged. He turned and walked out.

For weeks after it was as if two voices were arguing in my head.

One voice said, *Where is God now that you need Him? Where was He when you were a little girl and needed a loving father instead of an alcoholic?* And I would think, *What's the point of trying anymore? If I'm just trash, why don't I just go out and smoke dope and drink and sleep around like a lot of other kids?*

But another thought would vie. I pictured Carol Maier and her family sitting together in church. Even in a congregation full of good people, they stood out. How I wanted a family like that one day—a family based on truth and not lies.

Then, from somewhere at the back of my thoughts, the other voice would speak. *The truth shall set you free.*

Somehow I became aware I was the one who had the power to choose between truth and a lie, between life and death. I could blame God, quit the church, throw away my Bible. I could live an immoral life, always searching for love. Or . . .

Or I could do something to prevent my father's ugly prediction from coming true. I could tell the truth and be set free. Even if it killed me.

My chance came early in December when my grade report came home from school. This time, Mom confronted me. "Something's going on with you. Would you mind telling me why your marks have dropped?"

My stomach hurt suddenly. Why was it so hard to tell the truth? Maybe a lie would shield us all from the pain. But I took a deep breath. And the truth came out. All of it.

Mother watched me, unblinking, until I was silent. I waited for her to slap me, to call me a liar. Instead, she began to sob.

When Dad came home, there was a tremendous fight. Screaming. Bitter, hate-filled words. Roger and David had come in from school and we sat unmoving in the living room. Though David and Roger were nearly teenagers by then, their wide, frightened eyes made them look like little boys. I wanted to hug them but could not budge as the shouting rose. Then all was silent.

Strangely, months passed, and a fragile atmosphere held us. A year later the final, rotting plank fell through.

A week before Christmas, when I was sixteen, Mom, the boys, and I were out when Daddy left home. We came in to find his closet empty. He had taken all of our money.

That night in the darkness, I lay motionless in bed. Sleet tapped against my window. There would be no presents, no Christmas at our house. There was almost no money for food. I felt cold and had to fight off waves of self-pity.

Silently, I prayed. *Father, my dad is gone. My family has fallen apart. I'm a Christian. Why is all of this happening?*

Now I saw that the way I had chosen—the way of truth—was not an easy road. But I knew that living a lie, as my father had for so many years, eventually brought destruction. I had to cling to the fact that Mom's pain, and Roger's and David's and my own, resulted from choices Dad had made long ago. My telling the truth only short-circuited his life of lies.

I could not sleep that night. Not right away. The sleet turned to large flakes of snow that brushed the window. And all I could think was the fact that, despite the pain, I had stumbled across a life-governing principle.

Clearly, the path I would choose to walk from now on was up to me. Maybe our lives were going to be difficult, but as long as I held onto the truth, I would never have to be a victim again.

5

TERRY:
Mountains of Difficulty

A s much as I'd shocked my family that Sunday night in October, when I'd left my drunken friends to kneel at the altar of Dad's church, an even bigger surprise came that night at home.

"I'm not going back to the university on Monday," I'd told Dad resolutely. "I want you to get me into Bible school."

We were standing in the kitchen of the parsonage—the same room where Dad had knocked me down twice for defying his authority. Mother's eyes widened. Dad's eyes rimmed with tears, but he didn't cry. "What did you just say?"

"I want to preach. Can you get me into Bible school next week?" I'm sure Mom and Dad thought this was characteristic of my hot-and-cold personality. Nevertheless, the very next morning, Dad got on the phone. Even though we were weeks into the semester, I was accepted.

Eager though I was, Bible school turned out to be a

battleground. I went to a school in Saskatoon first, only to find the atmosphere confining. The only thing that kept me going was becoming best friends with Brian Stiller, who sang with me in a gospel quartet.

In fact, it was my renewed love of gospel music that caused me to transfer to Northwest Bible College in Edmonton. Primarily, I had come to join the school's new quartet, which did faster music, like the Blackwoods. Traveling with the group on weekends, I preached at small churches, which gave me much-needed confidence.

After graduation in 1963 I was troubled. Several churches had offered me a pulpit, even though I was yet to be formally ordained, but I felt restless. I stayed in Edmonton for the next six months, working in a hardware store and praying for clear direction. None came. By November, I thought a growing sense of being "lost" would crush me.

One Wednesday evening, after the midweek service in a church I was attending, I continued to kneel at the altar rail, praying. Out came my frustration, the hungry feeling that I had to find God's will and *do* it.

As I prayed, a Scripture circled through my head. "Woe is me, for I am undone. . . . " Over and over, I prayed the words of Isaiah. Then the Lord's question resounded within: "Whom shall I send? And who will go for us?"

I nearly shouted out, "Here am I! Send me!" Strangely, I felt that the words weren't coming from *me*, but that God's Spirit was praying them *through* me.

When I stepped out into the cool November air that night, I wondered what it all meant. Unexpectedly, a name came to mind: *Dennis Bjorgan.* How curious. I'd lost track of Dennis years before after moving from Prince Albert where we'd been "bad boys" together. Even more strange was the next thought: *You and Dennis are going to be in ministry together.* I shook my head.

The next day, to my complete shock, a letter showed up

in my mailbox, and neatly penned above the return address was the name Dennis Bjorgan.

I tore into it and pulled out the single sheet of paper. Scanning the page, my shock turned to amazement. Dennis had written, "I can't escape the conviction that you and I are to form an evangelistic team and go on the road. Do you sing or play an instrument?"

Forever after, I had a hard time relating the experience to others. Who would believe such a farfetched story? Dennis and I formed a gospel duet—like a Christian Everly brothers. Our idea was to reach young people with the new, upbeat style of music—Dennis on guitar, me on bass—backed by a solid call to commitment to Jesus Christ.

For all of 1964 and into the early months of 1965, we traveled and preached all over Canada's backwoods where, as Dennis jokingly put it, we played to "crowds of four," before graduating to larger rallies in the eastern cities. We saw hundreds coming to Christ—heady stuff for two twenty-one-year-old men. We even made contact with a pastor in South Africa and were considering a tour later in the fall.

On an April morning, back in Edmonton, I made my way to the Central Tabernacle where ordination services were about to begin. The air was clear and there was something curious—special—about this day. My mind raced ahead, though. I felt I was on the threshold of that worldwide mission I'd been promised.

Quickening my pace I stepped inside the tabernacle just as the school president began the invocation. I sat among the other graduates, impatient for the speeches to be over. Finally, as the service closed, we were invited to come forward to be prayed for by the older pastors of our denomination. It seemed like a formality—and, frankly, I was ready to leave.

With the others, however, I walked to the front and

knelt, knitting my fingers together to keep them from drumming the wooden altar rail. I wanted to get back on the road with Dennis.

One by one, men from the audience came down the aisle. One stood behind the guy who was kneeling beside me. I heard him whisper a prayer of blessing over this other young pastor-to-be.

My knees were beginning to hurt. I wished someone would hurry up and pray for me.

Still I waited. Twenty minutes passed. Thirty. The crowd at the altar thinned. As people in the congregation finished praying they, too, got up and left the tabernacle. The place was getting empty.

Now my back ached. I felt warm around the collar and fidgety. Closing my eyes, I prayed silently, *Lord, someone must have a word to encourage me.*

When I opened my eyes a few minutes later, I didn't see anyone left in the whole sanctuary. No one had come for me!

Embarrassed, I started to get up—but a movement near the back of the sanctuary stopped me. A man with silver-gray hair, a pastor I had known, was making his way toward me.

When he reached my side, he placed his hand on my shoulder. "Young man, God has a very unusual, world-wide ministry for you. I think you already know this. I want to encourage you to follow that call. But," he paused, as if considering, "you are going to face *mountains* of difficulty. I see them rising high—but I also see the Holy Spirit moving before you. Don't give in to fear. God will open the way."

As I walked out of the tabernacle that day, I was amazed and delighted: His words echoed Dwight McLaughlin's prayer of six years before, which I'd all but forgotten.

For the rest of that summer, the old pastor's message

weighed on me: *mountains of difficulty*. Who wanted to hear that? I finally shelved it in favor of getting on with the business at hand.

Five months later, in September 1965, Dennis and I headed for South Africa on a steamship loaded with lumber from Newfoundland. Arriving in Cape Town Harbor I got my first glimpse of Table Mountain, gray and looming in the clouds.

Our one contact there opened the way to other churches, so for a full year we slept in strange beds, ate unusual new foods, and were in constant search of a mailbox for Dennis' letters home to his girlfriend. Most important was the personal growth. If my bass playing improved only slightly, I got more confident preaching. We found ourselves playing before thousands at a time. Everything fell into place so easily I had to chuckle. *Mountains of difficulty?* I was having a ball.

After ten months Dennis made the big announcement. He was tired of licking stamps. "I'm in love, Terry. And I'm going home to get married."

Upon returning to Canada in the summer of 1966, Dennis got engaged and the team broke up. I went to my family's current home in Medicine Hat to plan my next move. Now I had Bible school, my "shingle" from ordination, *and* experience. I felt excited, ready for a bigger ministry.

In Medicine Hat I was in for a big letdown.

My first morning at home, Dad dropped the question he'd evidently tucked in his head the moment he knew I was coming. Over breakfast, he said, "It sure would be nice to have an associate pastor to work with me this summer." He grinned. "What do you say, Terry?"

Strong feelings for this man I admired so much swelled in my chest. I hardly hesitated. "Yes, Dad," I said. "I'd like that a lot."

And so, for one of the first times in my life, my dad and

I would be working together, on the same team, for the short time I planned to be in Medicine Hat.

One immediate problem was money. The Africa trip was a faith venture. Dennis and I had lived day-to-day, meal-to-meal, and came home with just a jingle of change in our pockets. The solution came through one of the church elders, a man named Ed Stahl.

The first time I met Ed it was like shaking hands with quiet lightning. In Hatton, fifty miles from Medicine Hat, he owned thirteen square miles of land, where he ran five hundred Herefords. In his fifties and graying slightly, there was nevertheless a bright youthfulness about him and a quality I could not put my finger on. I was glad when he asked me to work for him. As part of the agreement, I could live in a small house on his property.

So rather than touring the world, I spent the rest of 1966 as a country pastor and farm hand—with one eye always set beyond Medicine Hat, beyond Canada. I preached many Sundays in Dad's church; I dedicated chubby-legged babies, posing for pictures on the church steps with proud young parents; I whispered comforting words at graveside services. Weekdays, I worked the farm with my brother Clayton, whom Ed also hired, throwing seventy-five-pound hay bales onto a wagon till our backs ached. Sometimes, in a burst of craziness, Clayton and I chased coyotes across the open land in a battered pickup truck. Early mornings I read Scripture, alone on the front porch of the tenant house, the cool airflows lifting the scent of dew on the fields.

But where was my dream? I was getting edgy, wanting to take a new, bigger musical group on the road.

Throughout the fall I talked to people in the church about my idea. Whenever I tried to explain my dream of a contemporary gospel team I met with blank looks. Once a man even shrugged and said, "A group like that'll never make a go in Canada."

A damp, stifled feeling draped itself over me that winter.

One day, early in spring 1967, I decided to discuss my discouragement with Ed. In the months I'd worked for him, he had listened to my ideas about a new kind of music ministry, and had gained my respect. Not only was he a fine cattle breeder, but he could not speak the name Jesus without his eyes misting. He often walked the fields, lost in prayer. His apparent communion with God was often startling.

The day I wanted to talk with Ed, he drove me out to a certain field in his pickup truck. "I asked the Lord to show me a new well site," he explained, as we got out.

That God would direct him to water hidden in the rock strata beneath the earth was as matter-of-fact to Ed as branding a Hereford. Tramping along at his side through the Russian wild rye grass, I had to smile: In jeans and a faded workshirt he looked anything but the prophet.

"It's about the group," I began. Ed scanned the horizon and I wondered if he heard me. "Young people are listening to the Beatles and the Rolling Stones. I know we can reach them with a new music for Jesus. But things just aren't going right."

Ed had stopped at the top of a grassy knoll. I pressed him. "What do you think?"

"I think this is it," he smiled.

"What?"

"This is where we drill the new well," Ed went on calmly. Glancing across the fields I could see no apparent fault lines that distinguished the site at all. Then he turned and walked back to the pickup. "Let's set some dynamite."

Feeling hurt that he'd ignored me, I watched as Ed showed me how to set the charge. As far as I could tell this was no place to blast a well. Then we dropped back behind some trees. Even with fingers stuffed in my ears, I jumped when the roar of dynamite blew large rocks high in the air.

When we examined the crater it was bone dry. "Huh," Ed sniffed. "Guess this one'll take two charges." Was he still holding onto the idea that God had told him there was water here? I bit my tongue.

We set off another charge.

This time when we reached the edge of the hole, a small trickle of water was collecting in a little circle of mud at the bottom. But still no gusher. "Get a shovel from the truck, Terry," Ed directed.

Half-grudgingly, I obeyed.

As I scraped away the dirt, however, the trickle of water increased as if I were opening a tap. In a few minutes, my boots and socks were wet. Climbing out, I continued to shovel until the water had risen almost to the top of the hole.

Looking satisfied, Ed motioned for me to get into the truck. "I'll let it run awhile and we can cap it later," he said, revving the engine. I was speechless.

"How did you know where to blast?" I plied him.

"The same way that you're going to know God's plan for you," he came back. So he hadn't been ignoring me!

"The hidden things are all known to God," he went on. "Sometimes He hides a dream in our hearts—an unusual, challenging dream like the one He's given you. Don't be afraid of big dreams, Terry. That's what God has for you. But don't forget that He may use difficulties and challenges to toughen you along the way. The tough times get us ready for even bigger things."

He paused, as if he were going to say something but thought better of it. "Just learn to listen. And don't run out ahead of God."

After that day, Ed's uncanny accuracy in blasting the

well made me think twice about his counsel. I was hooked on all his talk about dreaming the big dreams of God. If only he hadn't mentioned *difficulties!* Why did that word have to keep cropping up? And I wondered what he'd meant to tell me when he stopped himself. Still, it was Ed's positive spirit that I focused on. That alone kept me going through the summer.

In August I heard that the American evangelist Oral Roberts would be holding a series of meetings in the Edmonton arena the following month. I'd listened to a couple of his tapes on an old reel-to-reel recorder and was amazed at his oratory. Naturally, I was also curious about his healing ministry.

On a Friday in September I drove the eight-hour, 350-mile trip back to Edmonton arriving just before the evening service. Inside, the arena was alive with excitement.

One thing especially caught my attention. On the platform, before Roberts spoke, a young musician was playing an organ the best I'd ever heard, the kind of up-tempo gospel music I could get into. His name, according to the program, was Larry Dalton.

When Oral Roberts was introduced, I was taken by this handsome man with the neatly combed hair and Midwestern accent. He introduced his sermon topic, Saul on the Damascus road, and I was hooked immediately. Throughout the evening he directed Saul's question at us: "Lord, what will You have me to do?" It felt like an arrow straight to my heart.

He also spoke about his belief that our generation would carry the Gospel to the whole world. I was captivated by Roberts' expansive thinking. When he finished he left me with a renewed hunger to be part of God's great evangelistic plan for the world.

When the meeting closed I tried to ease my way through the crowds jamming the aisles and lobby. I had to be back in Medicine Hat on Saturday and wanted to get started on the all-night drive home. I was charged by Roberts' bold challenge and ready to go home and try to get my singing group fired up. At least that was my intent.

Near the lobby doors were several tables with stacks of brochures. Even though I was in a hurry, I stopped at one and surveyed the piles. There was a pamphlet about Oral Roberts University, founded two years before in Tulsa, Oklahoma. On the front was a picture of the campus's tall, modernistic prayer tower. Impressive. The pamphlet said the school's purpose was to prepare Christian young people for a far greater ministry than Roberts would ever have himself.

Now that's some vision, I mused.

Tucking the pamphlet into my jacket pocket I started out the door to the parking lot. A thought took me unawares: *You are going to go to Oral Roberts University.*

I walked across the lot to my car fending off the crazy notion. I'd already been to Bible school, preached hundreds of times, traveled through Canada and even in Africa. How could I possibly think of going to a university now?

But as I drove the dark highways home the thought about going to Oral Roberts University kept buzzing my head like a pesky fly. Hours later, when I drove up the road to Ed Stahl's farm, dawn was pouring a golden light on the autumn hills with their red-gold poplars. And I was unhappy.

Lord, I prayed, *I want to go out on the road. You know I'm dying to preach. I don't want to go to school again.* Besides that, I had no money. And Tulsa sounded like the end of the world.

One week passed. Two weeks. And that inner direction would not leave me. I agonized.

On a clear October morning Ed and I drove a pickup truck full of new fence posts into the fields to set up a new line. We worked through the morning, gouging holes in the moist earth, backhanding sweat off our brows as the sun grew warmer toward noon. Just before lunch I thought I should mention the persistent idea about ORU to someone. Ed was a man whose judgment I trusted. And he was practical.

He'd just hoisted another post out of the pickup and was handing it to me when I said, "You know, Ed, I've had this crazy thought for a month. I'm convinced God wants me to go to Oral Roberts University. I don't know how I'm going to do it, because—"

The fence post fell with a thud, just missing my foot.

"Get in the truck," Ed ordered, smiling.

"Are you all right?"

"Fine. Just get in."

We left our digging tools and posts and drove across the field. A few minutes later Ed slowed and stopped on a small knoll. "This is the spot."

We got out of the truck. All was quiet except for the slight wind that cut through my jacket. There Ed told me what he'd hesitated to tell me before. Even before I went to hear Oral Roberts, Ed said he had been walking across this field, praying as he usually did when he was alone on the land. "And I received a message from the Lord, Terry."

"He spoke to you?"

Ed looked at me with a level gaze. "I know some Christians get nervous when you talk about things like this. But on this spot I heard the voice of an angel: 'Terry is going to go to Oral Roberts University.'

"*And*," he added when I opened my mouth to protest, "He told me that I am to pay your way. I knew I wasn't to tell you any of this until the Lord got through to you Himself."

Angels? Well, maybe that was just Ed's way of putting it. But if the confirmation that I was to go to ORU had come from anyone other than Ed Stahl I might have questioned it. That evening I wrote a letter to the university asking for an application.

More important, as I awaited a reply from Tulsa, I thought I saw the vague outlines of what God was teaching me about this impossible vision that had a grip on me.

Perhaps the old pastor who had prayed for me at my ordination was right and there were "mountains of difficulty" to overcome on the way. Maybe I was just topping my first one. I'd felt so stifled when other Christians shook their heads at the idea of a musical group touring the world with the good news of the Gospel. I'd been listening to people say it wouldn't work, somehow wanting their approval. Maybe the mountain I'd faced was their unbelief and its dampening effect.

What had helped me overcome that dour thinking was Ed Stahl's belief in following God's dream—even if it meant taking an illogical side trip like going back to school.

Just after Christmas, I learned that I was accepted for ORU's spring semester. The first week of January I said goodbye to Ed—and to my family. Lois had recently been married and I had just enough time to visit her and her husband, Lorne. When Mom, Dad, and Clayton drove me to the airport in Calgary we all seemed to sense that this was a different kind of departure, that "home" for me would be elsewhere from now on.

As the flight to Tulsa took off, I kept reminding myself of Ed's final counsel: *You need to leave here, Terry. Trust His Spirit. There are no sidetracks in God.*

I clung to those words because I still had no earthly desire to go to ORU and did not see how this fit into my plans for a traveling gospel music team. Reluctant as I was to admit it, though, I had the undeniable feeling of standing on the threshold of a new challenge that would demand my all.

6

TERRY:
Surprise Visit

The January wind whipped snow-devils across the campus of Oral Roberts University as I made my way to the semester's opening chapel service. Stamping the slush from my feet, I went inside. The chapel hummed with the sound of old friends greeting one another after the winter holidays.

Quickly I found a seat. Four months before, in Edmonton, I'd seen Roberts as a "miracle man," a superstar passing through my skyway. Now I was trusting that something he and his school had to offer me was going to affect my life's path.

President Roberts welcomed us and then began to talk about the purpose for his founding the university.

"I heard the Lord telling me," he began, " 'You are going to raise up your students to hear My voice, to go where My light is dim and My voice is heard small. Their work will exceed yours.' "

I listened eagerly to the rest of his talk. The thought of

70

going where God's light was dim captivated me. That's what I wanted to do.

In the days following that inspiring message, however, I felt the cold dreariness of the Oklahoma winter. And I woke up to the realities of sharing a dorm with younger guys just out of high school while I was almost twenty-five! To boot, I had entered as a junior and, to complete academic requirements, had been tossed into a third-year French course where no English was spoken.

Midway through January, I found myself trudging across the sleet-swept campus on a gray morning. Under one arm was my French book and in my head a voice whispered with an accusing bite: *You were stupid to come here.*

The accusation stung like the tiny pellets of ice that whipped my face.

My classes that day and in the weeks following were sheer misery. Halfheartedly, I accepted an invitation and led the song service in morning chapel. Someone had heard that I'd held a musical devotion in our dorm and they needed a fill-in. Not for a moment did I suspect anything would come of it.

By the first week of March as we neared mid-terms I was ready to quit. My grades were fine (even in French), but my heart was champing to be out on the road again.

One night, alone in my room, I began to pray. I felt I was right back where I was the night five years before when I'd prayed, "Here am I, send me." Only now I prayed, "Here am I—get me out!" I hated wasting time, I told God, when I could be out serving Him. Around four A.M., I fell heavily into bed.

When the alarm rang, just a few hours later, I had to make myself get up and face the day. Soon I grabbed my books and was out the door. In the dorm lobby was a message for me: "Please see Ron Smith immediately."

Hurrying along the sidewalks, I made my way to Ron

Smith's office. He was Oral Roberts' crusade director. What could he possibly want with me?

In a few minutes I was standing in Smith's office. He came right to the point.

"Terry, Oral's songleader has resigned and we're right in the middle of a busy tour schedule. I understand that you've traveled, and I've heard you in chapel. I think you're the man to travel with Oral."

A bomb could not have shaken me more. Oral Roberts didn't know me from a bar of soap. Yet, right after telling God I was ready to quit, He was honoring me with a position on Roberts' team.

When I left Smith's office, I went straight to Gene Eland, the head of the music department. Dennis Bjorgan had taught me how to play bass guitar and I wanted to audition for The Collegians, a group of forty-two students that would perform in the overseas crusades that summer. The fact that The Collegians performed intricate stage music and I could not even read music didn't stop me for a moment. I practiced every free minute until my thumb blistered—and got a spot with the group.

The rest of that semester I fell into a frenzied schedule. Early mornings I locked myself in a practice room, sheet music and bass guitar in hand. Between classes I studied and practiced with The Collegians. Weekends, I hopped a plane headed for the next crusade. I became the group's student minister, which meant leading devotions, some minor counseling, and preaching occasionally. I never anticipated, as summer approached, that my life was about to be radically altered.

On a June morning, The Collegians were bused to the airport to begin a tour of nine countries in Europe, Scandinavia, and the Middle East with Oral. As we filed up the narrow stairs to the plane I hoped to finagle a seat near a new friend. Her name was Jan D'Arpa.

I'd "noticed" Jan on the spring weekend bus trips. She was an excellent soloist, with a sultry alto voice. She was pretty and slender with dark hair, high cheekbones, and an olive complexion. Warmth and life and enthusiasm lit her eyes, especially when she sang. During the long hours on the highway I'd discovered in Jan a deeply sincere Christian who loved God and His work.

As we slipped into our seats on the plane, however, Jan chose to sit with some girlfriends. That would make the conquest all the more fun.

Our first stop was England. Oral Roberts preached and we performed. And for me, something important was happening inwardly.

British young people were tightly in the grip of the rock music craze. The Stones, the Beatles, the Byrds, Petula Clark, and a raft of others were churning out international hits. Teenagers in bell-bottoms and bright paisley prints even turned up at our concerts—though our sound could hardly be called rock. I was impressed all over again that music was becoming an "international language" among young people.

And I had the growing awareness that this tour was the schooling for which I'd been sent to ORU. Working in a large group was much tougher, of course, than living out of a suitcase with Dennis. Mentally, I made notes.

After a short series of concerts, we wound up in London for a weekend off.

On the first morning, I wanted to see downtown London—as much of it as I could pack in on such a short stay—and pick up a postcard for the folks in Medicine Hat. Others decided to visit the British Museum or certain galleries. As teams of two and three collected and went off together I was suddenly faced with a delightful prospect: Jan and I were left in the lobby together!

That day became a blur of walking and talking. Together,

we sauntered beneath the carved stone arches of Westminster Abbey, craned our necks at the lofted statue of Lord Nelson in Trafalgar Square and visited Buckingham Palace. After, I wanted to catch a double-decker bus to Piccadilly.

With mock sternness, Jan stopped me. "First, we eat lunch. I'm starving! Where do you get all your energy, Terry?"

Looking at my watch, my face went red. I'd been dragging her around London for hours. "Oh, Jan, I'm sorry—" I faltered.

"I'm not complaining," she replied, a spark dancing in her eyes.

We moved up the sidewalk and our fingers brushed. An ignition key turned in my chest. I slid my hand into hers. Our fingers knitted.

I would never clearly remember what we talked about that afternoon because something beyond words passed between us.

When the tour moved on to continental Europe, Jan and I were never far apart. Oral had gone on to Kenya and would rejoin us in the Middle East at the end of our travels. Now it was my job to perform with The Collegians and to preach in churches large and small as we moved slowly northward. Midway through the summer we reached Scandinavia, performing in Norway, Denmark, Sweden, and, lastly, Finland. Then we were to move south again and on to Israel.

We performed in Salem Church in Helsinki and the charm of that old port city on the Baltic Sea touched me. Then we learned that there was a cancellation, allowing for a three-day break in our schedule. I thought perhaps Jan and I could enjoy some romantic wharf-side restaurants together.

But someone checked with a travel agency and returned

with the news that we could book tickets on a ferry that crossed the Baltic's eastern spur to Estonia. With our student visas we could make a brief "tourist" visit to the U.S.S.R.

And suddenly, there was that tingle—the one I used to get when I sensed danger! I hadn't felt that since I was a crazy kid blowing up outhouses in Canada. I couldn't wait.

Very early on Sunday morning, we trooped down to the docks and boarded. The sea and sunless sky blended in a steel gray at the horizon. Gulls called, and the smell of salt spray and diesel exhaust from the ship's engine met us as the ferry slipped its mooring. Standing at the rail, I looked at Jan and the other girls, all wrapped in sweaters against the chill air. The guys, who were usually clowning, were silent.

In several hours we saw the skyline of Estonia's ancient port city, Tallinn. A pale sun colored the haze with gold as the ferry churned into the harbor. Our mood had eased a little.

When we got to the dock in Tallinn, however, I began to feel the enormity of what we were doing. Inside the port station, guards silently herded us into several lines. One by one, we stepped up to the passport window, which was something like a small booth open on two sides.

When I stepped inside, I was surprised. The back and ceiling of the "booth" were really mirrors. Nervously, I slid my passport through the bars. At first, the young man behind the counter did not even look up.

"Good morning," I ventured.

He looked up, not at me, but at the mirror overhead. I began to feel like a specimen under a microscope.

I tried again. "Do you speak English?"

Now his eyes met mine with a look of pure disdain. Nervously, I cleared my throat. His eyes never left me. I wanted to squirm. Why did those eyes make me feel so guilty?

After a minute or more he shoved the passport into my hand and looked away. If he was trying to make a point— that we were being watched—he'd scored with me.

We were assigned an official Intourist guide who would stay with us in our assigned hotel. He was a rail-thin man of about forty-five. During the bus ride to the hotel he lit one cigarette after another.

"For your safety," he said, with a heavy accent and the sterility of a tape-recorded message, "you will leave your passports at the registration desk."

There was an uneasy shifting among the students but I nodded at him. Jan caught my eye and I winked to give her assurance.

At the hotel we were directed to leave our suitcases in our rooms. We would be escorted to a church to see "freedom of religion in the U.S.S.R." Our guide told us he'd selected Oleviste Baptist Church at the center of town, an old church built by Lutherans in the Middle Ages.

Once our things were safely stowed in our rooms we were led outside. Walking along the busy sidewalks we got our first good look at Tallinn.

Cobbled streets ran crookedly between shops and houses of hewn beams and mortar. We passed open-air *kiosks* where old ladies in bright kerchiefs sold fish, vegetables, black bread. Flowers were everywhere. On one street corner, as we waited for the light to change, a pretty blonde girl was selling newspaper cones full of yellow and white daisies.

I smiled at her, thinking I would buy some for Jan after church. For just an instant the girl's eyes darted toward mine. Then she dropped her gaze to the sidewalk.

In fact everyone we passed exchanged hasty glances with us, only to look away quickly. Forever after I would think of this as "the country of the eyes." What was hidden in the hearts of these people that a look might betray?

Turning one more corner I was amazed to see Oleviste Church, a soaring stone structure, and the huge crowd jamming the street around it. Quiet, orderly, the group had gathered on the church steps, apparently unable to get inside.

"You see," said our escort, "the churches are full every Sunday. Everyone who wishes to do so may worship."

His words surprised me. I had not expected public shows of faith to be allowed in the Soviet Union.

Then I saw them. Uniformed policemen with machine guns rimmed the crowd. I was about to ask the obvious question but our companion spoke up again.

"Inside, your group will sit in a section set up just for you."

One of the guys called out, "Can't we meet some of the people?"

"I regret that it is not possible," said our escort pleasantly.

"Why not?" The question was too sharp.

"Soviet law does not allow for foreign guests to make religious statements," he replied. "To visit here is enough—yes?"

I jumped in. "Yes. Please take us in."

Inside, the church was packed. As our escort led us down the long aisle every head turned and a murmur rose. We were led up front where we were seated. Some thirty feet divided us from the mass of upturned faces. Women in colorfully printed *babushkas* and men in drab jackets stared at us somberly as if across an invisible barrier. I noticed there were few young people.

The moment we were seated the service began. Everything—the Scripture readings, the hymns, and the sermon—was in Estonian. All we could do was to stare at the silent worshipers who paid no attention to the service, but stared back at us. The empty floor between us seemed like a no-man's-land.

When the pastor finished his sermon there was a moment's lull. All was silent. Then, faintly, a melody rose. Heads turned toward one old woman, her face seamed with wrinkles, who was singing in a frail voice.

Hesitantly, others joined her—I could not quite catch the song. Then I knew it!

Some in our group had joined in English:

On a hill far away
stood an old rugged cross
the emblem of suffering and shame . . .

The pastor clutched his pulpit, as if he might pass out. I had joined in, too, tears starting down my face.

And I love that old cross
where the dearest and best
For a world of lost sinners was slain.

When we finished the pastor closed the service as quickly as propriety would allow. Then we were hurried out between the rows of worshipers, between the crowds in the street, which the police parted to let us through. Our escort was tight-lipped.

Returning to my hotel room, I was seething. That transcendant moment in the church had done something inside me. Pacing back and forth, I saw faces in my mind—the old woman courageously offering her love song to Jesus in Estonian, the crowd in the street who hoped to catch even the echoes of worship, the pretty flower seller who could not brave a look at me.

For the first time in my life I was feeling the oppressive nature of the Soviet system. Tourists, churches—everything was claustrophobically monitored by the state.

I was still feeling that frustration the next evening when there was a knock at my hotel room door. Dale Anderson and Bo Melin, two Collegians, came in. By the looks on their faces I knew something was up.

"There was a guy hanging around in the lobby a little while ago," Dale explained. "We didn't realize he was watching us but suddenly he came up and wanted to talk."

"Talk?" This didn't sound good.

Bo jumped in. "He said he's a *believer*. They're having a secret meeting tonight. He asked if a couple of us would meet him downstairs in one hour."

Glancing out the window I could see it was getting dark. I knew it was crucial, for the safety of the whole team and the reputation of the ministry we represented, that we not mess up. And how would we be able to slip by our chain-smoking escort?

But the daring of it lured me. "Let's go," I said.

An hour later, at the appointed time, Dale, Bo, and I sauntered into the lobby. The desk clerk was shuffling papers and didn't look up. No one was in sight.

Casually, we stepped outside. Streetlights cast deep shadows along the silent sidewalk. At once a large figure emerged from a dark corner and stepped to our side.

"This is the guy," Dale whispered, shaking hands. "His name is Andrus."

An imposing man, Andrus had black hair and a thick beard. In the dim light, he appeared to be in his early 20s. I offered my hand. "Hi, my name is—"

His finger flew to his lips. Carefully, he gestured at something behind him. Or rather some*one*. Looking beyond him, I saw another figure.

On the street corner stood a man in a trenchcoat with a

hat pulled low over his eyes, the glowing stub of a cigarette between his lips. The crazy thing was that he was watching us through dark glasses. In another setting it might have seemed silly, but this was the Soviet Union and we were being watched.

"Follow me," Andrus ordered. "Do what I do."

We followed him to the far corner and, at a distance, so did our spy. At the corner, Andrus leaned against a post and did not even look at us. In almost five minutes a bus pulled up. Two old women with shopping bags lumbered out the front door, while the back door through which passengers entered stood open before us.

"Wait," Andrus whispered. Our trenchcoated friend was pretending to study something in a darkened shop window not fifty feet away.

In another few seconds the bus engine revved and, just as the doors were about to close, Andrus said, "Now!"

We jumped, barely squeezing through the back door as the bus rolled forward. Through the back window I watched our spy lose his cigarette as he chased after us.

In two blocks, the bus turned a corner. In a few blocks more, we got out. Andrus immediately hailed a cab. Leaning over the front seat, he regaled the poor driver through a series of turns. Finally, we got out on a dismal side street. From there, we hiked in silence for about a mile until we reached an apartment building. Andrus directed us to enter without a sound.

We tiptoed, my adrenalin pumping, up a dark stairway and then along a hallway. Passing one door I heard a baby crying and somewhere a radio blared. All at once, Andrus opened a door and pushed the three of us inside. When he closed it, I heard the bolt slide into place. I realized I had no idea where I was.

The room we had entered was pitch black. Something very heavy must have covered the windows. The air felt

close, and we picked our way across the room, bumping
into legs as we went. We found a place against a wall and
sat down on the floor between other bodies. How many
were here, I couldn't tell.

We had not spoken since we entered the building. Now
Andrus whispered, "The American Christians are here."

For more than an hour we were plied with whispered
questions. What was God doing in America? What was
happening with Oral Roberts' healing ministry? Every answer brought another question, as if our invisible hosts
were starved for any encouragement from the West.

At one point a truck rumbled up outside. A deathly
silence fell. I could feel the tense breathing of the person
next to me. Someone lifted a window shade and whispered in Estonian. In English, Andrus repeated, "It's not
the police."

Apparently Andrus decided we were safe. He reached
up and hit a switch. Blinking in the sudden light, I saw
that the small room was crowded with about thirty young
people.

For another hour or more Andrus and his friends—who
remained anonymous—began to tell us about the underground church that was spreading throughout the Soviet
Union. Weekly, more young hearts were coming to Jesus
Christ and they were eager to evangelize. The sanctioned
or "registered" churches, like the one we'd been taken to,
were mostly attended by older men and women who had
tired of struggling with the government and wanted to be
left in peace. Meetings like this one were held in apart-
ments or in isolated forests across the land. My heart began to ache for these young people.

But something else touched me more deeply.

Andrus took us into his tiny kitchen where he removed
a secret panel inside a cabinet. As he worked, he said,
"The police raid my apartment—three times in four

months. But they never find this." He pulled out several manuscripts of Christian books and a Bible.

When Andrus had replaced the panel he stood up and faced me. It was the first time I'd gotten a look at him in full light. It was not the handsomeness that impressed me now, but his eyes . . . !

They burned with a living fire. While I had rebelled against church and God so much of my life, failing in my commitments, here was a young man willing to die for Christ if necessary.

As the meeting closed Andrus asked if I would pray for the healing of the sick. By then I was painfully aware of how puny my faith was. I mumbled a prayer, feeling such shame. Shortly afterward the meeting ended.

That night, after a taxi ride back to our hotel, I was sleepless. When the morning light grew I got up to pack. My mind and heart were numb with a type of grief I'd never felt before. Not sorrow for myself, but for the suffering of these Christians.

At the ferry we were treated to one final surprise. The pier was crowded with young people—some of them I recognized from Andrus' apartment—each one bearing a colorful bouquet of flowers.

We had barely stepped from the bus when they surrounded us, hugging, weeping, offering their flowers. One young woman shyly hugged me. Remembering the New Testament in my jacket pocket I quickly slipped it out and pressed it into her hand. Quietly, I told the others to do the same.

When the ferry pulled out of Tallinn Harbor the waving figures on the dock grew smaller and smaller. My chest heaved painfully. Jan, who was at my side, wept openly. She had such a tender heart.

"I'm coming back here to preach someday," I vowed,

my voice husky with emotion. "I don't know how I'll do it, but I'm coming back."

Jan could only smile and nod. Leaning against me, she squeezed my hand.

7

SHIRLEY:
Meeting of the Hearts

The insight I'd had on that snowy December night after my father left home proved completely accurate: Choosing to tell Mom the truth about Dad's abuse did set us free from the strange grip of his personality. However, it also made our lives very hard for a long time to come.

One immediate effect was that I had to take on even more responsibility for myself and the boys. Mom got a job, but it didn't pay much. Legal papers were filed against Dad, seeking support. Months and months passed and not much money came in. I took weekend jobs and then, in my senior year, got out of school at noon to work a part-time job to help buy my clothes.

When I graduated from high school I found a job in downtown Portland and moved into an apartment with Carol Maier who also took an office job. She was still my dearest friend and her parents' house was home to me. All during those tough years, when my mother, brothers, and

84

I struggled just to survive, Carl and Lois Maier became surrogate parents, always ready to listen, offering guidance and encouragement. In the summer of 1969, as my parents' divorce was dragging to an unhappy close, I leaned on them more and more for emotional support. The crumbling of my own family was nearly complete.

And as a young woman trying to make her way in the world I often felt unsteady, especially when it came to men. That was why, on a hot evening in June, I left work and drove straight to the Maiers'. On the phone the night before, I had told Carl I needed to talk. In the background, I heard Lois ask him to invite Carol and me "home" for supper.

At the front door Lois greeted me with a hug. "Carl's changing," she said, ushering me into the family room, "and Carol's not home yet. Why don't you wait here, while I check on the roast."

Sinking into an armchair I nervously picked at my fingernails. Now that I was here I wasn't sure I could explain what was bothering me. Part of it was Ron, whom I'd been dating for some time. He was demanding so much of my time. When I wanted to go out with my girlfriends, for instance, he said little, but acted resentful.

Yet I realized that wasn't the only problem.

Even after Dad left, I could not escape the emotional effects of his abuse for a long, long time. Many nights his face haunted my dreams. As I sat there, hearing Lois move about the kitchen, the same nightmare I'd had for months played before my eyes.

He stood at the door of my room, silently turning the lock. His fingers curled on the handle of a gun. He aimed it at my head. "If you tell anyone, Shirley, so help me God. . . ."

Sitting in the Maiers' family room my heart began pounding just at the memory—the way it did when I woke trembling at night. I'd prayed so many times, saying, *Fa-*

ther, I know You can take away this hurt. But I'm so angry. Why did he do those things to me?

I didn't know how I could overcome the pain of my past.

Now, as the Maiers seated themselves on the sofa opposite me, we exchanged some pleasantries and talked about the retreat our church was having for young single adults coming up in mid-August. Then Carl smiled at me. "What's on your mind, Shirley?"

Out came the jumbled thoughts: how Ron was getting too serious, even talking about marriage. He was a nice Christian guy, but he made me feel closed in. I'd even tried to let him know that he should back off a little. Just two weeks before, the musical group called Living Sound had performed at church. Their vibrance and sense of mission stuck with me, and I'd told Ron I wanted to spend my life with a man who was in the ministry—knowing that Ron was planning a career in engineering.

"You didn't tell him *that!*" Lois interrupted with a disbelieving smile.

I reddened. "Was I too blunt?"

Carl chuckled. "That's our Shirley. She's nothing if she's not direct."

"But I don't want to mislead him," I explained hastily. "I thought he should know the truth."

"That means a lot to you, doesn't it?" he replied. When I looked puzzled, he pursued it. "The truth, I mean. You don't like people who seem to be one thing on the surface when they're something else underneath."

I had to grin. They knew me only too well.

He continued. "And maybe—now I'm not trying to play armchair psychologist—but maybe that's why you're holding out: to meet a guy who *really* wants to serve God with his whole heart."

Lois leaned close. "Look, Shirley, you've had to grow

up fast, but you're still only eighteen. Take your time. Date other guys if you want. Maybe your relationship with Ron is too limiting. Healthy relationships are the kind that stretch you, challenge you. Those are the relationships God uses to shape us."

I'd always found great wisdom in Lois' soft-spoken words. Yet I still felt confused. "I just don't want to hurt Ron. But," I conceded, "I don't think our relationship is right."

"Perhaps," Carl added, "one of the problems is this. You can't believe that God wants you to have a good relationship as much as you want to have one—as if you're not 'worthy.' Now you can believe that lie, or you can choose to trust God."

We chatted for a few more minutes concluding that it would be good for both Ron and me to date others. Carol came in, and we had an enjoyable, relaxing supper.

As we drove back to the apartment that night, it was Carl Maier's statement about trusting God that repeated in my head.

Negotiating the dark streets, humid summer air blowing into the car window, I thought about people in the Bible, which I'd been studying more. Abraham, for instance, was a man who really trusted God. God had spoken to him, Abraham believed what God said, and acted on it in faith. He seemed to *know* that God would come through always.

I wondered, *Do I really have faith? If not, how do I get it?*

Perhaps what I had was not *faith* at all. I knew that Jesus had died for me, that I was born again, and because His blood was shed for my sins I had a place in heaven. And I knew God helped people. I wondered, though, what my part was. To pray differently? To do something different? I didn't know.

By the time we got home I decided that, at best, what I

had was half-faith. Hope. I *hoped* God would answer my prayers, like the prayer that I would one day have a good Christian husband and family. But I did not *know*, the way Abraham knew.

These thoughts and questions, though I didn't realize it then, were my first true launchings into deeper spiritual waters.

Two months later, in mid-August, my relationship with Ron was still stuck—that is, I wanted to back off to get perspective on my feelings and he wanted to get more serious. I knew, somehow, that the young adult retreat had to be a time of decision.

On the Friday evening Ron and I made the hour drive to the Pacific coast together, I kept the conversation light. At the retreat lodge, located on a sandy bluff above the ocean, my roommates were already lugging suitcases and guitars inside. Ron took my things from the car and gave me a peck on the cheek, which I did not return.

That evening, the retreat opened with a time of relaxation around the fireplace in the lodge's great room. Small knots of people gathered around on sofas and chairs, and I was chatting with some girlfriends by the fire keeping my distance from Ron.

As we talked, our retreat leader, Jim Arnold, came up and introduced himself.

Because our church was fairly large I'd never gotten to know Jim, a twenty-six-year-old salesman who'd been coming to our church since he moved to Portland from Minneapolis. He was tall, big-framed, blond, and blue-eyed with a boyish face.

He chatted with us for just a few minutes and I found myself interested in what he had to say when the group talked later about living the Christian life.

"I know that God will give His best to us when we give our best to Him. But it takes commitment of everything—

our possessions, our boyfriends and girlfriends, money. It means putting aside our own goals and ambitions."

I could tell he was really serious about his faith, and I liked him right away.

On Saturday morning, over coffee and eggs, I was talking with several girlfriends. Talk centered on Jim. Someone hinted that the church secretary had staked her claim on him. So had most of the other single women. He rarely dated anyone from the church, though. Too bad, someone else said, because he was the best "catch" around—a success in business, a committed Christian, and good-looking. But did he have a girlfriend back in Minneapolis? Someone thought so. No one knew.

As we finished our breakfast, I marveled. With all this "intrigue" going on, where had I been? It seemed I was the only eligible female in the church who wasn't chasing Jim Arnold. No matter. Someone *that* fantastic was 'way out of my league. He wouldn't give me a second look. Besides, he was eight years older.

That evening, with these thoughts in mind, I came face-to-face again with "Mr. Fantastic" himself.

The ocean was calm and the first stars shining as we collected driftwood for a cookout on the dunes. I was walking with a close friend, Mary Jo, when we met Jim and another guy along a path to the beach. We stopped and chatted casually. I was attracted to the strong line of his jaw, the mischievous liveliness of his eyes. The banter ended and we moved on.

Just out of earshot, Mary Jo turned excitedly. "Shirley! He couldn't take his eyes off you! I'll bet he asks you out."

"Well, if he does," I parried, "just don't tell the church secretary." Secretly, I hoped he would.

Sunday morning, when the retreat was over, I was folding some blouses and jeans in the suitcase when Ron came to say he'd be ready to leave in an hour. When he left, I knew he'd want to talk about our relationship. Squeezing the suitcase closed, I decided to take a final walk along the breakers to think.

At the beach, I took off my sandals and sank my feet in the warm sand. The surf was light, the breeze cool. It was then I saw Jim coming down the path, a golf bag slung over his shoulder. He waved and walked toward me.

"Do you really think there's enough time to play eighteen holes?" I teased.

He set his clubs in the sand. "Oh, I was just going to practice my putt," he replied, smiling. "Perfect place for a sandtrap, isn't it? How about you?"

"Just walking."

"Mind if I join you?"

I hesitated. Ron would be looking for me. "What about your putt?"

He responded by laying his clubs beside a tuft of sea oats. We began walking at the ocean's edge as the white foam washed at our ankles.

The conversation was humorous, really. It was obvious at once that both of us were cautious about venturing too much personal information. We seemed like two little children who once had touched a red-hot stove. Or maybe I was imagining it. For a long while, it was "name-rank-and-serial-number" only—until we hit upon a mutual love.

The moment Jim mentioned his desire to learn how to be Christ's instrument in ministering to people the conversation got rolling.

"I'm finding that the Christian life doesn't stop with being born again and filled with the Spirit," Jim said emphatically. "It's making choices every step of the way. Each one leads you closer to God, or farther away."

Choices. I was really on his wavelength now.

We walked for quite a while, the sound of waves and crying gulls surrounding our conversation. Then I happened to glance at my wristwatch. We'd been talking for over two hours!—and Ron was waiting at the lodge.

As we hurried back along the beach, Jim told me he sold dental equipment and that he made sales calls in the downtown area where I worked. I was nervous and scarcely paid attention.

Needless to say, the ride home with Ron was uncomfortably quiet. Of course, I apologized for keeping him waiting. At the same time I felt a stirring of happiness.

Upon returning to Portland my chance meeting with Jim on the beach led to a fast-growing friendship. Jim surprised me by calling my office one morning and inviting me to lunch. My one-hour break turned into two-and-a-half delightful hours, for which I had to make some heavy apologies at the office.

One Friday night Jim invited me out to a concert. On the way home, he brought up Ron.

"Do you have a commitment to him?" Jim asked. He sounded casual but I picked up other signals.

I took a deep breath. "No, we have no commitments."

Shortly thereafter Jim called the apartment on a Saturday morning. He had planned a day at Mount St. Helens, and could I be ready in, say, an hour? Carol smiled at me as I hung up the phone. "And here's my friend Shirley being courted by the best-looking bachelor in the church!"

"Carol, we're just good friends."

She rolled her eyes. "Come on. I can see what's happening here."

And so could I.

Jim and I talked and laughed all the way to Mount St. Helens. We hiked to Spirit Lake where we skipped stones on the water, shattering the blue mirror that reflected the first hints of autumn reds and golds. Above us the snow-cowled mountain capped the forest with unspeakable majesty. When he slipped his hand into mine a confusion of feelings ran through me. I had been wanting him to hold my hand. So why did I feel uncomfortable?

It took me a few minutes to relax with Jim's hand in mine. The rest of the day was beautiful. And later, when he kissed me, I was overwhelmed. This seemed like a gift, handmade by God, and just for me.

But there was still the matter of Ron. That week I got up the courage to tell him about Jim, hoping he would allow me the freedom to date both of them. His face clouded. For a long time he begged me to reconsider, but it came down to this: I had to choose between them. I hadn't wanted that to happen.

Later, Jim and I met at a park. As we walked I told him about the conversation, how hurt and disappointed Ron was with my answer: I had decided I would see Jim.

Jim cleared his throat nervously.

"Do you think I handled it wrong?" I asked.

Gently, he squeezed my arm. "No," he said reassuringly, "I'm glad you're as up-front as you are, Shirley. There is one wrinkle we have to think about, though."

"What's that?"

"Well," he explained, "since I work with the young adults it might be difficult if it's known that I'm dating one of the women in the group. See what I'm getting at?"

I frowned. "I hadn't thought of it that way, but I guess so."

He put his arm around me as we walked. "Hey, come on. Don't look upset. I'm real happy that you and Ron have cooled it. I'm just saying we ought to keep this to ourselves for a while."

I hadn't expected this. Why should we sneak around together? On the other hand, I certainly didn't want to cause any problems in the group. Maybe he was right. "Okay," I conceded.

We stopped at a little shop for an ice cream cone. Then

walked some more. When Jim kissed me goodnight I could not relax in his arms. His request clouded the evening for me. Still, I resolved not to let a petty thing spoil my happiness.

From then on we saw each other constantly. Only in church did we keep our distance. We did a lot of fun things together—quietly, that is. Since Jim loved golf, I watched him play in a tournament. We enjoyed driving in the mountains. We were affectionate. And yet, there was one major hurdle.

As Jim and I got closer his gentleness made it easy to tell him about my hopes and dreams, about my conviction that I would marry someone with an interest in the ministry. He was warm and accepting. The thing I noticed, however, was that something was stirring inside Jim, something he would not share with me.

Just before Thanksgiving I determined that there *was* some cloud between us. He kept part of himself in reserve somehow. Jim's widowed mother, his sister, and two brothers lived in Minneapolis and he was going to be with them for the holiday. Rather than allow the shadow to remain over the long holiday weekend, I decided we had to talk about it.

On our way out one evening, I said, "Jim, have I done something to offend you?"

By the dashboard lights I could see his smile. "Of course not."

"Well, then, I want to know what you're really afraid of," I said, surprised at my own boldness.

"Afraid?" Jim shifted uneasily in his seat.

"I just don't get it," I insisted. "It's not just the church group and the jealousy thing. I've tried to come up with other reasons why you're keeping your distance. And do you know what I think?"

I could almost hear Jim gulp. "What?"

"I think you're falling in love with me. And I *know* I'm in love with you. But I want you to trust me—to *talk* to me, for cryin' out loud. And you won't.

"If that startles you," I went on, "then I'm sorry. It's just that I was brought up with so much dishonesty." Jim looked at me, curious, but I avoided going any further. "Now you've got something on your mind. And we owe each other honest communication."

Jim was silent, staring ahead at the busy street. "Shirley," he said at last, "to tell you the truth, since that's what you want, I need time to think about us."

Evidently the subject was closed. For the rest of the evening he would only talk about other things. Inwardly I felt terrible. Maybe I'd blown one of the best things that ever happened to me. But the dishonesty—even if it was for supposedly *good* reasons—bothered me. I'd seen too much pain from covering things up. Wasn't it always better to be honest and face the consequences?

On Tuesday morning, the day before he was to fly to Minnesota, Jim phoned and asked me out to dinner that night. I accepted even though his voice sounded restrained. That evening when he picked me up after work he could hardly look at me. Once we were seated in the restaurant he fidgeted with his napkin. After asking a few questions about my day he finally looked me in the eyes. I was ready for the worst.

"Shirley, I'm in love with you."

Tears rose suddenly and my throat was tight. Jim slid his hand across the linen tablecloth and touched my fingers.

He went on, his eyes never leaving mine. "It's just that—well, I'm older than you. And it's important that I marry the right person."

"Marry?" I blurted. "Jim, I love you, but we've just

known each other a few months, and besides, I'm not in any hurry."

"What I'm trying to say—oh, I can't really explain it, Shirley. But it's important to me that we keep our relationship private for now. Can you trust me in that?"

Trust. Why did Jim have such a knack for touching the important issues inside me?

"Okay," I said at last, squeezing his hand. "I love you—*and* I trust you."

After Jim had left me off at my apartment my mood lightened. I went to my room and, as I got ready for bed, my thoughts turned to God. *Father,* I prayed, *this whole thing is too wonderful. Not only is Jim a strong Christian but You seem to be using him to get at those deep places inside me.*

Laying my head on the pillow, I switched off the light, still thanking God for the way our relationship was growing. Then the thought hit me: *If you want to grow closer to Jim you'll have to be honest with him, too, and tell him about the past.*

That, of course, meant opening up to Jim about my dad's abuse. I panicked. What if he was horrified? Disgusted? *Why that, Lord?* I prayed.

Before the words had cleared my head, I knew the answer. Months before, Carl Maier had put his finger right on my problem—*trust.*

I could trust God that He had brought Jim into my life, or I could choose not to trust Him. I could become vulnerable and tell Jim about those painful childhood experiences, or keep them to myself. To my chagrin I recalled that I was the one who had just been steamed up about honesty in our relationship.

Still I protested. *It would be easier if Jim had opened up and told me why we had to keep our relationship quiet.*

Again, I sensed an inner response. *You can't worry about the choices other people make. You do what's right.*

Gradually, while this dialogue went on, a warm peacefulness had washed into me. Panic ebbed away. As I fell asleep I resolved—reluctantly—that I would soon tell Jim about my past.

Whatever his response I knew it would tell me a lot about him—and about our future.

8

SHIRLEY:
Obstacles

Several months went by before I felt brave enough to open up with Jim about my past.

We were continuing to keep our relationship quiet. I was warming to him more and more, enjoying his humor. We were even able to pray about things together, like problems at work, or problems friends at church were having.

I invited Jim to supper one evening in early spring of 1970. I felt it was now or never.

When the doorbell rang, I was still arranging cut flowers in a vase on the table. Nervously, I straightened the candles and gave the china and silverware a final once-over look. I wanted everything to be perfect.

Jim was in a chipper mood. I wanted to forget about telling him and just enjoy his company. As we ate I stole glances at him. His cheeks dimpled when he laughed or smiled. And I loved his blue eyes. So many times I'd seen them reflect the joy or pain others were feeling. Would he have the same compassion for me?

I didn't realize until just that moment what a risk this was—how devastating a rejection would be.

When supper was over, I stalled. I fussed with the dishes. I made another pot of coffee. Finally I got up my courage and settled beside him on the sofa. "Jim, there's something I need to tell you. It's personal—and kind of difficult."

His eyebrows went up questioningly. At other times Jim lightened a serious mood with a quip, but not tonight. "Okay," he said gently. "I'm listening."

Getting the story out was even more excruciating than I'd expected. I'd hoped I could do it without crying. But no. When I finished Jim's big hand enveloped mine, which brought more tears.

"You know," he said quietly, tracing my hand with one finger, "I have to admit, Shirley. I've wondered."

It was hard to speak. "Wondered what?"

"Well, sometimes—not always, but every once in a while—you act like you're scared of me. Sometimes I'll take your hand or put my arm around you and you tense up. Now I understand why. But Shirley"—and now I saw tears in his eyes—"don't you know that *I* would never hurt you?"

That brought fresh tears. When I could find my voice at all I assured Jim that my reactions had nothing to do with him. I knew I still had deep feelings about my father.

"What kind of feelings?" he prompted.

"I have a hard time forgiving him—" My voice choked. "In fact, I *hate* my father for what he did to me. And I hate him for what he did to Mom and the boys." The intensity of my answer surprised me. "But I'm a Christian and I'm not supposed to hate. On the other hand, God sees my heart so there's no point in pretending. Oh, I just don't know what to do."

Jim did not try to counsel me. Nor did he merely sympathize and let me off the hook.

"Shirley," he said at one point, "I know that what I'm going to say can sound cheap and easy. But you have to forgive your father. Not just with words but in a way that will show you've forgiven him. It's not just for his sake, but for yours. You have to overcome this hatred before you'll ever be really free with a man."

We both fell silent, as if stunned by the truth and the intimacy of Jim's words. Nervously, Jim lightened the moment. "At least we're in this together," he smiled.

That made me smile, too.

After that evening I was able to relax with Jim, to enjoy the warmth of his arms around me. If this was to be a time of inner growth, I was happy that Jim would be part of it.

Mostly, my admiration for Jim grew throughout that summer and fall, and before Christmas we began to talk about marriage. Since Jim had insisted we keep our relationship quiet, his suggestion that we make a public proclamation delighted me. Our young adults group was planning a ski retreat on Valentine's Day weekend. We agreed that would be a perfect time and setting.

So on February 14, shortly before my twentieth birthday, Jim stood before the group at supper and invited them all to our wedding in November. We were congratulated, kissed, and hugged. And the feeling of having Jim beside me, openly at last, without apology, his arm around my waist, was wonderful.

But I wasn't prepared for the visible dismay on many faces. Some friends, I knew, were rightly disappointed that we had kept our relationship such a secret. And more than a few women, I suspected, were flat-out upset.

And back in Portland, just a week or two after our announcement, I learned that several people in the church were questioning whether or not our engagement was right. People who were close to Ron were startled, of course, since they'd already paired us for marriage. I was more troubled when I overheard the comment that Jim was too old for me.

When I told Jim about it, I was upset.

He was typically nonchalant. "People talk, Shirley."

"But these are Christians—"

He held up his hand. "That doesn't matter. People always disappoint you. Keep your eyes on the Lord."

Of course I'd heard that a thousand times. Grudgingly, I had to agree he was right.

Jim changed the subject immediately to tell me about a phone conversation he'd just had with Buddy Harrison, one of his best friends. Buddy's wife, Pat, was the daughter of the evangelist and teacher Kenneth Hagin of Tulsa, Oklahoma. The Harrisons now lived in Tulsa and Buddy worked with his father-in-law's ministry.

"Buddy said he'll be happy to be my best man," Jim said, beaming. "He and Pat will definitely be here in November."

Jim's calmness helped me to relax. I would need to lean on him more in the coming weeks. For me, what should have been a joyous time was about to become an obstacle course.

As I made plans, choosing gowns and a color scheme, I kept dodging one very important decision: Who would give me away? Carl Maier was my first choice. But what about my dad? Even thinking about asking him made my stomach turn. As a woman, how *could* I ask him? As a Christian, how could I *not*? Why did everything have to involve hard choices?

When I talked about it with Jim he had already mulled over the situation. And he didn't hesitate in his response. "You can't insult your father."

Maybe, subconsciously, I was trying to find a different

opinion when I decided to talk it over with Carl. Seated in his family room I was overwhelmed with emotion. I cared about this family so much.

"You don't know how much I want you to walk me down the aisle."

As ever, his gentle eyes and soft response said more than words. "And I'd love to do it. You know you're like a daughter to us. But I understand. You have to do what's right. That's the way the Lord would have it."

There was one more thing Carl said to me that day. In the turmoil of the moment I hardly let the words sink in. He was concerned for some reason about Jim, and he wanted me to be sure I was doing the right thing. My mind was on other things. I assured him that Jim and I loved each other, and hastily dismissed the comment.

After talking to Carl I faced the difficult conclusion: For my own spiritual health, as well as Dad's, it was imperative that I honor Dad and ask him to give me away at our wedding.

In the four years since Dad had left us our contact had been occasional, mostly on holidays. He was remarried and still living in Portland. The visits had been understandably stiff. Could I really face him now with this important request? Jim and I decided it was best that we see him together.

There was another big obstacle, however, that neither of us foresaw.

We had not really had a chance to discuss our wedding plans with Mom. She had taken a liking to Jim months before when they first met. When she and her new husband, Milt, invited Jim and me to dinner at their home, I had in my head a list of things that had yet to be done. We really had to get busy and shop for my bridal dress, decide on a menu for the reception, and finalize the family guest list.

Over supper Mom listened quietly as I explained the plans so far. I hardly touched my food. Jim talked quietly with Milt. Mom was spooning a second helping of casserole onto Jim's plate when she asked who was going to escort me down the aisle.

Gingerly, I lifted my water glass and wet my lips. "Well, actually," I forged ahead brightly, "I'm going to ask Dad to give me away."

I know it was hard for Mom to understand my reasons after all we'd been through. Milt, who obviously wanted to shield her from the upset of seeing Dad at the church, jumped in. He was adamant: If my father and his new wife came to the wedding *at all*, they were not coming. Mom nodded in agreement. When I tried to explain, they interrupted.

Right in the middle of it all Jim quietly pushed back his chair and stood up. "Folks, I don't mean to be rude, but Shirley has made a decision. I'm behind her all the way."

Mother seemed embarrassed and stunned, but only for a moment. Then she tried again to talk me out of my decision.

Jim interrupted. "Shirley, it looks like we ought to be going. Perhaps we can come back and talk about this some other time."

Driving away, I was miserable. The decision about my dad was difficult enough, I complained. Why did I have to run into this roadblock, too?

"Because you're doing the right thing, Shirley," Jim said, squeezing my hand. "Whenever we obey God, we'll be tested."

At that moment I was so proud of Jim—the gentle strength he'd just shown at Mom's, his insight and encouragement. How I would need his strength when it was time to see Dad.

And so, as summer came, Jim and I worked through

wedding details, deciding where to put up out-of-town guests like his family and the Harrisons. And almost daily we prayed for me to find the strength to face my dad.

The strange thing was that, as hard as I prayed, I didn't feel any different. I was expecting to wake up one sunny morning and find that God had poured in a gallon of supernatural grace and love. Midway through the summer I talked with Jim about my angry feelings, which had not softened one iota.

"I don't get it," I complained. "God must know I'm willing to do the right thing. Why doesn't He change my attitude? How can I put on a Pollyanna smile and say, 'Daddy, dear, I love you so much. Please honor me by walking me down the aisle on my wedding day.' I can't be a phony."

Jim nodded. "Maybe a little honesty wouldn't hurt." And then he grinned. "But just a *little*, Shirley. We want to leave the man in one piece."

I almost socked him—but it made me smile. Jim was already used to my bluntness.

On the day that Dad had agreed to meet us I nearly backed out.

That morning I made toast for breakfast—and then couldn't eat it. My hands were clammy. Jim picked me up and as we drove to Dad's house a million frightening thoughts bombarded me. *What if he begins to call me horrible names in front of Jim? Or what if he's nice and tries to hug me?* The thought of either happening made me nauseous.

We found the house easily and parked at the curb. Jim rang the bell and while we waited for someone to answer I took deep breaths to steady myself.

The door swung open and there stood my dad.

He looked the same, except for a flatness in his eyes. He couldn't look at us directly, but he was polite and ushered us into the living room.

When we were seated he spoke so timidly I could hardly picture him as the raving tyrant I remembered. Maybe it was the presence of Jim, who was bigger and taller than he. When Dad lit a cigarette I noticed his hands shaking. Suddenly, I was aware that this pathetic man was not the looming monster of my nightmares.

For a few minutes we caught up on family small talk and I told him about my job. When the talk came around to our wedding plans, conversation faltered. Dad fumbled to light a second cigarette and puffed furiously. I felt a pain so deep I could hardly open my mouth.

Catching Jim's eye I could tell he was feeling the anguish with me. Something—I had to focus on something. Jim's hand rested on top of mine, its weight and warmth covering my fingers. This small gesture brought a surge of courage.

Forcing myself to speak, I said, "Dad, we both know some things happened in the past that were hurtful and ugly. We can't deny that or pretend it didn't happen. But that's over. And I've come to ask if you would give me away at my wedding."

He stared from me to Jim, his face reddening. He must have realized that Jim knew everything. Obviously it was painful for him to be exposed before another man. The cigarette hung limply in his fingers, dropping ashes on the carpet between his feet.

Then his mouth trembled and tears spilled down his cheeks. "Thank you, Shirley. I know I don't deserve to have anything to do with you. But you don't know how happy this makes me."

I must be honest. I was numb to his tears. And we did not stay long after that. As we got up to leave I brought the conversation back to a less threatening level, telling Dad where to go to be fitted for his tuxedo.

"Shirley," he said, before letting us go. "Let me do

something for you. I'd like to buy your wedding dress."
I almost refused—but something stopped me. In his better moments Dad was so generous. I knew it was important for him to *give.*

"All right, Dad," I conceded. "Thanks."

Then, just as I reached for the door, Dad gently seized
my shoulders. Wrapping his arms around me, he pulled
me to himself. For just a moment he squeezed me and
whispered, "I'm so sorry, Shirley." Then he released me.

On the way home Jim was quiet, allowing me to be
alone with my thoughts. I still felt no warmth for my father. And yet I had to acknowledge that my act of obedience—no, call it a sacrifice—had touched my father at some
very personal level.

I hadn't the emotional energy at that moment to think
about grand spiritual insights from the experience. But my
action that day would bring far-ranging results I could not
imagine just then.

I only felt that facing Dad was like cresting a mountain.
After that everything leading up to the wedding *had* to be
a snap. Shortly Jim and I would be together, building our
own life and growing in the Lord.

By fall I couldn't take my eyes off the calendar and eagerly penciled off each day. Something seemed to be on
Jim's mind. He became distant but I supposed he was as
nervous as I and, in the hubbub of last-minute arrange-
ments, ignored it.

The morning I arrived at church in my bridal gown—
that chilly and damp November day—I stepped from the
car as if in a dream. Though Carol and my other atten-
dants fussed with my dress and veil, they seemed far-off.
With one finger I traced a white rosebud in my bouquet. It
seemed too perfect to be real.

I wish everything else had been as perfect as the pretty
trappings. First, there was Mom. Even though she had

agreed to come she had let me know, just that morning, how upset she was that Dad was going to be *at* the wedding, let alone *in* it.

And, waiting for me inside the church, was Dad. My heart pounded as the girls helped me make my way inside.

In the foyer were David, Roger, and Buddy Harrison, all of them dapper and smiling in their tuxedos. David and Roger had grown to be handsome and angular teenagers. They hugged me, which gave me another ounce of courage somehow.

It was when I saw Dad again that I almost wished I *had* bowed to Mom's pressure.

He took my arm in his and kissed me gently on the cheek. "You're beautiful, Shirley."

His touch and those words hurt so deeply. In my head I still saw it—*the locked door, the gun.* I didn't need this. Not now.

Fighting down the images, I stepped with Dad through the open sanctuary doors. The organist saw us, struck the first chords, and the crowd rose to its feet. To me it was a blur of colors and music, but for the one person I'd set my eyes on.

Jim stood beaming at the far end of the aisle. Dad's hand felt cold as clay, and my smile must have looked like paint on a plaster mannequin. Never did a walk seem so long.

At the front of the church we stopped. When Dad lifted my veil his face was streaked with tears. His lips touched my cheek. For an instant, I felt a pang of love. Later I would recognize it as forgiveness.

Then I turned and Jim's hand was waiting. Our fingers touched.

The days surrounding our wedding should have been among the happiest of my life.

On our wedding night Jim insisted that we get up at the

crack of dawn to drive Buddy and Pat to the airport. Then we stayed in Portland two more days to visit with his family before they returned to Minneapolis. I didn't understand what was happening. Finally we left for a week in Reno and southern California.

On our honeymoon I was suddenly, painfully, aware that Jim had been distant toward me for almost a month before our wedding. He was gentle, as usual—except for one thing.

Then, and in the weeks to come, he hardly touched me.

9

TERRY: Living Sound

Settling into the fall '68 semester at ORU was impossible after our tour of Europe and the Middle East. I now charged between the practice room and my senior classes with plans perking in my head. We had returned just a week before classes began and I had the feeling that something big and exciting was about to break for me.

The fact that a bunch of young people could go where we'd gone convinced me my idea was right: I was going to put together a musical group and hit the road again, and soon.

But before that happened, there was this certain personal matter I had to resolve involving a very special lady.

On that summer tour, and especially in Estonia, I'd seen a depth of compassion in Jan. In her gutsy alto solos I could hear her love for Jesus. And there had been that very special moment in Jerusalem. . . .

It had been evening, late in August, and very hot. The group was staying at the King David Hotel. Jan and I had taken a walk after supper at dusk.

We wandered between the ancient stone walls of the old city hand in hand. The sellers of bread, almonds, pastries, postcards, souvenirs, and fruit were closing their small shops and stalls for the day. We dodged a man in a *kaffiyeh* who offered to take our picture with his camel—for a fee. When we wandered out through St. Stephen's Gate in the Eastern wall, the stars had come out but there was no moon. Across the way, on the Mount of Olives, lights from the two great churches blazed.

We left the road, which led steeply downhill, walking along the grass outside the wall. In the pitch dark I couldn't tell but thought we were in a kind of park with lots of stone benches. The one we sat on was awfully uncomfortable. All that mattered to me at the moment was the softness of Jan's hand.

My lips brushed her cheek.

Yaww.

A second after that horrible sound erupted from the dark behind us, Jan's scream nearly split my eardrum. She jumped into my arms, clinging to me. My scalp tingled.

Yaww. The noise jolted us again—something like a dog with its tail in a meat grinder.

Then from the darkness a lop-eared creature shuffled toward us. We let out our breath. A donkey.

Jan and I held each other and had a good laugh. And in my heart, I thanked the donkey.

We got another surprise the next day when, riding out of Jerusalem on our tour bus, we passed the "park" again. Jan winced. "Oh no, Terry! Look."

What we'd been seated on was not a stone bench but a tomb surrounded by hundreds of other tombs that spread across the eastern hillside. Jan's deep, hearty laugh filled the bus.

Now, three weeks later, I was in a college classroom and could not concentrate on the lectures. Jan's face, her bright eyes, and mellow laugh—they were on my mind all the time. I'd never felt this way about anyone. And I wasn't one to waste time.

Early in October, Jan and I were invited to the home of some friends for dinner. For days I paced my dorm room, planning for the moment. I loved her, she said she loved me. The next move was simple.

On the brisk fall evening we pulled up in front of our friends' home I shut off the motor but did not make a move to open the door. I was hoping we could make an important announcement at dinner.

"Terry?" Jan prompted, looking at me quizzically. "Aren't we getting out?"

"Not just yet," I replied. It took some rambling before I could express my feelings. Jan listened, probably unaware of what I was leading up to. Finally, I just came out with it. "I've fallen in love. I want to marry you."

Jan's eyes got moist. A few silent moments passed. She sniffed and I felt my palms getting damp as I waited for that important one-word answer. But Jan surprised me.

"Terry, you're so sure of things," she said, rummaging in her purse for a tissue. "I need a little time."

I started to protest. "No, Terry, listen," she insisted. "I know you're called to a travel ministry. Your head is full of plans. I admire that. But anyone who marries you will have to sacrifice a lot. You'll be on the road. Money will be tight. There won't be much time together—even less when kids come along. Maybe it sounds selfish, but I've always wanted a nice, quiet family. And then you came along."

I didn't know what to say. Jan insisted she needed some time. She would not say more. And so dinner that night was not the celebration I'd planned.

For the next few days classes were lost on me. Notebook propped open, a pencil limp in my fingers, I alternately prayed and tried to guess what was going on in Jan's head. Why hadn't I considered the matter from her viewpoint? I understood why she had reservations.

Just after the tour Jan and I stopped briefly in Tampa, Florida, to meet her parents. Albert and Marion D'Arpa welcomed me warmly into their lovely home. Jan was showered with hugs and kisses. During her visit her folks asked if she had enough spending money and clothes and if the new car they'd bought her was running well.

And here you are, I chastised myself, *offering a crazy, uncertain kind of life to a girl who's been provided for and protected by good Christian parents.*

By the end of the week, when Jan had agreed to see me, I'd concocted a jillion reasons why she was going to turn me down. And all of them catalogued through my brain when she faced me again.

I knew that Jan was committed to Christ above all, however, so I was sure she would give me a prayerful answer. I would trust whatever she said.

And she said, "Yes, Terry. I guess I'm ready for this.

"At least," she quickly added, "I *hope* I'm ready."

I threw my arms around her and held her tightly.

Just three months later, at the end of January 1969, we were married in Jan's home church in Tampa. The D'Arpas, with so little notice, pulled off a beautiful wedding and reception for us. My family flew in from Medicine Hat and Dad performed the ceremony. Clayton, who was now in college, was my best man.

Returning from our honeymoon we moved our few unmatched pieces of furniture into an apartment off-campus. So began our last semester at ORU. Jan was student teaching at a local grade school. And my thoughts were already ten steps ahead of our upcoming graduation.

In mid-February I couldn't sit still any longer. Now that I had all this experience leading a team, how long was I supposed to wait? It was time to move out.

The first person I talked to was Larry Dalton. Larry was the talented organist I'd first heard at the Oral Roberts crusade in Edmonton more than a year before. He was also a member of The Collegians, and we'd become close friends. He listened carefully as I explained the idea.

It was simply this: Secular rock music had taken a downward turn openly promoting drugs, Eastern religions, and "free sex." Rock stars who opposed America's involvement in Vietnam were stirring up college students to burn classroom buildings. We, on the other hand, had seen that a team of turned-on-to-Jesus college people could reach teenage audiences with the Gospel through contemporary music. I had in mind a smaller, more flexible group than the team traveling with Oral Roberts.

As I talked, Larry nodded. "Count me in, Terry."

On the spot, we joined forces. Larry would be the group's musical leader. I would be responsible for spiritual direction.

Immediately we went to others on campus—those who, we knew, shared our concern that even Christian kids were being anesthetized by the music of the drug culture. They needed to hear the call to commitment. Within days we had an excited team of sixteen, including Jan and me. Pooling our instruments and sound equipment we began practicing together. Someone came up with a name, Living Sound.

In just days, the dream that had swirled for years in the mists of my mind became a clear-cut reality. Just to see them practicing together gave me a sense of awe.

These guys and girls who came from all over the U.S. and Canada were fine Christians. Most of the guys had muttonchop whiskers, which were popular just then. And a couple of girls wore their hair teased up in a beehive. We practiced contemporary songs by Ralph Carmichael, like "Reach Out to Jesus" and "All My Life," some black spirituals, like "He's My Rock, My Sword, My Shield" in which Jan sang solo. And the musical blend! My feet were barely touching the ground.

Another man who had become influential in my life was Gene Eland, head of ORU's music department. "Kids definitely need this ministry, Terry," he told me when I explained what we were doing. "There are so many bad things for them to get into. But I know you can reach them."

In our excitement Larry and I decided to contact pastors who had connection with the university, asking if we might come and perform one weekend soon. Our main idea at first was that, if we had appearances to prepare for, the group's sound would shape up faster.

But bigger things were in store for us.

Our very first engagement was in a Baptist church in Kansas City. We were seated in the choir during the opening hymns. My head was bowed as I prayed about my sermon.

A forceful thought took me by surprise: *Take the team to Africa.*

My eyes came open. I stared down at my folded hands. *Lord . . . ?* I began, questioningly. But the thought came again. *Take Living Sound to Africa.*

Now I looked up at the fifteen team members seated around me. Most had their eyes closed in prayer. It occurred to me for the first time that I was their spiritual leader in this venture, and they were not only trusting God, but trusting *me.*

Objections poured into my head: *What about airfare? Where is all that money going to come from? And the logistics— moving equipment, planning an itinerary. How could we coordinate such an enormous task?* It was one thing for Dennis and me to travel through Africa, but leading a whole team in was quite a different story.

Africa. Specifically, South Africa. The thought would not leave me alone.

I was aware that the pastor had stood up and given a brief introduction. The service was ours.

Driving back to Tulsa Sunday night after the service I didn't say much. And back at the apartment that night, Jan unpacked our suitcase. "All right, Terry," she said, carrying my shirts to the closet, "why are you so quiet? For a first time out we sounded pretty good. I thought you'd be talking my ear off all the way home."

I sat down on the edge of the bed. "Jan, come sit here," I said, patting the place beside me. "I want to try out an idea on you."

When I told her I could see Jan was scared. But, in her trusting way, she replied, "If that's what God is telling you, honey, I'm with you all the way."

Her blank-check kind of faith made me feel the weight of responsibility even more. The response of the team members would be a crucial test, too.

When I called the group together the next morning, a heavy silence hung while I explained the plan. This time I got bold enough to say that I really believed this to be God's will for the group.

Someone asked how we would raise the money. I was ready with an answer. We would tour churches in America and Canada all summer and save every penny for plane tickets, food, and travel in Africa.

Evidently my enthusiasm that morning was infectious. Within days, having prayed, the first few team members committed to making the trip. Those who were underclassmen took a little longer. For them it would mean taking a year out of school, a big sacrifice. Yet two months later all but one had the same reply: We were going to Africa!

When school was out in May we set out on a South-

114

western swing that took us through New Mexico, Arizona, and up the coast of California. I was happy when Clayton decided to join us for the summer, too.

Mostly we had a lot of fun, staying in the homes of Christian families along the way. In Oregon, Bo Melin, one of the guys who had come to the underground church meeting with me in Estonia, met a girl named Paula, and they began a courtship by correspondence.

There were some less happy moments, though, for Jan and me. For one thing we were hoarding every cent, each of us living on only about four dollars a week for personal necessities. Even though Jan was good about the whole thing, it wasn't the easiest way to spend the first summer of our marriage. And sticking to a tight schedule sometimes made me snappish. For instance, in her laid-back way, Jan sometimes took a little more time getting dressed before a concert than I thought necessary. I was patient with the other women. But I guess I expected more of Jan. After all, she was married to the "spiritual leader" of the group. We had to set an example.

A few times the strain made me question whether I was cut out to be a leader at all—like the Sunday evening in Portland when a sarcastic remark really hurt Jan just before a concert. Though I apologized, I had a hard time that night telling the people who packed the sanctuary that they could be "new creatures in Christ." That evening I got my first dose of doubt: Was there something wrong in the way I was handling things? Was I pushing too hard to succeed?

At the end of September we had done it. We had raised enough money to fly the team to South Africa and begin our tour there. A friend in Little Rock, Arkansas, offered to house us for a couple of weeks while we rested up. For me there was little relaxation, though. I had to buy tickets, write to African contacts, and send out visa applications. In a matter of weeks we would be on our way.

Immediately circumstances began to turn against us.

It started early in October with the letter that arrived from the South African consulate. News had traveled around the world about student anti-war riots on U.S. campuses, and when the South Africans learned we were a student group they apparently decided not to take any chances: Our visas were denied.

Quickly I came up with the idea to get some of the officials at ORU to pull strings with their contacts in Washington. But on the trip to Tulsa with our drummer, Ron Hallden, I was in a car accident. The vehicle, which we'd borrowed, was totaled. When we finally reached ORU, my arm was cradled in a sling against my bruised ribs. Another surprise awaited me.

Oral Roberts had gotten wind of the fact that underclassmen were dropping out of school to follow me to Africa. He wasn't happy when he talked to me. His correction was strong. I felt terrible. Then, to my relief, his face grew kind, concerned. "You really have a strong call of God on your life, don't you?"

At the moment I felt like something the cat dragged in. But I replied, "Yes, sir. I do."

Perhaps, looking at me, he remembered what it was like to be a young, eager maverick. He'd faced opposition all the time. In the end he gave me his blessing.

As I limped out of President Roberts' office that day I was more determined than ever to get the team to Africa— no matter what it took.

All I could think of was finding another way into Africa, and on the trip back to Little Rock I hit upon a new plan: We would try going to Rhodesia first. Then after we had toured there for a while the South Africans would see our good intentions and let us in. When I relayed that suggestion to the group, the plan was unanimously approved.

So on the afternoon of December 15 we flew to JFK International Airport in New York. That evening we were to board an overnight flight bound for Rhodesia.

We sat inside the airport, shivering because of the freezing temperatures outside. It felt odd to be wearing light cotton clothes and tennis shoes when everyone else was in boots and overcoats—but after all, it would be blazing summer in Africa. We'd sent all of our equipment and clothing ahead of us by ship because it was cheaper. Since the weather was mild and sunny when we'd flown out from the Midwest none of us had even worn a sweater.

We had a couple of hours to kill before the flight to Salisbury, Rhodesia's capital. Jan and I decided to grab a bite together in a sandwich shop. When we'd chosen a booth, Jan looked wistful, talking about her folks and our friends in Tulsa, how she would miss them during the year we'd be in Africa.

But I could think of only one thing: My dream was so close, so nearly real. In just hours, I'd be standing on African soil with my own team of gospel singers. I could picture myself next fall, telling the enrapt students and professors at ORU about the thousands who had come to Christ. In that mental scene I felt so good about myself. I hoped Oral Roberts would be there. . . .

"Terry?" Jan squeezed my hand and looked at me across the booth.

I hadn't heard a word she'd said.

10

TERRY: Disaster

After the overseas flight, I should have been exhausted. A few passengers, who were going on to the plane's final destination in Mozambique, were still trying to sleep as the gray of dawn filled the cabin. Jan was dozing, her head against my shoulder. But I'd been awake all night, excited, congratulating myself on the clever way we had sidestepped the South African government by going to Rhodesia.

I was also hoping our things had been shipped up from Johannesburg since we had a meeting the next evening. The pilot's announcement interrupted my thoughts. "In just a few minutes we will be landing in Salisbury. Those passengers who are continuing on this flight. . . ."

From the rows in front of us a few team members turned to me, each one grinning. I motioned to Larry Dalton, who slipped out of his seat.

He crouched in the aisle beside me just as Jan awoke. Even in a rumpled dress, her dark hair mussed, she looked gorgeous.

"Let's get the group together and pray," I suggested. Jan yawned and nodded and Larry went to rouse the others.

Shortly, the other fourteen Living Sound members were crammed into seats all around us. We tried to keep our voices low, but excitement edged our prayers.

"God," I declared, squeezing Jan's hand, "we praise You that South Africa has refused to let us come. We know that You are going to show Your glory through our work in Rhodesia. We know this is our ticket into South Africa."

Momentarily, when the pilot asked that we fasten our seat belts for landing, my prayer was punctuated with some hearty amens.

When the plane taxied to a halt on the runway I nearly dragged Jan after me as I threaded my way to the door. At the head of the stairs I squinted at the brilliant equatorial sunlight. A blast of hot tropical air rushed into the air-conditioned cabin. I'd forgotten how stifling African summers were. Holding Jan's hand tightly, I hurried down the steps to the tarmac.

We were halfway to the terminal doors when I recognized the pastor from Salisbury in whose church we were meeting tomorrow. He waved excitedly at Jan and me from an observation deck on the airport roof.

And at the same moment someone called, "Terry Law! Please identify yourself." Standing outside the terminal in crisp, all-white summer uniforms were three or four customs officers. When I raised my hand, one of them walked toward us.

"You are Terry Law?"

"Yes."

In his hand was a sheet of paper, which he now held up for me to examine. "And are these people with you?"

It was a list of names—all the men and women in Living

Sound, a few of whom had come up behind Jan and me. I shrugged. "Yes, they're with me. Where did you get these names?"

"I am under orders to tell you that you will not be allowed into our country."

This had to be a joke. "What regulation have we broken?"

"No regulation," the officer said bluntly. "But you are not entering our country. We have arranged with the airlines to send you on to Mozambique."

All the team members were around me now. In the oppressive heat I was already sweating through my shirt. Jan evidently saw my jaw muscles tightening and she was telling me to stay calm. "There's no way we're leaving," I said emphatically.

The officer glared. "I don't want to get tough with you, Mr. Law, but if you don't get back on that plane, we'll make you go."

And so we were forced back up the stairs into the plane. When I caught a final glimpse of the pastor who had come to meet us, my anger dissolved into a sick feeling.

All during the flight to Mozambique I was in turmoil. What had we done to be treated so rudely? It would be a long time before I knew the answer to that question. And in the meantime what were we going to do about our clothes and equipment? More immediately, what was I going to do with the group in Mozambique?

Jan, who knew I was still seething, was quiet for most of the flight. Only once, she ventured, timidly, "It will all work out, honey."

I was too irritated to answer.

We landed in Beira, a port city on the Indian Ocean. The temperature was almost 110 degrees, and the humidity stifling. Quickly, we found a hotel. By then, I'd developed a two-pronged attack.

The first thing to do was contact the Rhodesian Embassy and get them to reverse their decision. Not only that, I made a trans-Atlantic call to some university friends who had political contacts. I didn't care who got us into Rhodesia, the Holy Spirit or a U.S. senator. I only knew that our hard-earned money was going fast. I didn't even have time to deal with the emotional shock and the question of why we'd been kicked out.

Since we were in Mozambique without visas I also had to contact a city police inspector for permission to stay in Beira a few days until we could get into Rhodesia.

The inspector was a pudgy little man. Someone had made the mistake of giving him a badge. His heavily lidded eyes drooped with obvious disinterest. He flashed a pair of stubby fingers at me. "Two days," he said abruptly. I was dismissed.

The second line of attack was to pray. During the day, I sent the others off to the beach, while I haunted government offices and placed phone calls. Evenings, we would gather for prayer. But we had another problem.

How should we pray?

It was *God's* purpose that we preach the Gospel in Africa. But should we *thank* Him for the present mess we were in, knowing that He would bring good out of it? We'd read we should do that very thing in a popular book on praise we had studied. I was having a hard time buying that at the moment, but did not admit it. Other books we'd been studying told us to "claim in faith" exactly what we wanted God to do. Should we pray that the phone would ring, and the embassy would be on the line, granting our entry? Or should we pray and "bind" demon spirits who were warring against us in heavenly realms, as another book taught? None of the books told us how to know when to use which technique.

What we wound up with was spiritual smorgasbord. In

Jesus' name, we declared our dominion over the powers of darkness. We thanked God we were stranded. We cheered. We rebuked Satan as we had never heard anyone rebuke him before.

And each day, the embassy official remained stone-faced. And I had to go back and beg the little "tin dictator" of Beira for "one more day—please," thinking every minute of the precious funds we were wasting.

For three weeks, the deadlock continued. All the while, the $14,000 we'd raised on tour slowly sifted out of our pockets. New Years Day 1970 found us still in Mozam-bique. At some point, I became convinced that God really wanted to perform a miracle—something unusual that would amaze these penny-ante officials. So the morning the inspector told us we were being deported to New York in two hours, I didn't even flinch.

Even as taxis whisked us to the airport, I said blithely, "We might as well go along with them and see what God's going to do. He never loses."

At the airport, no officials from the consulate ran up to say, "Beg your pardon for the inconvenience," as I ex-pected. So God must have something even more dramatic in store. *This plane won't get off the ground,* I told myself, as we trooped up the steps. *We'll have a flat tire or something.*

We taxied out the runway, pausing at the end for take-off clearance. I smiled and winked at Jan. *Any second now,* I mused. *Maybe they'll radio the pilot and tell him to let us off the plane.*

The jet engines roared. We eased forward quickly gain-ing in speed as I shot silent prayers heavenward. *C'mon, God. Do it. Now!*

Then we felt the lift. We were off the ground—headed back to New York. Jan, at my side, smiled nervously.

I thought my heart was being crushed.

Seated all around us, the team sat in silence. Later, when

the stewardess came, balancing a tray of complimentary Cokes, no one accepted.

About the only one who spoke to me during that long, long flight besides Jan was Bo Melin. Several hours after takeoff and halfway across Africa, Bo suddenly came and squatted beside me in the aisle.

If I had ever seen any brightness and idealism in Bo's eyes, it was dead now. "Terry," he mumbled, "I just don't think I'll ever be able to trust God again."

And as if that didn't hurt enough, landing at JFK airport in New York was even more painful.

Leaving Mozambique, the temperature was over 100 degrees. New York, on January 8, the morning we landed, was deadlocked in a punishing blizzard.

We hurried through the movable tunnel that linked the plane to the terminal. Most of the men were in short sleeves and the women in summer shifts. Trotting at my side, Jan shivered as swirls of snow blew on us around the expansion joints. It did not feel much warmer inside the terminal. A radio was playing as we passed a snack bar, and the announcer reported that, so far, it was the coldest winter in 99 years. No one had to tell me that.

We found seats in a lounge area. The huge panes of glass all around us shivered with the pounding winds. Between the gusts of wind-driven snow, we saw the gaunt gray trees outside right themselves before the next shaking blast Every few minutes the glass doors would open allowing another muffled and snow-covered form to enter with a swirl of snow and dead leaves.

But none of this could match the cold desolation I felt inside. I had bravely faced the surly customs official in Rhodesia, and even the little "dictator" in Mozambique. Now I was nearly overwhelmed by the conflicts going on in me.

First, though, I had to decide what to do. Wasn't *I* the

leader of these shivering men and women who had no place to go? We didn't even know where our clothes were. Worse, none of our friends even knew we were in New York, because *I* had announced to everyone who knew us—not to mention churches full of people all across North America—that God had told *me* we were to go to Africa. With these accusations beating at me, I slunk over to a pay phone to make some calls. Fortunately a regent of ORU, a Mr. Cardone, lived in Philadelphia. Since he knew many organizations in Philly, he quickly contacted an inner-city ministry, which agreed to put us up for a time until we could figure out what to do. Then Jim Gilbert, a singer from Baltimore, called his dad, who arranged for taxis for the two-hour trip to Philadelphia.

After the phone exchanges, I went to the lounge area where the others sat sipping cups of hot coffee to keep warm. Briefly, I laid out the plan—Mr. Cardone's plan. What right had I to take any credit, even to insinuate that I could be their leader? Everyone nodded silently when I told them to sit tight. Was it my imagination or did they really avoid looking at me? I excused myself and disappeared into the men's room.

Despite the numbness in my fingers I went to a sink and bent over to splash cold water on my face. When I stood up, I saw my face reflected in the mirror—and the eyes were like bullets.

You're a failure, Law. Inside, you always knew you couldn't do anything worthwhile. You were destined to fail. Why did you have to drag these others down with you?

Still the eyes penetrated me. Not just my own, suddenly, but others, too. I gripped the sink, the cool solidity of the porcelain bowl steadying me as I saw my father's eyes. How often were they veiled in disappointment, disapproval? There were others—Oral Roberts, Gene Eland, scores of friends and teachers at the university. I saw in the eyes of each one the same sad judgment: *Despite all your big talk, Terry Law is a big zero.*

When I finally left the men's room I shuffled around the terminal avoiding even Jan as much as possible.

About an hour later, the taxis rolled up. The women ran out first, screaming as the icy wind bit their bare arms, followed by the guys. I came last, nearly slipping on the glazed sidewalk. The taxi drivers stared disbelievingly. The foolishness of the scene stung me. With snow pelting my face, I prayed one more time, from the bottom of my heart. *Lord, I will never preach again. It's over.*

If only it *were* over.

The ministry in Philadelphia that had agreed to take us in was a drug rehabilitation center on a busy street. Outside, *un*rehabilitated pushers and prostitutes jive-talked to passersby. Though we were grateful to have *any*where to go at this point, life inside the center was dismal, at least for us.

Despite the fact that we were not addicts, we were subjected to all of the center's strict rules. Men and women could not sit, eat, or talk with each other. I suppose it made sense, to some degree, since most of the women off the streets had been prostitutes. But I had to argue with the director of the program about letting Jan and me sleep in the same room. Begrudgingly, he agreed—but we were not allowed to eat at the same table.

Two weeks later, on January 21, our first wedding anniversary, we were still stranded there. What we were to do, I had no idea. At breakfast, Jan looked over at me from the women's table and ventured a wink. Her brave smile was worse than a look of hatred. *She had it so good before she married you,* I lashed myself. *Some life you've given her.* My misery was complete.

A couple of mornings after, we all shuffled into the Saturday morning chapel service—"compulsory," of course.

I happened to sit beside Bo. Since I still had trouble looking at him, I focused on Jan who was seated over with the
women. I hardly listened as the director introduced the
morning's speaker. His name was Whittle, the pastor of
an Evangelical Free Church in Minneapolis. For some reason he had come here from Minneapolis with his wife just
to speak at this center. I couldn't imagine why anyone
would do that. But then, nothing was clear to me at the
moment.

Mrs. Whittle stood in front of us, accompanied by a
woman who played the mission's banged-up piano, and
began to sing. Her first words caught me off-guard:

> *I don't need to understand,*
> *I just need to hold His hand. . . .*

Goosebumps crawled up my arms. The song went on in
that vein and several in the group started sniffling.

When she'd finished, Reverend Whittle stood up. "This
morning, I know there are people here who have come to
the bottom of themselves. You feel as if you can't trust
God anymore."

Beside me, Bo winced. I didn't dare look at him.

Reverend Whittle continued, saying that we often set
out to work for God, to "do great things" for Him. Then
we seem to fail. "We all love success," he said, "but sometimes at the very rock bottom of failure we find God Himself—not God as we try to control Him, but God in His
own sovereign and mighty power. Then the life of victory
can truly begin."

I could hardly see through the blur of tears. Larry, Jan,
and the others were sobbing. I'd been too hard on the
director. I'd have to thank him for telling this man our
story and bringing him here just to encourage us.

As soon as the chapel service was over I bolted from my

seat. Grabbing Reverend Whittle by the hand I pulled him aside.

"What you said really helped us," I told him, wiping my eyes with the back of my hand. "I mean, after what we've been through."

He smiled at me politely. "After what you've been through?"

"You know," I prompted. "Getting kicked out of South Africa. Losing our luggage. I'm Terry Law."

"I'm sorry, I've never heard of you," he said.

"My group is Living Sound. Didn't they tell you about us?"

"No. Who are you?"

As I told him our sorry story, Reverend Whittle's mouth fell open.

"So you're the ones!" he blurted. "We've got to talk somewhere. Bring your group up to our room right away."

And once there he began to tell us in detail the most incredible story.

Reverend Whittle explained that a year ago he and his wife had experienced a deepening of their spiritual lives. They had committed themselves to listening to God more closely and obeying inner directions that came to them. Usually the directions involved someone in their church who needed help.

A couple of weeks before, on January 8—immediately, I noted the date; Living Sound had been returning from Mozambique—his wife had been at home alone during the day praying quietly as she went about her housework. She had folded some clothes and was taking them down the hallway to their room when suddenly she stopped dead. The most unusual thought was bombarding her. She and her husband were to go to Philadelphia. They didn't even know anyone in Philadelphia.

"When she told me," Reverend Whittle chuckled, "I

said, 'If the Lord told you that, fine. But He hasn't told me.' "

Just days later, he continued, he was preaching from his pulpit on Sunday morning when the words faltered in his mouth. *Philadelphia,* said the inner voice. He stuttered. *Someone there needs you.*

At home he and his wife decided that if God wanted them to go east for some unknown reason they would give Him one day. Dialing an airline ticket agent, they booked a flight for Friday afternoon, returning Saturday.

"Last night when we landed at the airport we had no idea where to go," he said, smiling. "We flipped through the yellow pages and I felt compelled to call this center. The director said he would be glad to have us speak at chapel this morning. I had no idea what to say until the moment I got up. You don't know how dumb I felt."

Yes, I did know how dumb he felt. Inside I was a landslide of feelings and impossible questions. Could God really have sent them all this way just to talk to us? Did He love us *that* much? Could it be that He still had work for us to do?

When I filled Reverend Whittle in on all that had happened to us—from the turndown by the South African government to the snowstorm at JFK—my voice kept breaking.

My face was red and stained with tears when, at the end, he said, "So you *are* the ones we were sent here for."

Seizing my hand he ducked his head and began to pray. First quietly, then loudly. Suddenly he opened his eyes, looking me full in the face. "The Lord has a message for you. You are going to be in the Johannesburg airport in seven days."

I blinked. Then I looked at Larry Dalton, who looked like he wanted to roll his eyes. "Sir—uh—you don't understand," I said. "We don't have any money. We don't have any tickets or visas."

"The Lord says you'll be there in a week," he insisted.

We talked for sometime more, and then they had to prepare to leave for the airport again. When I walked downstairs with Jan and the others I had a sinking feeling.

I wanted so badly to believe. But Pastor Whittle's message seemed impossible. Stuck here in this dismal place, however, could I dare to *not* believe?

When we discussed it as a group, there were smiles, some head-nodding. No cheers. I couldn't blame them. And yet I wanted to believe. Somewhere inside I found the smallest bit of courage to say, "Okay, Lord, it sounds pretty wild to me, but we put it in Your hands. If You want to get us into South Africa we're willing to go." I didn't want to mess things up by barging ahead on my own again.

And on Monday things began to happen—fast. Sometime after breakfast the director called me into his office to take a long-distance call.

A man was phoning from the U.S. State Department. "We've been trying to locate you. The South African government has just granted your visas. They've telexed them to New York. You can pick them up at immigration at the airport."

I stifled a laugh. "You don't have any spare tax money lying around that you'd like to buy our tickets with, do you?"

He did not laugh.

But the group did when I told them about the call. Spirits were picking up.

On Thursday we came totally unglued. Again, I was summoned to the phone. The caller identified himself as an official from an international airline and my ears began to burn. He would not identify the individual who had contacted him about us. He was calling to offer us tickets to Johannesburg on his airline. The only condition was that we never disclose the airline's identity because they'd be swamped with requests for free rides. Would I accept the offer?

I almost shouted a hearty *yes, sir!*—when I caught myself.

"I hope this doesn't sound ungrateful, but South Africa will not allow you to enter the country without proof—return tickets or something—to show you have a way out."

"We can guarantee a return flight for all of you. When would you like to leave?"

There is no way to describe the cloud of joy on which we stepped off the plane in Johannesburg that Saturday—seven days after Reverend Whittle had received that message from the Lord. No way to describe the feeling of stepping out into the hot sunshine of a South African summer.

Happily, we were reunited with our equipment and clothes. We practiced hastily, accepting an invitation to perform for a week at an all-white high school in Klerksdorp, sixty miles from Johannesburg. The principal, a Christian, informed us that most of the 1,000 students there were on drugs.

After the Spirit-led adventure we'd been through our singing and sharing were unusually vibrant—but none of us imagined for an instant that *we* were the cause of what happened at Klerksdorp. In one week 650 students gave their lives to Christ, many of them quitting drugs on the spot. People from the neighboring town of Potchefstroom began coming to our evening meetings, and a hundred people a night were answering our call to commitment.

So it went from town to town for the next six weeks.

More people came to Christ than in our whole previous summer of traveling in the U.S.

I was still marveling one Sunday morning just before I was to speak at a large church. I was alone in a small prayer room behind the platform. Living Sound had nearly finished singing.

While I was praying I thought about the silence of God. I was going to speak that morning about the Syrophoenician woman in Matthew 15 who came to Jesus to ask that He heal her daughter. Despite her weeping and begging, Jesus was silent. But because of her persistent faith Jesus granted her request.

Kneeling, my face to the carpet, I reviewed what I'd be saying to this congregation about the things I'd learned during the silence of God through which we'd just come.

I saw now for the first time that when my prayers had gone unanswered I was not interested in God's approval as much as I wanted to be admired by others—my dad, Oral Roberts. I'd been trying so hard, underneath it all, to be *somebody* in their eyes.

Second, having heard God's voice, I'd then taken off and run away with the idea on my own. I'd ignored circumstances and the wise counsel of leaders like Oral Roberts. Now I saw that, if God had some plan for me and Living Sound, it was crucial that I do things *His* way. Only then could I lead the team wherever He wanted us to go.

It was then I became conscious of the feeling—peace, warmth, awe, and mystery—the sense of God's presence. Words formed once again in the quiet of my worshiping heart. They could not have been clearer. I was stunned.

Still on my knees I heard the singing stop. Larry Dalton was speaking. I knew they'd be calling me out to speak in a moment.

How could I tell them, after the tough things we'd just

gone through, that those obstacles were nothing compared to the mountains ahead? *Mountains of difficulty.*

How could I tell them that Africa was only a preliminary step—that God had just whispered a further direction in my heart?

I am sending you behind the Iron Curtain.

11

SHIRLEY:
The Walls Come Down

The sun glowed through the summer morning haze, making the trees at the far end of the golf course look ghost-like. The air was cool, but the sun felt hot and I wished I'd worn a lighter blouse.

Jim was preparing to tee off, oblivious to everything but the ball on the ground in front of him.

I studied his face, shadowed beneath the visor, as he got ready to drive. Jim was a better-than-amateur golfer, and had chosen an iron to loft the ball over the small hill between us and the green beside the stand of trees some two hundred yards away. He shifted his feet, but his eyes were frozen. Only the faint flicker of a shoulder muscle told me he was about to swing. I wondered what was going on in his head.

How often I'd wondered that in the eight months we'd been married. Jim could talk to me about golf, explaining the reasons you used different clubs. He never minded my tagging along on an occasional Saturday, like today. And we could fill up dinner conversations with office chat. Jim's customers were charmed by his warmth and humor, and he was selling more dental equipment than most of the company's other salesmen. He was so successful that the company offered him a better sales district in Texas, though I was against leaving Portland.

But our communication rarely touched any deeper levels. I couldn't understand it. Jim had listened to all the painful intimacies of my past, and had stood by me in facing my father. What had happened to the closeness we'd felt before our marriage? At dinner parties or in church Jim would slip his arm around my shoulder or hold my hand. *Then* he was affectionate, gentle. When we were alone at home, however, a distance opened up between us. Evenings, when the television went off and he'd finished the paper, he rarely paid any attention to me. Lying at his side in bed, as his breathing slipped into a gentle rhythm, I moved from disappointment to rejection.

Jim's sudden movement—the fluid coiling of his body and the *swoop* of the club before it struck the ball—stirred me from my thoughts. In the distance the tiny speck of white bounced not ten feet from the green.

"What a drive!" he crowed. We climbed into the golf cart and he patted my knee.

"That was excellent, hon," I responded. I *wanted* to sound enthusiastic. Inside, though, I'd determined that we were not going to *just* talk golf all day. It meant waiting for the right moment.

When Jim had finished nine holes, he was just under par. That put a spring in his step as he went into the clubhouse to change. Glancing into the coffee shop I saw that the place was empty, and chose a table by the windows. When Jim found me there a few minutes later he was still analyzing his game.

"If I keep the right touch on those long putts I've got a

good chance of winning that tournament next month," he said, accepting a glass of milk from the waitress.

I smiled. "From the way you looked today you ought to do well."

The waitress walked away and disappeared into the kitchen. Neither of us spoke for a few moments.

"Shirley, what was wrong today?" Jim said at last.

"*Today?*" It came out more sharply than I'd intended. Maybe I was feeling more than rejection. Jim frowned—as though he wished he hadn't asked.

"I'm sorry," I fumbled. "I just don't understand what's happened between us. We were so affectionate before we got married. What's changed? Why can't we be lovers? If you have a problem, why can't we—"

"I don't have a problem," he interrupted. Too late, I knew I'd misstepped.

"I meant, if *we* have a problem. It's *our* problem."

"Shirley, there's no problem."

"Then I have a problem," I insisted. "I'm not satisfied with the way things are between us."

"Look, honey," he said quietly, "can we discuss this later?"

There was a flat silence.

"Okay," I backed off. "Let's go home."

So my hope of talking things out that day was crippled. In fact, once I had brought up the subject, the walls of silence seemed even thicker. Among Christian friends, in our adult Sunday school class, we probably looked like the ideal Christian couple with a successful marriage. But the hidden truth was that the physical aspect of our relationship was strictly limited to Jim's terms. I felt in a fog as to what I should do.

About a month after my failed attempt I was alone in the office, busily grinding through a mound of paperwork. I hadn't been thinking about Jim just then, not consciously at any rate. Unexpectedly, his face was before me.

Gripping my pencil in both hands, I snapped it.

How could this happen, God? My frustration spilled out in a silent prayer. *This is so unreal. First I'm abused by my father. Now I don't know how to relate to my husband. What have I done? How can I get Jim to talk to me?*

I could get angry at God, but what good did it do? It certainly didn't make me feel better. With my face sunk forward into my hands, I prayed over and over, *What am I supposed to do?*

Later that afternoon, as I drove home through rush-hour traffic, an unexpected thing happened. One minute I was concentrating on the red sports car that kept cutting in and out of my lane and the next moment I was thinking about Carl Maier. Jim and I had not spent much time with the Maiers recently. But I could not get my mind off that conversation when Carl had expressed a concern about Jim before we married.

Checking the rearview mirror, I swung into the far lane and, at the next corner, turned off. Carl would be on his way home, too. This subject was a little embarrassing, of course, and I didn't want to betray Jim in any way. Suddenly, though, I knew I had to talk to Carl.

Fortunately, he was home already when I arrived. I made some feeble excuse about "dropping in to say hello." When Carl asked a "How's-married-life-treating-you?" sort of question, I seized the opportunity.

Casually I asked, "You know, you said something once that puzzled me. When I was trying to decide about asking my dad to give me away at the wedding, you were concerned about Jim. I wasn't paying attention then, but I've wondered about it since."

Carl pursed his lips thoughtfully. "Maybe it was wrong for me to bring it up then. I'm not positive why I've been concerned for Jim—not entirely anyway. But he kept such a careful distance between himself and women. Now that's not unusual for some bachelors. . . ."

Inwardly, I winced: *A careful distance.* Carl had no idea the accuracy of his perception.

"Maybe," he was saying, "I'm concerned because I know Jim's been considering the ministry. At least the idea of working for one. If he's serious, he's probably going to be tested. Since you're his wife, you'll be affected, too. People in the ministry can face added strain on their marriages."

Momentarily, I told Carl I had to get along. He patted me on the shoulder as I stepped outside. "I'll be praying for you and Jim, Shirley."

Praying. All the way home that word hounded me. If I looked back, my track record for answered prayer wasn't very good. How I'd wanted a decent family, a father who didn't drink or beat my mother or abuse me. How I'd wanted intimacy—a *good* marriage. I was almost afraid that, when I prayed, it would boomerang and I'd get just the opposite.

Later that evening, as Jim disappeared behind a copy of the *Wall Street Journal*, fragments of memory—small incidents with Jim—began to come together.

First, there had been the talk about his reluctance to date women in the church, and then his insistence that we keep our relationship hush-hush. I wasn't comfortable with the idea, but it made some sense then. Had he been avoiding closeness all along and I'd missed the signals? Was he, belatedly, turned off by what he knew of my past? Why did he marry me at all?

All that week I fought off those questions and tried to focus on the mound of credit card applications on my desk. I was miserable and confused. At times, guilt feelings I'd had as a girl returned. Maybe *I* was somehow to blame. Even worse I was tempted to think, *Maybe there are some people whose prayers don't get answered. Maybe God has favorite children—and I'm not one of them.*

Immediately, I rebelled at that idea. For one thing I knew the Bible well enough to know that that wasn't true. Even more, I detested such self-pitying ideas. One thing I knew for sure, though, I couldn't handle the feeling of rejection. So half the time I prayed, comforted in knowing that Carl Maier was praying for us, too. And the rest of the time I tried to fight my way through the inner fog to decide what my next move should be.

About two weeks later I was in my office when an unusual thought struck me with such force I froze.

It was a rainy afternoon and I was carrying an armful of folders to the file when I happened to catch a glimpse of the gray sky and drizzly streets outside—a typical day in Portland. Jim disliked this climate. Once in a while, he'd ask if I was ready to move. But to me, this was home.

In that split second it was as though someone had torn away a curtain. I stared out the window. The streets, the buildings, everything looked alien. Suddenly, fiercely, I did not want to live in Oregon another minute.

All the way home that day, I tried to understand the swiftness of my change-of-mind. Was God telling me something? Maybe moving would give us a new start.

That evening Jim kept eyeing me across the table. Finally, he set down his fork. "That's a suspicious-looking grin," he said lightly.

I laughed. "I've made a decision. You've said you'd like to move. And today the strangest feeling came over me. I'm ready to leave as soon as you are."

"You're joking."

"No, I mean it," I replied.

That smile I loved so much immediately dimpled his

cheeks. "All right, then. Turn in your resignation tomorrow. We'll leave in two weeks."

I couldn't believe it—my cautious, conservative husband, making such a radical decision. He reached across the table and took my hand.

The next day Jim went into action so fast that I quickly saw how much he'd wanted to leave, and how generous he'd been not to force me into an unwanted move. First thing in the morning he asked his boss if the company's offer to make him a regional manager in San Antonio was still good. It was. Jim accepted.

Just that quickly, the decision was made.

After that, I fed on Jim's momentum. We barely had time for proper farewells. Perhaps the sheer flurry of packing made it a little easier to say goodbye to Mom, Roger and David, Carol and her folks, and all our other friends.

Then the morning came in September when our car was loaded with suitcases—and we were on the road. It seemed unbelievable.

During that long drive I had lots of time to think. *Lord,* I prayed silently, reviewing the events since that rainy afternoon just weeks before, *this sure is a bold step. I believe You helped us make the decision.* Then, as a P.S., I added, *I'm going to trust You that things will work out.*

On the way to Texas we'd planned to stop in Tulsa to spend some time with Buddy and Pat Harrison whom we had not seen since our wedding. Almost immediately upon our arrival there it seemed that our decision was not only bold but involved some extraordinary timing.

The morning we drove into Tulsa I decided that fall, with its searing heat and sun-scorched grass, was not going to be my favorite time of year in the Midwest.

I was travel-weary and hot when we knocked on the Harrisons' door. But the moment Buddy and Pat greeted us, my dour mood vanished.

Jim was a blond giant next to Buddy, who was short, with a barrel chest. He was boisterous, funny, and outgoing. I could see why he and Jim were friends. Pat, with her soft blue eyes, seemed a little shy. Then she enfolded me in her arms, graciously leading us inside. And from that first moment I knew she was a truly caring person.

Maybe it was the joy of two old friends getting together again. Maybe it was the happiness I felt at finding another couple with whom I felt completely at ease. A special chemistry sizzled between us. With great enthusiasm, they told us about Hagin Ministries, which was beginning to have an impact nationally and internationally. I knew Kenneth Hagin was Pat's father, but now I learned that he had been healed miraculously of a serious illness, and his teaching was largely based on the scriptural principles about faith he'd first discovered during that experience.

On our second morning in Tulsa we also learned over breakfast that the ministry's manager had just resigned. Buddy, as the head administrator, was going in early to help pick up the slack. Jim perked up.

"How about taking me to the office with you today?" he offered. "Shirley and Pat might like a little time together. And maybe I can do a little volunteer work for you."

Buddy grinned. "Okay—as long you don't con the staff into running off to play golf!"

Not only did Jim work with Buddy that day, but for the next three mornings he was up early, shaved, and ready to go. And in the evenings, as Jim and Buddy discussed their day at work, I could tell how happy Jim was to be involved with a Christian organization.

At the end of the week, the four of us were relaxing together in the living room when Buddy sprang his idea. "You'd make a great office manager, Jim. Pat and I would love to have you and Shirley stay on in Tulsa. What do you think?"

Jim looked at me. In my heart, I marveled at the timing. If we'd come a week later the position might have been filled. To me, this was the hand of God beckoning Jim into ministry, something I wanted very much. And I'd told Jim the night before that I'd never seen him happier. Now I just smiled. The decision had to be his alone.

He shrugged. "Well, Shirley seems happy. And I can't say the idea hasn't crossed my mind this week. So—the answer's yes."

I kissed Jim on the cheek. So leaving Portland *was* a right move. Maybe we were on a new threshold, a second beginning.

The following Monday, Jim called his company's office in San Antonio to explain why he wasn't coming after all. They tried offering him more money but Jim's mind was fixed.

For the first couple of weeks we stayed with the Harrisons until we were able to find a small apartment. One morning, a few weeks after Jim started working with the ministry, I watched him pull out of the parking lot. The sun was so hot it had burned off the dew before eight. I thought, *Lord, only weeks ago we were in a different world. I can't believe how our lives changed, practically overnight.*

At least the outward circumstances had changed. One rocky area remained. I guess I expected that, once we were involved in a ministry, our spiritual lives and our relationship would skyrocket. Perhaps that high expectation set me up for the near-crash that came.

Jim, of course, was the hit of the office. And in the new church we attended, he found friends immediately. Soon he was being asked to speak at businessmen's prayer breakfasts. But a numbing realization grew: Between us personally, nothing had changed in the slightest. Our physical relationship was still subject to his control. One evening late in October I tried carefully to discuss it again.

We'd been out to dinner together and talked about various things: There was news from old friends in Portland; Brother Hagin was planning a new school, Rhema Bible Institute; and we made plans for a Saturday fishing trip, since Jim had taken to the sport.

It was around ten when we pulled into the parking lot outside the apartment. It was a balmy night and, when Jim turned off the car, we sat listening to the chorus of crickets. Jim took my hand. "I enjoy talking to you," he remarked quietly.

"I enjoy listening."

He dropped my hand. "Shirley, why do you do that?"

"Do what?"

"Sometimes you make it sound like I monopolize—oh, forget it."

"No, Jim," I insisted. "Tell me."

He did not reply.

"Are you upset because I said I enjoy listening?"

"Yeah. You do a fair amount of talking yourself."

I'd been stuffing too many feelings inside for too long. "Well, Jim, there's one thing I wish we *could* talk about. Us. We never do." My voice was level, but cool—even so, I wished I could stop myself. "You might as well know it, if you don't already. Sometimes I feel used."

For a long time, only night sounds riddled our silence. Then, almost in a whisper, Jim said, "I don't know what it is."

That was as far as we could go. Hardly speaking, we went inside.

From that night on two thoughts began to dominate my waking hours.

The first was this: Somehow I'd imagined that taking a bold step, moving, would help us leave our problems behind. But hadn't I learned from my mother's experience when she thought leaving North Dakota would make a teetotaler out of Dad? Yet taking bold steps was something I'd had to do all my life: challenging Dad when he brutalized Mom or the boys, being a "good" girl when I could have gone along with the crowd, being a surrogate mother to Roger and David, asking Dad to be in the wedding.

I felt that I had sacrificed so much, even leaving my home to try to find a new life with Jim. And it wasn't working.

That depressed me greatly and brought an avalanche of questions. When *does* God intervene? Once we've done our part, been obedient, when does He begin to act on our behalf?

And the second thought that filled my days was more depressing. Perhaps the only answer was to get out of the marriage. Divorce was something I hated, but I considered separation. I didn't know what to do. I felt so out of control.

More months passed and, by summer of 1973, nothing changed except my attitude. I was twenty-two. Most of my life, I'd fought to survive. I wanted peace; to be loved. And though we hadn't been married two years I wanted to leave Jim.

When Buddy Harrison called me one morning I assumed he and Pat wanted us to come over for the evening. But I was surprised when, after chatting a few minutes, he said, "Shirley, this is difficult. But I have to ask. Are you and Jim having problems?"

I'd never have betrayed the intimacy of our relationship—especially with Jim's best friend—but all my defenses were gone. The whole story came out: the rejections, the attempts at dialogue. Buddy gave me his perspective on Jim, admitting that Jim had always put up a wall when it came to personal matters.

"It's one thing between friends," I replied, "but if he won't work on our marriage, I can't take it any longer."

"Are you saying you want a divorce?"

"No. But I can't believe things are going to change."

"Can you believe that *God* wants you to have a good marriage?" he asked.

That stopped me. *I* wanted a good marriage. And I knew God wanted marriages to be healthy. "I want to believe," I admitted. "But—no, I don't have faith like that."

Buddy prodded gently. "Do you mind if Pat and I pray for you and Jim? Because we have faith for your marriage."

"No," I shrugged. "I'd like that."

We talked a few minutes longer and, as we finished, Buddy said resolutely, "With God, nothing is impossible. That's His word to us."

That evening, talking on a deep level seemed anything but possible. Jim came home and plopped in front of the TV all evening, while I hid in our room with a book. Later, when he crawled into bed, turning his back to me, that said it all. I went to the kitchen for a glass of iced tea. When I came back he'd already dozed off.

Miserably, I slipped beneath the covers, reaching to turn off the light on my night table.

Jim started.

"It's just me," I said.

He rubbed his eyes. "No. It wasn't you. I had just a flicker of a dream—but it was awful."

Jim was shaken. He said that the moment he fell asleep he saw himself as a salesman, knocking on a series of doors. At the first door, I was right beside him. He made a few more sales calls and, as he was about to knock on another door, he suddenly realized I was no longer at his side.

In the few moments it took Jim to relay those details, tears had begun to fill his eyes. "And when I turned to look for you," he said, "you were far away. I called and you said, 'Jim, I've gone as far as I can go with you. Shirley, I can't believe it. It's the same dream I had a week before we were married."

Suddenly, the tears were sliding down his face. To my astonishment, he said, "I've kept a distance between us. It was wrong. At least you should know why."

Most of what I learned is better held in confidence. But one painful story in particular helped me begin to understand.

Before Jim moved from Minneapolis, he had been in love with a young woman named Roberta. They had gone to the same church for years and dated when they were teenagers. Roberta seemed troubled, often depressed and secretive. Jim's reaction was to lavish her with affection and always do the things she wanted to do, hoping his love would ease her inner pain, whatever it was. When they got older, she refused his proposal. But one evening, when he tried to talk about marriage again, she made a shocking confession.

Roberta told him, without a twinge of remorse, that she was seeing a married man in the church. They had been sleeping together. Jim had been a convenient cover. If he insisted on getting serious, however, he had to know why she would never marry him.

"It was foolish—and unfair to you," he whispered, "but after Roberta, I *couldn't* let a woman get close to me like she did. Before we got married, I panicked. I hardened myself to any of your needs. Can you forgive me?"

His arms were around me then, his tears dampening my hair. Never had I thought him a stronger man than at that moment.

We talked far into the night. And healing came.

The next morning, Jim gave me an extra-tight squeeze as we kissed goodbye. He was backing the car out the driveway when I remembered Buddy and Pat.

Just the day before, Buddy had talked to me about faith. Jim's sudden willingness to talk *had* to be a result of their prayers. Even before I met Jim, I'd wondered about faith. What was this faith that Buddy and Pat had discovered? What did they know about the Scriptures that I had obviously missed?

Jim's car disappeared down the street and, still warmed with a new joy and hope, I knew I was on the verge of discovery.

12

SHIRLEY:
This Thing Called Faith

Only by contrast did I fully realize how far apart Jim and I had been emotionally.

Following Jim's disclosure about the past, we could not spend enough time together. It was like he was a new person—or rather the person I had believed him to be all along. Jim had developed a love for fishing so we planned special Saturdays just for the two of us: I packed fried chicken, salads, and cold sodas, and would sun myself in the boat while Jim reeled in bass and croppies. Jim also picked up the hobby of buying used cars to fix and resell and I enjoyed handing him tools as he worked.

We were falling in love in a whole new way. It was interesting that, once our physical relationship got straightened out, we began to grow much stronger together spiritually. Now the spiritual leadership and strength in Jim that had drawn me to him initially began to show, and I marveled at what God had done.

Certainly, before, there had been answers to prayer. I'd

applied for a job at a bank in Tulsa in their MasterCard department and been told they had no openings. As I prayed though, the company reversed its decision and created a position, placing me in charge of other sales people.

Still, it was the change in our marriage that opened my eyes. Though Jim always talked to me about the need to develop a stronger faith, it was through our relationship with the Harrisons and the Hagins that I began to make sense of ideas I'd been trying to put together for some time.

During this time, Jim and I had many long conversations with Buddy and Pat, whose prayers had been so instrumental in turning our marriage around. Buddy, in fact, pastored a lively and growing church in Tulsa, which we attended. As we talked, I started to understand on a deeper level what faith is.

For instance, I knew I was "born again." By that, I meant, first, that I believed the Bible to be the Word of God. And the Bible said Jesus shed His blood for our sins—He took our sins on Himself and died in our place. The Bible promised that all who trust in Christ will be saved.

As I thought about it though, there were days when I didn't *feel* like a Christian. Days when I didn't even act like a Christian. On those days, was my salvation wiped out? No. Because we live by faith, not by feelings. That was a line I'd heard preachers use for years.

Then what about all the other promises in the Bible?

Some of God's promises, I knew, were conditional—like in 2 Chronicles, where it says, "*If* My people will humble themselves and pray, I will heal their land." God's fulfilling His promise depended on obedience.

Still, as a businesswoman, I saw this "covenant" almost like a business transaction: "You do this, and I'll do that." For the first time I saw very clearly that God is a covenant-keeping God. If He's given us a promise in His Word, He'll keep it.

One night Jim and I were driving back to our apartment after one of these conversations and a forceful thought grabbed me. *What's the most impossible thing I can pray for?*

An answer leaped readily to mind: that my dad would come to Christ. I felt so confused about him still. I wanted to love him—I just didn't know how. Still, I knew the Bible said that God is love. The next thought really shook me: *God loves my dad.*

Jim picked up on my silence. "What are you thinking about?"

I told him. "But it's hard to have faith that my dad will ever give his life to God."

Jim thought for a minute. "You know that the Gospel of John says that 'God is not willing that any should perish.' If you're willing to believe that Scripture on behalf of your dad, I'll agree with you."

"But God isn't going to override my father's will in this," I replied, thinking out loud. "It's Dad's decision, isn't it? And as far as I can tell, he isn't the least bit interested in God."

Jim persisted. "Jesus told us in John 15:7, 'If you abide in me and my words abide in you, you shall ask whatever you will, and it shall be done for you.'

"Shirley," he said, glancing at me, "it's one of those big choices again. You can choose to believe Jesus' word, and pray in faith for your dad, or not. Your faith is what releases His power."

Suddenly I had a new thought: I'd never considered that I could pray for Dad's *will* to change. Maybe that was my first step.

It was beginning to make sense. The funny thing was, if this line of thought had been presented to me five years ago, I wasn't sure I'd have been ready to accept it. But now, I could see no other way.

That night I did begin to pray for Dad, though it was not easy. In days to come I would have to wrestle with old feelings of hostility, making a conscious choice to pray for Dad when I did not feel like it. But I was committed.

And as fall arrived in Tulsa I had a chance to test my new understanding of faith in a different way.

An early cold front came in, bringing chilling rains and a flu epidemic.

One drizzly, cold Monday morning, both Jim and I awoke with sore throats. Jim's eyes were glassy with fever. My face was hot and I ached all over. Both Jim and I had important work to get done. Rolling over, I forced myself to stand, feeling tipsy.

"I'm going to make us some hot tea with honey," I muttered. "Then we'll call our offices and tell them we're not coming today."

Jim sat up. "No. I'm going to get well."

I stared at him. "What are you talking about?"

"What we've been learning," he replied hoarsely. "The Bible says in Isaiah 53, 'By His stripes we are healed.' Just before you got up, that verse came to mind. I think we're supposed to agree that, when Jesus died on the cross, He took our sickness upon Himself as well as our sins. If we believe that verse, we'll be well today."

My head was swimming and I wasn't sure I'd make it to the kitchen, let alone put in a day's work. Then something occurred to me: *This is when I need to have faith. Not when I'm feeling up. But when I'm not feeling like it.*

"Okay," I replied, folding my arms. "You pray."

Jim's prayer was simple, "Thank You, Lord, that Your Word says we're healed. Amen."

"That's it?"

"That's all we need," he replied, throwing off the covers.

"But I still feel terrible."

"Don't think about the way you feel. Just keep thanking God that you're well."

"I just don't know. . . ."

Jim was in the bathroom already, getting out his razor. He called back, "You can gripe about your sore throat—or you can fix your thoughts on the fact that our God is a healing God. It's up to you."

Jim's attitude, I thought, was a little flippant. Sulking, I didn't reply as Jim finished shaving and stepped into the shower. I thought he could have shown a little sympathy. *You can set your mind on the Truth,* that other, inner voice interrupted again, *or you can go back to bed and wallow in self-pity.*

That got my attention. "All right," I called, over the rush of the shower. "By His stripes I *am* healed."

Minutes later I was in the kitchen, stirring honey into my just-made tea, when I realized my throat did not hurt. Incredulous, I hurried back down the hall to tell Jim, when he rushed out of the bedroom in his robe.

"I feel great," he announced. His eyes looked bright and the huskiness was gone from his voice.

"I'm getting there," I added. "The sore throat is gone, but my head is still warm. Not as bad as it was, though."

"Just keep repeating what the Bible says: I'm healed, in the name of Jesus," Jim instructed.

I decided to skip the tea and just get dressed. By the time I'd curled my hair and dabbed on some makeup, I must have repeated the verse from Isaiah fifty times. Going back out to the kitchen, I found Jim scrambling eggs.

"It's unbelievable," I marveled, practically gaping at Jim, "but I feel super."

Jim pointed the spatula at me. "Believe it," he said, smiling.

Even after that experience, I have to admit, I still had trouble with this new idea of a faith that challenges and wins. Two days after we were healed of the flu I almost got myself to believe that we'd talked ourselves into feeling better. But I rejected that idea when I witnessed the many close friends and co-workers who were laid up with the flu that fall, while neither Jim nor I had so much as a scratchy throat or a stuffy nose.

That experience, in the fall of 1973, opened broader vistas in terms of my spiritual growth in the next two years. For one thing, I began to view the problems I faced as opportunities to grow in faith.

I also learned, however, that the idea of trusting God's promises—really *counting* on them—made some people upset.

One place where this became painfully obvious was in the Hagins' ministry, which grew rapidly throughout the mid-'70s. I was saddened at the unfair criticisms leveled at them by other Christians. And I was amazed at the family's response to Jesus' command in Matthew 5 to "bless those who curse you." Time after time, Buddy, Pat, and the Hagins would forgive their critics, praying for God's blessing upon them. Their example caused me to pray for this kind of divine love for my own father.

One thing became very clear to me as I watched them. The biggest battleground, I saw, is not the everyday world where hasty and unkind words are spoken, where husbands and wives argue, where tragic accidents happen, where illness threatens to drain the joy of living. The real battleground is in the soul of each one of us. There, the *decisions* that govern our lives are made.

I got another glimpse—for me, a shocking glimpse—into that "other reality" in September 1975.

Jim was out of town one Saturday when the phone rang. I lifted the receiver.

"Shirley?" It sounded like—but no! In the past four years I'd only spoken to him on rare occasions.

At the other end of the line, my father was sobbing.

"Dad? What's wrong?"

In somewhat garbled speech he told me his second wife was divorcing him. Then his voice cracked. "Shirley, I'm so sorry for the way I treated you and your mom and the boys. I'm just no good."

He's been drinking, I thought, and almost hung up in disgust. He'd said he was sorry in the past, but his words seemed so empty. But did that matter? I'd forgiven him, hadn't I?

"Shirley, do you forgive me? Please?"

Unexpectedly, a wave of compassion came over me for this broken, hurting man.

Before I could answer, he said in a low voice, "I've got a gun here. I'm going to kill myself."

"Dad—don't." Where was this sudden love coming from?

I kept him on the phone just long enough to learn that he was in a hotel in Portland. Then I made him hang up, promising I'd call him back on my nickel.

Quickly, I phoned Roger and David and told them to get to the hotel and see that Dad was on a plane to Tulsa. "We'll cover the ticket. Just don't let him out of your sight."

What followed was a long phone conversation with Dad, interrupted by my brothers' arrival at the hotel. Then there was a call from the Portland airport. Dad was on his way.

My head was swimming when I met him coming off the plane that evening. More years of hard living had grayed him considerably. But it was the dullness in his eyes, the slight stoop of his shoulders that told me Dad was a broken man.

Driving home I kept remembering my prayer of two years before. We had believed my dad would come to Christ. I felt so off-kilter now. Had God allowed events in Dad's life to bring him to his knees? How impossible it seemed—and how I wanted it to be true.

Jim returned the next day. It was then Dad told us an incredible story. He'd had to change planes in Denver. When he got off the airplane he made up his mind to exchange the tickets I'd bought for a ticket back to Portland.

"The craziest thing happened," he said shaking his head. "I hadn't been in that ticket line two minutes when some lady walked up to me and said, 'Wherever you're headed, you better get on that plane and go there.' What do you make of that?"

Jim and I looked at each other. Had God intervened in some dramatic way to get Dad to us? Just the thought gave me more hope that he was here for a special reason.

The following evening we took Dad out for supper, then stopped at Buddy and Pat's to visit. We were all in the living room chatting. Buddy, I believe, asked Dad an innocent question, something so innocuous I cannot now recall it.

Dad seemed to deflate before our eyes. "I'm a failure," he said, his head sinking forward. "I've failed Shirley . . . her mother . . . the boys."

Again I felt such unusual warmth for him—an honest love. Gently, I replied, "You have every reason to feel the way you do. But"—I felt a fullness in my throat—"I love you."

Buddy asked him, "Mr. Paintner, you were a church man for so many years, you must have heard the Gospel. Did you ever give your life to Christ?"

"No," Dad said, still looking at the floor.

"Why was that?" Buddy prompted, quietly.

Dad's shoulders began to heave. "Because I smoked! I'd always thought that if you smoked, you couldn't be a Christian. I tried to quit so many times but—I guess I'm just weak."

Buddy, in his gentle pastoral manner, talked to Dad for some time, explaining the free gift of salvation in Jesus Christ. Then he led Dad in a prayer and I saw my father open his heart to accept God's forgiveness.

When they finished, Dad was crying. I'd wanted to go touch him, but couldn't. Buddy looked over at me. "Shirley, go touch your father and pray with him."

I stood and walked toward Dad, my legs feeling like rubber. Timidly, I stretched out my hand, not knowing if I could really go through with this. The moment my fingers touched his shoulder an amazing thing happened. Warmth and love flooded into me.

Embracing my dad, we wept together.

Dad stayed only till the end of the week. Then he returned to Portland. But the love I'd wanted for him was now in me! It was as if I'd had a logjam inside and somehow God's power had blown it away the moment I'd acted in obedience. In time to come, as we shared phone calls and letters, a very natural love continued to flow between us.

Mostly, Dad's unexpected visit, his coming to Christ made me wonder. I'd heard Christians talk about "spiritual warfare." Paul talked about battling "against powers and principalities and rulers of the unseen world." Had we—the Harrisons, Jim, and I—broken some unseen force with our prayers? More disturbing, I wondered what would have happened to Dad if I'd refused to pray.

I decided that there must be something to this "spiritual warfare." It did not enter my head that the experience with Dad was preparation for what was to come.

Two weeks after Dad's visit, I walked out of a downtown bank, having just made a successful sales call. I should have felt great. Instead I felt—what was it? *Unsettled* was the word that came to mind. But why?

All the way back to the office, I tried to push the feeling aside. Dad had called me three times since he got home to talk about the Bible and his rebirth. Jim was happily fixing his used cars. We were settled in our jobs. . . .

My hands tightened on the wheel. Come to think of it, Jim had hardly talked about the ministry at all lately. My questions brought only one-word answers. But the past two years with Jim had been so wonderful. Was this unsettled feeling, so contrary to evidence, some sort of spiritual nudge?

That evening after supper, Jim was hidden behind the newspaper when I asked if we could talk. He folded back a corner. "Sure. What's on your mind?"

I didn't want to sound "super-spiritual," but. . . "You're thinking about leaving the ministry, aren't you?"

Jim's jaw dropped. The paper fell across his lap. "What makes you think that?"

"I'm just sensing that there's some change coming."

He folded up the paper. "Odd that you should bring it up. I do feel like I'm ready for a change. I was waiting for just the right time to talk to you about it."

Then Jim explained that he'd felt restless for several months. He thought he needed to be out on his own for once, to run his own business. He wanted to open a used car dealership. "It's something I just have to do."

"What about the ministry?" I pursued.

"Who knows? Maybe God's leading me into a ministry of my own or something. You'd be happy about that, wouldn't you?"

Typical of Jim, he had a plan worked out—even a potential location in Tulsa for his business. When we finished, there was little for me to say, really. Though the unsettled feeling I'd had earlier did not leave, I knew this was a crucial time and felt I needed to support him.

Very shortly, Jim terminated his position with the Hagins' ministry and opened his own automobile dealership. It was small at first. But Jim was like a magnet when it came to customers. And he put one hundred percent of himself into everything. In a matter of months, he was running a profitable small business. We were finally able to buy a home of our own.

For most of 1976 I accepted this "sidetrack"—which was how I thought of it—as a time of preparation for the next step. Jim had so much knowledge of the Bible, so much personal charisma that I knew he'd be great in ministry. He even doubled his time for prayer and Bible reading. Inside, I grew more unsettled and couldn't understand why.

After Jim opened the business, I noticed that he also began reading many books on success: successful time and money management, success at sales, success in relationships.

Only later was I able to pinpoint the day that something changed. I scarcely noticed at the time.

Bounding in from work one evening, he gave me an extra tight squeeze.

"You're in a great mood," I smiled.

"Someone paid me a great compliment today."

I kissed him. "I'm not surprised."

"I was closing a deal with a guy, a stockbroker. He said I had finesse and an excellent mind with finances. He said I'd make a great broker."

My heart skipped. "That's interesting, dear," I replied. "But I don't know too many stockbrokers in the ministry."

Jim released me from his arms, still smiling. "Yeah," he said. Nothing else.

We didn't talk about it any more that evening. And I couldn't understand my deepening uneasiness.

After that, however, Jim's preoccupation disturbed me, even though he never missed church and continued to read his Bible daily. That October, as our fourth anniversary approached, I felt it was time to start our family. When I talked to Jim about it, he got a strange look.

"I don't know if having kids is a good idea, honey You know, I've always had this funny feeling that I wouldn't live to be forty."

I didn't like to hear that kind of talk, and steered the conversation back to having children. Jim shrugged, and agreed it was probably time.

Later in the month Jim came home and announced that he'd registered us for—no surprise—a one-day seminar on "developing winning attitudes" at a local Sheraton Hotel. The man teaching the seminar was a Christian. I'd been meaning to talk to Jim about this preoccupation with the success books, but he was so excited I decided our talk could wait.

If only I'd followed my instincts.

On Saturday morning, as we walked into the lobby of the Sheraton, Jim noticed the seminar leader. Laying a hand on my back, Jim guided me to him.

The speaker, whom I'll call Mr. Barnes, was talking to the *consierge*. He was in his 40s, boyishly handsome, every hair in place, and dressed in a tailored suit of expensive gray herringbone. When Jim introduced me to Mr. Barnes, he extended his hand cordially. I noticed the diamond ring and a thick gold bracelet.

With perfect poise he inquired about our work and where we lived. His brow furrowed with concern as Jim mentioned he was looking for new direction. Squeezing Jim's shoulder with one hand, he said, "With a pretty wife like this at your side, it's a cinch you're headed for the top, my friend."

That annoyed me. But I smiled. Jim ushered me into the meeting room, which was appointed in crystal chandeliers and richly flocked wallpaper, and jammed with about two hundred people. Mr. Barnes' delivery was smooth. The audience was laughing at his jokes. I was getting more unhappy by the minute without the slightest clue as to why.

"No matter what your goal, you can *reach* it.

"Let's say that you need a new car. So does one of your friends. Now you'd both love a new red Jaguar. You say, 'All I can afford is a Dodge.' But your friend says, 'I can *have* the Jaguar. I can give up some time with my family and work harder.' And he *will* have it!

"And you? Where will you be?" Here Mr. Barnes let his shoulders droop and shuffled ape-like across the platform. "You'll be plodding along in your ol' Dodge."

Everyone laughed—except me.

Mr. Barnes leaned into the mike and said, with a conspiratorial hush, "Every one of us wants a nicer home and a better car. You can have it! The secret is this: You must meditate. Make up your mind to succeed. Lie on the floor each day. Close your eyes and think about your success."

Jim clapped heartily with the others. Tears welled up in my eyes, rolled down my cheeks. Now I knew why Mr. Barnes brought out revulsion in me. Maybe it was his ape imitation, but he was no longer the handsome, nattily dressed man. I could only see him as a hideously grinning monkey whose words were like groping fingers, grabbing at souls. Jim's soul.

At this point Mr. Barnes instructed everyone to lie on the floor while he put on a motivational tape. I excused myself and went out to the lobby.

An hour passed. I was still standing in a lonely corner when I heard someone come up to me from behind.

When I turned, the hard-set face of Mr. Barnes startled me. He glared. "Why don't you go home?"

Had he seen me crying and been annoyed? Or was it something else? Had our spirits somehow read each other?

Jim came up behind him just then, and his smile vanished when he heard my reply.

"I don't know who you *really* are. But you're not going to harm my husband. I'm going to stay right here and pray against everything you're trying to do."

Mr. Barnes, of course, had seen Jim. He didn't respond, but abruptly walked away.

Jim shocked me. He was furious.

"Who do you think you are?" Jim glared at me angrily. "You have no right to talk to him like that!"

"Honey," I pleaded, "his words are a trap. You don't see it. The enemy is using this man. If you listen to what he's teaching, you're on dangerous ground."

"He gives me good things," Jim shot back. "Something to hang onto."

Before I could say another word, he turned and walked away from me.

The rest of the day, I sat at Jim's side and prayed silently.

And when we got home that evening, Jim wanted to talk. "I saw you in a different light today, Shirley."

"What was that?" I asked, puzzled.

"You see something I don't see. A different reality, maybe." He paused, considering. "You have to know this, though—until *I* see it, I can't go along with you. But I do appreciate you."

He kissed me on top of my head. The subject was closed.

That was not quite the end of it, though.

A week later we went out to dinner with an older couple we'd met while Jim was with the Hagins. Mama and Papa Goodwin had captivated us with their old-time, plainspoken love for God. Later, while we were talking, Mama Goodwin suddenly leaned forward, staring at Jim. "When you were talking the strangest feeling came over me. Something is trying to affix itself to you. That's the only way I can explain it."

Jim shot a glance at me. "That's strange. Shirley told me the same thing."

Mama Goodwin went on, telling Jim he was at a major crossroad. "You need to do what the Lord wants you to do."

That, I thought, would drive the nail home.

And following that, Jim did let up on the success bit. Or maybe it was just that my attention was suddenly drawn elsewhere.

In November, after our anniversary, I discovered that I was pregnant. I'd suspected, but didn't tell Jim until I was sure. I was thankful that he didn't mention his horrible prophecy but held me tightly in his arms.

Three months later, in February, when Tulsa was being whipped by frigid winds and the radio promised freezing rain, Jim came home one evening with a surprise for me.

"I've decided to sell the car business and become a stockbroker, honey," he announced.

How do you describe the feeling of warning bells ringing inside of you when on the surface nothing appears to be wrong? He was a thirty-two-year-old adult. I couldn't expect him to run his life according to my "feelings."

"I know it's what you want to do," I managed. "I'm happy for you."

He hugged me and smiled, as if he couldn't even see my questioning look.

And that was the beginning of the greatest fight I'd ever faced—more terrifying than anything I'd ever known.

Soon I would be fighting, not only for my husband's spiritual well-being, but for his very life.

=== 13 ===

TERRY:
A Party in Poland

W hen Living Sound returned from touring South Africa at the end of 1970, we were happy, but exhausted. I knew also that we'd come to a major turning point.

It wasn't just the miracle God had performed to get us there after our first blazing defeat, or seeing thousands respond to our music and testimonies, though that was marvelous enough. More difficult was the knowledge that the fire we'd been through was only a preliminary, a purification. I couldn't forget the horrified look on Jan's face when, in that church in the high veldt outside Johannesburg, I announced that God had set before us a serious challenge: to carry His Word behind the Iron Curtain.

Leaving Africa's heat for the gray winter of Tulsa was a cold reawakening into the world of the everyday. Early one morning in January 1971, it was bitter cold outside our small apartment near ORU and not too warm inside. Jan was rinsing the coffeepot in the kitchen. Closing our bed-

163

room door, I got on my knees beside the bed to pray. The Iron Curtain mission was an enormous undertaking, and I had spent much time in prayer about it—particularly since I'd found out the reason we had been expelled from Africa the first time.

I had gone to the South African consulate in Johannesburg that late-summer morning to request an extension on our six-month visas. The revival sweeping the African churches was so explosive we had wanted more time there. When I had filled out the application and handed it to the official, he stared at it, then looked up at me in amazement. *"You* are Terry Law?"

I swallowed, remembering the expulsion at the airport in Rhodesia. "Yes, I am," I replied sheepishly.

Out came the most intriguing story. This man had been in the consulate in Rhodesia when Living Sound was expelled from the country. He'd learned that Rhodesian Prime Minister Ian Smith had been invited by a U.S. university to explain his racial policies, which appeared to be anti-black. The U.S. Immigration Department, however, in protest of his policies had refused him entry, an embarrassment that somehow never hit the papers.

Living Sound had landed in Salisbury just days after the incident. Smith had ordered that the next large group coming from the U.S. be turned away in retaliation.

When I'd left the consulate that morning, I'd had conflicting feelings. I was relieved at finally discovering we'd done nothing illegal to cause our eviction. But I had a strong sense that I'd been allowed to glimpse beyond everyday occurrences into a supernatural realm in which even the timing of politics could fall under the domain of powers and principalities. In other words, spiritual warfare could affect us more than we ever realized.

If that was the case, the confrontation at Salisbury was mild, certainly, to what we could expect if we tried to go behind the Iron Curtain. I was glad I had learned this tough lesson about waiting for the Lord's timing. That would be imperative now, especially since I'd had that glimpse of the power of the spiritual realm working against us.

"Terry? Breakfast is ready." Jan was now smiling at me from the bedroom door.

As I got up from my knees, I had one parting-shot prayer. Though I'd accepted the challenge from the Lord, I couldn't help but pray wistfully, *Couldn't You give this hard stuff to someone else?*

Breakfast fare was light since we'd returned to the U.S. with little in our pockets. Undaunted, Jan had used some light spices and bits of leftover ham to dress up the eggs. I felt so proud of her. I hoped I could express that to her someday.

Throughout the meal, Jan kept smiling as if she had a secret. I was preoccupied, however. Whether or not we went behind the Iron Curtain at some future time, there were immediate questions to answer. While Jan listened, I more or less thought out loud, considering what was to become of Living Sound in the wake of the Africa trip. Some members of the group would be leaving us to finish their degrees at ORU.

As Jan cleared away our plates, I rambled: "We need to regroup. Form another team. And we need a nonprofit organization behind us. I think we'll need a bus. . . ."

That's when Jan sidled up to me. Taking my hand, she searched my face. Her eyes glistened. "We'll also need a few other things this summer—like a crib."

I nearly tipped over the chair getting up to hug her. "When, honey?"

"In August." Wistfully, she added, "Sounds like your schedule's pretty full. I hope you'll be around."

I vowed that wild horses couldn't keep me away.

So 1971 *did* prove to be a big year—a year of "new births." Larry and I were occupied with two main thrusts: first, putting together a nonprofit organization, Living Sound International; second, auditioning singers and musicians for a new team and planning tours in the Caribbean and the southwestern U.S. By summer, we'd also raised money to buy an old Greyhound bus, which we'd need for domestic travel.

And in August, while Jan was visiting friends in Canada, she delivered a beautiful baby girl at Red Deer Hospital in Alberta, two weeks ahead of schedule. Misty was the name we'd chosen. Unfortunately, I'd gone south to Des Moines, Iowa, for an engagement with the team. When Jan's friends reached me by phone, I made hasty plans to fly north to be with her.

When I hung up I was beaming. "It's a girl!" I announced. "They say she has olive skin like Jan's."

One of Jan's girlfriends on the team asked, "How's Jan doing?"

"Oh, you know Jan—a real trooper. I'm sure she's fine," I remarked.

A look passed between two of the girls, which I did not miss. But I ignored it. Taking Jan and Misty to the Caribbean with Living Sound in the winter would make up for my not being there.

Even with all the changes in my life, that unsettling call to the Iron Curtain countries remained fresh in my mind. Sometimes I'd awaken at night, feeling the warmth of Jan beside me and listening to Misty's soft murmurs in the crib next to our bed. My palms would go icy. Staring at the dark ceiling, I'd pray, *Lord, it's so dangerous. How can we do what You've asked? It would take an army of angels to get us in there.*

Fortunately, I'd learned that, unless I wanted to lead the group into more near-disasters, Terry Law's barnstorming ideas about worldwide ministry had to be silenced in favor of God's step-by-step blueprints. I'd seen Him move supernaturally to get us into Africa, and I'd follow nothing less in this venture.

I refuse to push or manipulate our way in, I prayed. *If You really want us behind the Iron Curtain, You'll have to open the way.*

My prayers continued in that vein as the twenty-four members of the new Living Sound team—counting Misty—took to the road. For the next nine or ten months we toured the United States. We'd gotten a house trailer to make traveling "easier" with the baby. For poor Jan it became a grueling time. Money was always tight, the constant moving disrupted Misty's schedule. Then she began teething. The other women pitched in to help, but even so, I'd occasionally find Jan crying in a private moment. The best I could do was offer a feeble prayer of comfort and a hug.

We were traveling again in May of 1972 hoping to raise enough money for a fall tour in Europe, Israel, and Africa when I got one of the hugest surprises of my life.

Since we were on the road so much, we arranged for mail to be forwarded. One of our mail *rendezvous* was a small church in southern California where we were scheduled to sing for a youth rally one evening. Sure enough, a sack of mail was waiting for us in the church office when we arrived that afternoon. The university had sent it along.

We took the sack to the sanctuary. One by one, the team members collected their mail and spread out through the sanctuary. And I, when I had a chance to examine the small stack addressed to me, found my attention drawn to a very unusual-looking blue envelope, obviously from overseas, which had been addressed to Living Sound, Oral Roberts University, Tulsa, U.S.A.

167

What intrigued me most, as I carefully tore it open, was the postmark: Krakow, Poland.

The letter was in very broken English. I understood the shaky writing to say it was from a young man from the Jagiellonian University in Krakow, representing some sort of group for students. He'd met an American girl named Beverly—an exchange student from ORU studying Polish—who had told him about us. Somehow she'd heard we'd be touring Europe.

My hands were tingling. "Hey, everybody," I called, "put your mail down, and come listen to this."

When they'd gathered around me, my voice shook as I read the rest of the letter to them: We were officially invited to perform in Poland. At the bottom was a government stamp, which would allow us to get visas.

A ring of somber faces stared at me. All the newer members had learned about the call I'd heard in Africa. Now, two years later, without any finagling on my part, an official invitation!

The rest of the summer we excitedly shared our news at every performance. And in the fall, as we began our European tour in England, my heart was set on only one goal: Poland.

Weeks later, at the airport in Vienna, Jan handed our baby into the arms of our close friend Laura Shrock. From Austria, we'd be traveling east. Circumstances in Poland would be rough enough without the added worry of having eighteen-month-old Misty along. Laura was taking Misty south to Africa where friends in Johannesburg would put them up until we arrived in several weeks.

My heart ached as Misty innocently waved bye-bye, knowing she hadn't the slightest idea that thousands of miles would separate us before we could hold her again. When Laura left with Misty, Jan fought the tears. From the moment of Misty's birth, I'd known she was a natural mother. Inside, I marveled at her bravery in sacrificing a quiet home life for the work we had to do.

From Vienna, we traveled east by bus to Czechoslovakia. Though the so-called Iron Curtain is an invisible one, a certain coldness fell upon the group the moment we crossed into Communist territory. Not me. The closer we got to Poland, the old sense of adventure that drove me to do crazy and dangerous things set my adrenalin pumping.

Winding through the Carpathian Mountains, I was struck by the beauty of Poland. An early dusting of snow capped the high peaks above the red and gold carpet of hardwood forests. Jan was beside me at the window, watching charming alpine villages of thatch-roofed homes rush by.

Arriving in Krakow, I thought at once of Tallinn, the port city in Estonia where, four years before, both Jan and I first had our hearts touched by Christians under the thumb of mother Russia. The sidewalks were crowded with pedestrians. Though street peddlers were everywhere, selling flowers, fruit, and finely carved wooden plates and animals, few dared to look you in the eye for more than a moment. No matter, I was still flying high.

The Jagiellonian University impressed me at once with its massive, medieval stone buildings. It was near there that I finally met with our sponsors, three young men representing the student group. They'd arranged for Beverly Hubbard, the exchange student from ORU, to meet us, too. I was a little surprised by their formality with her because I'd assumed they all knew each other. Evidently not.

With Bev as our translator, I told them how happy we were to be their guests. Jokingly, I said I hoped the university officials would like our Western music.

One young man, who was especially stiff-faced, explained that they weren't expecting officials. This was for students only. He talked on, and I gathered that our act, as he put it, was to be presented in some sort of nightclub. We were performing for a party.

That's strange, I thought. *Inviting us to come all the way here for a. . . .* Tingles shot up my spine. Of course he wasn't talking about a private party.

By the look on Bev's face, I knew it had dawned on her, too, that these guys were leaders in the local student chapter of the People's Party of Poland. The name Living Sound did not connote anything Christian to them and Bev had told them we were a contemporary music group planning to tour Europe. The name Oral Roberts University where they'd written to us obviously meant nothing to them.

Now, Bev and I stared at each other, red-faced, realizing these guys weren't interested in winning souls for Jesus. We were here to play a concert at the Communist youth headquarters in southern Poland!

That night, in a hostel near the university, I paced the floor. Jan was obliged to stay in the women's dorm and I a men's building.

How could we have gotten into such a mess? I fumed. I'd been so petrified at what we'd fallen into, all I'd been able to do was politely excuse ourselves, saying we were tired from traveling.

As soon as we were away from our three Communist hosts, I asked Bev to get me a Polish history book written in English. Perhaps if I could "soft sell" our group to them, we wouldn't get kicked out of Poland, cause an international scandal, and go down in defeat as we had in Rhodesia.

That was my plan, at any rate.

The next afternoon, hours before our first "performance," we were escorted to the dingy brick nightclub where we set up our equipment. As I was waiting to do a sound check on the mikes, a skinny kid with his arm around a young girl pulled at my sleeve. "Do you have grass?"

"Uh, no," I said, nervously. I was astonished that, even here in Poland, drugs had apparently caught on.

The first concert was scheduled for five P.M. An hour before, we prayed. Jan's hand was perspiring as she held mine. We prayed for wisdom. Tact. All the songs we knew were about Jesus, so it wouldn't take them long to catch on to us. It was obvious by our prayers that all the twenty-two of us wanted was to get out with our skins.

Then came the curtain call. We moved out onto the stage in a dark, low-ceilinged hall. The air was blue with cigarette smoke. Beyond the glare of the spotlights, I could see that every table was packed and littered with liquor bottles and glasses. People stood along the walls as well. A roar went up from the crowd as the musicians picked up their instruments and the singers spread out across the stage. These people were expecting to have quite a bash.

As soon as we began to sing, I saw the confused looks on faces across the audience. Apparently, most of them understood English enough to realize what was coming off. After our third or fourth song I took the mike, hoping I'd remember some of the Polish history I'd read for my opening gambit.

Nervously, I started by saying how happy we were to be in Poland, the land of Copernicus and. . . . The faces were stony. I might as well have been lecturing on George Washington chopping down the cherry tree to students at Berkeley. Clearing my throat, I started over. The Polish were such heroic people to have survived so many invasions by unwanted foreign powers. . . .

A rustle went through the crowd. I stuttered to a halt. Jan's lips were moving in silent prayer. Sitting at the piano, Larry Dalton looked like he was going to swallow his tongue. From the edge of the curtain backstage, the three guys who'd met us yesterday stared angrily.

We were sunk. These students obviously expected us to

play Jimi Hendrix, Led Zeppelin, and the Grateful Dead. If we went on, they'd want our blood.

I don't know how to explain what happened next. I thought of Jesus and the cross—and suddenly these smoking, hard-drinking Communist young people mysteriously lost the enemy label I'd put on them. They were just trying to drown their emptiness in liquor and worldly philosophies like young people everywhere. I saw in my head an image of them all, standing beneath a blood-stained cross, the cross on which Jesus had died for them as He had for me. The fear was leaving me.

Holding the mike to my lips, I said loudly. "We aren't a rock band. That's not why we're here." I saw one girl in the group go pale. I'm sure she wanted to shut me up.

"We're here," I went on, "because we want to tell you how to find the way to true peace and happiness. Marx and Lenin said they knew the way—but they did not. There is only one way, and His name is Jesus Christ."

Behind me, the Living Sound team squirmed as I told the crowd they needed to make Jesus their Savior and allow Him to cleanse their sins with His blood. Each time I paused for a breath, silence hung heavily in the air like the blue haze of cigarette smoke. Ten minutes later, when I finished, every eye was glued on me. Where had this boldness come from? I'd been the uncommitted kid who couldn't refuse a cigarette. Turning, I walked offstage, leaving Larry to carry on the concert.

As I passed behind the curtain, two of the guys who'd been watching grabbed my arms roughly. They were furious. One of them said threateningly, "You come with us. We want to talk with you."

As they dragged me downstairs all I could think of was Jan's terrified look when they grabbed me, and of little Misty thousands of miles away. I thought of prison, too, and that, at least if they had me, they might let the others go.

In a cold little basement room, they shoved me down on a hardwood chair. Two other men came in cursing, and slammed the door behind them. Seating themselves at a table, all four of them glared at me.

One of them, a skinny blond man with a sallow complexion, became head interrogator. "We know you are CIA, come to embarrass us," he charged angrily. When I denied it, there was a fresh round of cursing.

For forty-five minutes, they bristled with questions, asking me probably a dozen times who my "contact" was. I repeated each time that we were a Christian group, preaching the Gospel in Europe. We had only come at their invitation, I reminded them, and offered to get the official letter.

As if to dismiss my claim, my interrogator demanded, "Why did you misrepresent yourselves?"

I took a deep breath. Calmly, I told them all again that we came in the name of Jesus Christ, and hadn't meant to misrepresent ourselves at all. As I had done upstairs, I explained the Gospel to them, wondering every second if they would fly into a rage.

When I was finished, the range of expressions was remarkable. There was red-faced embarrassment—also astonished looks that said, "I can't believe this guy has the nerve to sit here and tell us this stuff."

Then they spoke among themselves in Polish. There was some debate, and I began to shift nervously in my chair, supposing they were considering calling in the police.

At last, my skinny blond friend spoke, in nicer tones. He apologized for the questioning. Then he shocked me with his request: "We would like you to give a second show. But you don't talk. Just songs."

I was confused but too relieved to argue.

When I got upstairs, the hall was in an uproar. Living Sound had obviously finished the first "show," and one crowd was being hustled out to make way for a second. Joel Vesanen, our road manager, had followed us downstairs to see where they'd taken me. As we shouldered our way through the mob to get up onstage, he said, "They must have sold out both performances."

At once, it made sense to me. They'd sold tickets and made a lot of money on this benefit. Canceling the second show would halve their "take."

Suddenly my stomach wrenched. *We're singing to raise money for Communists.* I groaned inwardly.

When we got to the stage there was no time for anything but a reassuring glance at Jan. The crowd was shouting for music. Most of the guys on the team looked grim, and the girls looked like they wanted to cry. We were trapped.

The opening songs were terrible—stiff, a shade off-key. When it came to the usual break where I preached, I shook my head at Larry. He nodded, and went straight into the next set.

The group launched into the song, "Bright New World." I was miserable knowing that these young Communists would be furthering their cause with money we'd help them. . . .

My eye caught a movement on stage to my left, as the group sang.

> *Someday, a bright new wave will break upon the shore,*
> *and there'll be no sickness, no more sorrow,*
> *no more war. . . .**

---

* *Bright New World* by Flo Price © Copyright 1969 by Lexicon Music, Inc. ASCAP. All rights reserved. International copyright secured. Used by special permission.

At those words, one girl timidly lifted her hands in praise. Three others, including Jan, lifted their hands. But as they sang, it was the brightness on their faces . . . !

And little children never will go hungry anymore,
And there'll be a bright new morning over there!
There'll be a bright new world for us to share!

Now the others lifted their hands, caught up in worship. The heaviness in me lifted until—suddenly, I was filled with a sense of soaring. The musicians picked it up, too. I almost laughed out loud when our trombone player lifted one hand—and kept playing!

With voices of all ages praising God the three-in-One!

The electricity had the audience mesmerized. No catcalls when we finished that song; no one touched a glass of liquor or lit a cigarette as we finished the concert.

There was no doubt who was in control, even in this Communist stronghold. His love was overpowering.

Our "hosts" were waiting in the wings during the last song. At the final chorus I stepped in among the singers and said, as loudly as I dared, "The moment we're done, hit the floor. Fan out through the audience. Talk to everyone you can about Jesus before they catch us and throw us out."

The scene when we trooped off that stage was classic. Living Sound people were everywhere. The guys who had hauled me downstairs were trying to round us up and having no success. All across the room, the question was being asked, "Do you want to pray and receive Jesus into your heart?"

Perhaps the guys who'd sponsored us were too embarrassed to cause a scene, or maybe they figured none of these savvy young comrades would listen to our "fairytale" about Jesus' death and resurrection.

They let us stay well past midnight, talking to whoever would listen. Some were reluctant to make such a bold step in public. But seeds were sown. And several others did pray to accept Jesus that night—right there in a smoke-filled Communist youth club.

When we left, in the wee hours of the morning, feelings were running too high to sleep. Nearly dancing along the sidewalks, we found our way to an all-night Hungarian restaurant. The drowsy owner perked right up as this boisterous team of young Americans burst in. We laughed and talked and I somehow downed the hottest bowl of "soup laced with paprika." It was daybreak before we got back to our dorms.

We stayed only a few more days in Poland. Just before we left, we learned something interesting from Bev: The club leaders told her we were an embarrassment to them, not because of our message, but because we believed in Jesus so strongly we had been willing to risk our personal freedom and safety to tell others about Him, while most of them were Communists only so they could get material benefits out of the party.

What we did not know, as we left Poland, was that news of our bold witness had spread. Across town, someone had brought word to an influential leader in the Roman Catholic Church who would later draw the attention of the whole world. His name was Karol Cardinal Wojtyla.

It was only after we'd left Poland and made our tour through Israel to Africa, where we joyously united with Misty, that a flicker of insight came. I'd been too excited about the incident in Krakow to think clearly, but now I saw something dimly.

In the very midst of atheist ridicule, Jesus Christ had been miraculously honored. Paul's statement in Ephesians

176

would not leave me: "For we wrestle not against flesh and blood, but against powers and principalities and rulers of the unseen world." I saw that it was not the people who were our enemy, but something that wanted to bind them and crush us. But as God's love and power became transparent in us, shining out to the audience, it had blown a hole in political and ideological barriers.

In a very real sense, Jesus had triumphed over darkness. And it happened when we began to praise.

I mulled that over for a time, then tucked it away as an interesting lesson to share in between songs sometime. Wherever we traveled, I told the story happily. I couldn't know then this was another glimpse of that far-off dream Dwight McLaughlin had first showed me as a boy back in British Columbia, or that, one day, I would be in a kind of prison so deep and black that the light of God's love would be all but snuffed out.

One very small and interesting event marked that African tour for me.

Just before Christmas, at the very end of our tour, we went into Rhodesia to perform and preach in several churches. I was still smarting at the idea that two years before Ian Smith had used us as political pawns to embarrass the U.S., nearly wiping out my ministry. Now I felt a little smug that we were in his country after all.

We played in a chapel in Salisbury one evening and I gave my usual invitation: Anyone who wanted to receive Christ could come forward and one of us would pray with him. About sixty young people responded, including one young man who seemed especially troubled about the racial tension in Rhodesia. His interests seemed more political than spiritual, and I didn't spend a lot of time with him.

The next morning, the same young man sought me out at the house where Jan and I had spent the night. We went out and sat on the curb beside this busy downtown street to talk. He said his name was Alec, and he plied me with question after question about his newfound faith in Christ. From what little he told me about himself, I gathered he'd caused his family a lot of embarrassment by his rebellious behavior. Now he wanted to put things right with them, especially his dad.

Three hours after we began, we got up, shook hands, and he left me.

He was barely out of sight when a passerby on the sidewalk rushed up and said, "Do you know who that young man is?"

I shrugged. "No."

"He's Alec Smith," the man said excitedly, "the son of Ian Smith, our prime minister." He explained that Alec had been a rebel, outspoken against his father. His picture was constantly in the papers because of his troubles with drugs.

I was humbled and ashamed. Had the son of Rhodesia's prime minister bumped into me at random on the street, he might have gotten a different message from my lips. Yet God, in His infinite mercy and humor, had spoken through me, and led this young man to Himself.

Much later, in America, I would read news stories about the amazing turnaround in the life of Alec Smith, who now stood beside his father when revolution turned Rhodesia upside-down and dirty politics painted Smith as evil in the world press. No one could account for Alec's changed behavior.

But we had seen the truth behind the headlines: Jesus Christ knows no barriers.

14

TERRY:
Higher Mountains

When we returned to Tulsa in May 1973, having spent six months touring Africa, it was time for Living Sound to expand. My family was about to grow, too: In Africa, Jan had announced she was pregnant again.

The whole summer was spent working and planning. Larry and I deputized a second Living Sound team under the dual leadership of Joel Vesanen and Jim Gilbert. Both men showed good leadership qualities. Immediately, they planned a major trip, taking ten new singers and musicians to the Orient.

And in August, Jan and I were able to scrape together enough cash for a small down payment on a home. It was a little place, just a couple of miles out from ORU. The house needed cosmetic repairs and the lot called for nice trees and flowering shrubs. But it bordered on farmland and reminded me a little of Canada's solitude. We loved it.

The day we moved in, I unpacked boxes in the living room. Misty scooted into the kitchen where Jan was stacking dishes in the cupboards. I became aware of Misty's high-voiced cheery patter—and another sound. Jan was humming. Her rich alto tones expressed the most warm, contented sound I'd ever heard. I sensed Jan's great satisfaction in having her own "nest"—even though our kitchen table was literally a cardboard box. Smiling, I dug into another carton.

In November, however, shortly before the baby was due, I came home from the office to find Jan upset. I put my arms around her, feeling the fullness of the life within, and listened. With the ministry's growth, plus the new house, finances were tighter than usual. She'd been writing checks, only to find we had barely enough money to cover all our bills—and we still needed a winter coat for Misty.

"I know God will provide," she said bravely, leaning her head on my shoulder. "It's just so hard waiting sometimes."

I knew what she meant. We held one another and prayed.

About two weeks later, on November 17, Jan delivered a baby boy. Misty was cute, primly tucking blankets around our little blond-haired Scotty. But then, Jan was such a good mom. I was proud that Misty had her for a model.

The next spring, both Living Sound teams, one led by me, the other led by Joel and Jim, had hectic travel schedules. With Scotty only six months old, and Misty three, Jan couldn't travel with the team this year. But when we arranged some meetings in Tampa, it was a chance for her and the kids to see her folks. We expected a nice family visit—lots of picture-taking and kids bouncing on Grandpa's knee—not another strong encounter with God's Spirit.

One of our engagements in Tampa was at a Jesuit high school. The priests and brothers were polite, and the high school kids responsive. After, a priest from nearby St.

Paul's Church asked us to put on a concert there. I told him I'd consider and let him know.

The truth was, I tried to come up with a good excuse *not* to go the moment he turned his back. As a boy I'd been taught in my church that Roman Catholics were not going to be in heaven. So I had reasoned it was best here on earth to keep your distance.

But the priest's voice and his eager invitation kept coming back to me. For some reason, we had to go to that church. I phoned him and we set up a concert date.

Ten days later, Living Sound was singing for the first time in a Roman Catholic church. As the concert ended, I gave an altar call, saying that anyone who wanted to learn about a personal relationship with God should meet us at the front.

About twelve people came and sat in the front pew. A priest had come forward, too, and gone into the sacristy by himself. He went and knelt in the corner, head bowed, the black beads of a rosary clasped tightly in his hands. As I went toward him the crazy things I'd heard as a kid came back. If I laid hands on him to pray, would he be angry? *Lord,* I prayed, *what do I do now?*

Feeling timid, I stepped up beside him and gingerly set one hand on his shoulder.

The moment I touched him, that small, strong voice I knew all too well spoke clearly inside. I wanted to groan at what it said.

That night I was like a caged lion. While Jan slept, I paced the floor of our bedroom in the D'Arpas' home, trying to make peace with myself. A huge part of me fought that inner message I'd heard. What would my family and friends say? What would other evangelicals think? How would we be received?

At three A.M. I collapsed in bed. God had given me some unusual assignments, but this took the cake. Weary, I whispered, "Okay, Lord. I don't understand. But I'll do it."

The next evening, Living Sound performed at a Methodist church. In the middle of the service I got up to speak and took a deep breath before plunging in. "Folks, God spoke to me last night. He told me Living Sound is going to minister in the Roman Catholic church."

A murmur went through the audience. Jan shot me one of those "I-wish-I-didn't-have-to-learn-these-things-in-public" looks.

Immediately after, two team members cornered me in a Sunday school room, barraging me. "Do you know what you're doing? We don't believe the same things. . . ."

I'd learned my lesson about obeying God's voice. I cut in, trying to be gentle. "I've got to follow what the Spirit says. If you want to be part of Living Sound, fine. If not, that's your choice. But that's where this ministry is going."

The silence that fell was not an easy one.

Nor was there complete acceptance in the group as we left for another tour of Europe a month later, in June—our first big trip without Jan. A few on the Living Sound team had been reared, like me, in anti-Catholic environments. I picked up occasional rumblings, and hoped the issue wouldn't become a controversy. The plain fact was that after that initial conviction I had no idea how our ministry among Catholics was going to come about, or when.

This tour of Europe would climax in Lausanne, Switzerland, where we would perform at Billy Graham's Congress on World Evangelization. But before that, risky as it was, I knew I had to take the team back into Poland.

On Tuesday morning in the first week of June, anxiety shadowed each face as the ferry from Sweden landed on the Polish coast. No one knew we were coming; we had no bookings, just the address of a Bible school in Warsaw, given to us by someone in England. But the idea that we were free to do whatever the Holy Spirit directed gave me a rush of adrenalin. We set off by bus for Warsaw.

Once we'd hunted up the school, we were greeted at the front door by a young man who spoke fluent English. His name was Richard Pruszkowski. He knew of Living Sound because of our concerts in Krakow nearly two years ago. When I told him why we'd come, his mouth fell open. "We have seen very few Western missionaries. They don't come to Poland!"

That introduction was the ticket to our lodging. At least we had a foothold. Wednesday morning Richard happily offered to be our interpreter and "booking agent."

"There are two or three pastors nearby who would love you to sing and testify. Maybe I can arrange things." Then he paused, eyeing the group. "They don't have too many young people, mostly old ones. You must understand, Protestant churches are very small in Poland."

"To be honest," I explained, "God has called us to sing in Catholic churches."

His face fell. "Oh, no, you can't do that."

I couldn't believe that, even here behind the Iron Curtain, where Christians badly needed each other, they were divided. "Richard," I said flatly, "God has told me to go to Catholic churches. That's where we're going. Now what's the main Catholic church in Warsaw?"

Richard shook his head. "St. Anne's. The head priest is Father George Dombrowski. He speaks good English."

On the phone, Father George was delighted when I asked if we could come to his church. "Tomorrow evening, we have Mass. Why don't you come and sing after, at seven o'clock?"

Thursday afternoon, we hauled our equipment to St. Anne's, a fourteenth-century stone church in the heart of Warsaw. Richard had come along reluctantly. Some of the

Living Sound team had never set foot in a Catholic church.
I'd seen some of the great churches of Europe. Few were
more ornate.

Beautifully rendered frescoes covered the walls. Gilded
statues stood in corners and up front beside the altar.
Fifteen or twenty older people, women in black kerchiefs
and men with caps in hand, were kneeling in prayer. As
we bumped our heavy amplifiers over the cobbled floor,
heads turned. We neared the altar, and I saw some frown.

Father George bustled up to us as we began stringing
wire for the sound system. He said to me, "Tell your people they must remember to genuflect when they cross in
front of the altar."

Eyebrows shot up all around; I swallowed hard. Of
course. They believed that the physical presence of Christ
was in the Communion elements which, I now realized,
were inside a finely wrought golden container on the altar.

Father George retreated. I was getting questioning looks
from the team. "We have to be respectful," I insisted.
"Just do it."

So, we went back and forth, stringing wire, setting up
mikes and instruments, bowing each time we crossed in
front of the altar.

When we finished Father George treated us to a supper
of heavily spiced Polish sausage sandwiches in his small
apartment behind the church. Even though they appreci-
ated his kindness, I could see that few team members felt
comfortable.

When we walked out for the concert my jaw dropped.
The crowd was shoulder-to-shoulder! Mothers, fathers,
babies, young adults, grandparents—jammed into every
square foot, every aisle, corner, and window ledge.
Through the open doors and windows, I saw a large crowd
in the street, maybe three thousand altogether. With a
rope, someone had cordoned off a tiny space around our

instruments. We squeezed in, eye-to-eye with a row of college-aged young people.

From the opening song, the evening was charged with an other-worldly energy. One word is the same in every language—"Alleluia"—and when we sang that simple chorus, hands uplifted in praise, the tears flowed. Theirs and ours.

As we sang, I had an eye-opening realization. Evangelical Christians condemn Catholics for trying to work their way to heaven, yet I'd been raised in a Protestant denomination that taught basically the same idea. Other denominations and groups I'd brushed with in my travels had different sets of rules, methods of worship, even dress codes. But they all amounted to the same thing: someone's good idea of how to please God. The truth is, none is better, more inspired by God than another.

That evening, through Richard, I spoke about the blood of Jesus: how it continually cleansed me of my sins; that it was the only true way to God.

And when I invited people to come and commit their lives to Christ, it was like watching a wave gather on the ocean. People began pushing in from outside; from all corners of the church they came, squashing into the little sacristy. I pressed myself inside, followed by Richard— who was beaming with excitement—and led the crowd in prayer. Later we learned that some 360 had given their lives to Christ that night.

Perhaps the most key event of that trip came two days later. News about the concert had spread. By special invitation, we were escorted to the palace of Stefan Cardinal Wyszynski, the Catholic Primate of Poland.

The palace was gorgeous—thick Oriental carpets over gleaming inlaid floors, fine artwork covering the wood-paneled walls. But the Cardinal was far more impressive. Thin and gray-haired, he nonetheless charged into the room. As we talked, I sensed a spiritual authority in this man who had suffered for three years in prison for opposing the Communist regime. At the end of our visit, he prayed for each member of the team. Laying hands on me, he asked that I receive the boldness of Augustine in preaching the Gospel.

Just before he swept out of the room, he extended a surprise invitation: We were to come back to Poland as his special guests in the fall, to perform during Sacrasong, a one-week music festival in Warsaw, and also to tour the nation, singing in major cathedrals.

Traveling through West Germany on our way to Lausanne, the atmosphere in the group was one of excitement. I chuckled to myself: No one in Living Sound had balked for an instant when Wyszynski had laid hands on each and prayed a blessing.

I thought, too, about the insights gained on this trip. God had revealed in my heart one of the ugliest, most subtle obstacles to the Gospel: prejudice. I'd also seen the love of God for all His people, and witnessed how obedience, boldness, and the simple message of the cross overcomes even religious barriers. I couldn't wait to get home to tell Jan—and to raise money for our return in the fall.

As I walked through the front door at home, Jan and Misty nearly knocked me down with hugs and kisses. Nothing felt so good as holding the two of them and Scotty in my arms again. There was time that summer for only a short vacation in Medicine Hat, to visit my folks and to see Clayton and Lois and their families.

Then I plunged back into the work: We phoned anyone who'd ever supported us, explaining our opportunity to tour Poland. Almost miraculously, the money came in just in time for our September departure. I said goodbye to my family once more.

Driving into the heart of Poland, we felt as if a red carpet had been rolled out at our feet. We'd applied for visas to get into Russia, but they were denied. That didn't matter at the moment. The Poles welcomed us like celebrities, including Richard, who had become our main contact. In Warsaw, the top musicians and groups from all across Poland were waiting to jam with Living Sound. And then there were the crowds that came, the hunger for a word of spiritual encouragement etched on their faces.

Thousands came each night to the huge basilica in Warsaw, where we were honored as the featured performers. So many crowded in that people were passing out from the heat and closeness. Hundreds responded to the altar calls. Near Krakow, the response was just as breathtaking. The Franciscan cathedral, which normally seated 1,500, had overflowed. On our first night there, 7,000 had somehow managed to press inside, while another 2,000 stood outside in the rain, listening through the open windows as we sang and spoke about Jesus. I was told that some 1,800 prayed with us and opened their hearts to Christ that night.

And the whole time, I had the undeniable sense that I was being "carried" along—not speaking of my own accord; being spoken *through*. The Franciscan brothers timidly asked about the spiritual authority they felt when I opened the Bible to speak. They guessed I was older, forty-four or forty-five, and were incredulous when I said I was thirty-one. But no one was more amazed than I.

Only one small event was sobering.

Living Sound was staying in rooms at a monastery across the street from the cathedral. One morning, I was awakened by a knock on our door. It was still dark; my travel alarm said five A.M. Donning my bathrobe I opened the door a crack.

Out in the hall stood one of the brothers who lived at the monastery. Beside him was a young man. His hair and

187

clothes were disheveled. His eyes were red, as if he'd been crying all night. The brother apologized. "He won't leave until he talks to you."

I let him come in, still groggy. His confession woke me up fast.

He'd been assigned by the Communist Party to follow us and report on all our moves. "At first, I thought you were only an American stage show—the smiles, the fancy outfits. I thought you were American propaganda. But—" his voice choked, and his head fell forward. "Last night, when you spoke of Jesus, I made up my mind."

"What is it you have inside you?" he begged. "I need it. I'm so empty when I hear you speak."

For two hours, I led him through Scriptures. Then we knelt by my bed to pray. Of all the people who would open their hearts to Jesus during this trip to Poland, this young man's prayer of repentance moved me most deeply. Choosing Jesus meant a break from the Communist Party and all the power, position, and material comforts it promised. His decision might mean prison. But he prayed, quietly, "Jesus, You are now my Lord."

Moved as I was by his prayer, it also brought me back to reality. I'd decided that we were able to move so freely in Poland because we were sanctioned by the powerful Catholic Church. Now I wondered if that was the only reason, and whether we'd ever be able to come back.

As it turned out, in 1975 and 1976, Living Sound was invited back to Poland to perform at a religious festival at the huge Byzantine monastery in Czestochowa. We'd recorded two albums by then, and brought in copies, which we heard on Polish radio everywhere we went.

It was at this festival, in 1976, that an old memory came back.

When we walked onstage, the sight nearly took my breath away. In the vast field, stretching away from the onion-domed church at our backs, were some 300,000 people. The crowd stretched a half-mile in one directon, and nearly a mile in the other direction. Many had come on foot from cities, towns, and villages all over Poland.

We'd learned some songs in Polish by then. One song, "Jesus Is Here," was like a spiritual national anthem. When we began it, every hand went up. Across the field, men in gray suits joined upraised hands with women in bright skirts, all worshiping Jesus. The wonder of it gave me chills.

It was then the memory came back: *I was a fourteen-year-old boy again, sitting on a wooden bench in a barn-like tabernacle in British Columbia. Before me were hundreds of thousands of people whose language I didn't know. But we were worshiping God together. . . .*

My amplified voice echoing over that vast field, my dream became real. I preached a simple message from John 3:16: "For God so loved the world. . . ." Only one language speaks to every heart, the language of God's Spirit.

That year, 1976, was a landmark year in many other ways.

The ministry of Living Sound International exploded. We opened a European office in England and added a third team, with about nine new musicians and singers. All that year and the next, with Tulsa as our home base, I moved between the three Living Sound teams, which traveled around the globe.

Jan, Misty, and Scotty came with me whenever possible. Scotty was so tenderhearted that people took to him wherever we went. As Misty reached school age, though, taking them on trips was more difficult. Jan was just as content to be at home with the children. So I squeezed in time with the family between constant trips to Europe,

Africa, the Orient, or to some North American city where
Living Sound was performing.

Even though Living Sound touched every continent, I
felt the constant pull of the Iron Curtain countries.

In April of 1978, I was about to join a Living Sound team
at a crusade in Boise, Idaho, when I got an urgent phone
call from our office manager in Europe. His message was
so incredible, he had to tell me twice: "After four years of
applying, Terry, we've been granted a group visa into
Russia! We've got to pick them up in London right away."

When I hung up I knew we had to move fast or miss
getting into Russia. The problem was, cash was tight as
usual. I got on the plane to Boise, praying, *Lord, You've
opened the door. I'm trusting You to provide the way.*

The crusade was held in Boise Stadium, with thousands
in attendance. It was sponsored by a local pastor named
Roland Buck. He was about to publish a book claiming he
was being visited by angels with prophetic messages. I
was skeptical, though Pastor Buck appeared to be a very
sincere man. Mostly, I was delighted about the $10,000 the
crusade raised, which Pastor Buck turned over to Living
Sound when he learned about our chance to go into Russia.

While he was driving us to the airport, I asked him
questions about his book. His answers were gentle, direct.
He seemed levelheaded to me—but visiting angels?
Gordon Calmeyer, the team leader, said jokingly, "The
next time you talk to those angels, ask 'em what God has
in mind for Living Sound." My face reddened.

Pastor Buck just smiled and kept driving.

Our fourth and newest Living Sound team met me in
Helsinki for the bus trip into Russia. Having moved so
easily in and out of Poland, I assured the team as we
neared the border, that getting into Russia would be a
breeze.

At the border crossing, I stepped out. The June morning was still cool. Gray-uniformed guards with machine guns stood by. A half-mile of open land strewn with the metal cross-pieces of tank traps stretched before us. A customs official boarded the bus.

Stepping back outside, he said, "Everything comes off."

We sat in the customs hall as, one by one, every item was opened—guitar cases, camera bags, suitcases. They stirred a jar of peanut butter to see if we'd hidden anything in it. I chuckled because I'd made sure there wasn't so much as a Jesus sticker on the luggage.

About an hour into the search, a guard charged into the hall, waving a fistful of pamphlets. My heart sank. He'd found a whole box of Bible study guides, covered by the girls' long gowns. I'd missed it.

Two guards seized my arms.

They dragged me down a hallway, shoving me into a small windowless room with cement-block walls. Roughly, I was put into a straight-backed chair and photographed. Bright lights glared in my face. They accused me of being a smuggler. I tried not to shake, watching the cold glint of the guards' bayonets.

After a time, they shoved me back out into the hall where the group was seated. I was not allowed to talk to anyone. All I could do was pace—and pray.

Gradually, a calmness came over me. My racing heartbeat slowed. My shoulders relaxed. Inwardly, I heard, *It's going to be all right.* Such a strange thought in this cruel place.

After three hours I was taken back to the airless little room. This time a military interrogator came in, a large man with a chestful of medals. I noticed his huge scarred hands, the sadistic flicker in his eye.

He began speaking loudly, right in my face.

I held up my hand. He asked me if I had something to

say. Looking him in the eye, I asked, "Why are you afraid of me?"

He smirked. "I'm not afraid of you."

"Yes, you are."

"No, I'm not," he shot back.

"Do I have a gun? No. So why do your guards have guns? You're afraid of me," I challenged.

"I'm *not* afraid!"

His huge hands clenched. I didn't know if I should dare. "If you're not afraid, then you'll let us into your country."

"Yes, we will."

"Thank you, very much."

Eight hours after we should have "breezed" across the border, I rejoined the team. Our bus driver sped toward Leningrad and I was still scratching my head, not exactly sure what had happened in that cold, hostile little room.

In Leningrad, we were assigned an official "guide" named Marguerite. She led us through the Hermitage, Russia's premier art gallery. But I felt a drive to be elsewhere: in Tallinn on the coast of Estonia.

When we finally arrived in Tallinn, I recognized the towering spire of Oleviste Church where I'd performed with Oral Roberts' group ten years before. For the next couple of days we had to keep Marguerite occupied while sending members of the team in secret to make contact with believers.

Amazingly, we were able to set up an unannounced concert. After supper, on our third day in Tallinn, we somehow got rid of Marguerite for the evening. In small groups, we nonchalantly made our way to Oleviste. To my surprise, about 1,500 people—mostly young people—had invaded the church! The concert was joyous and emotional, Christians from East and West united in worship behind the backs of Communist authorities.

When it ended we were escorted to a back room where

tea and small cakes were being served. The leaders of the youth group pumped us for information about the West: Could we really preach so openly in America? Were there Christian young people in the U.S.?

I was hardly listening. There was someone I *had* to see— if he wasn't in prison, or worse. I knew it was risky. Leaning over to a young blonde girl named Natasha, I decided to test the water. "I was in the Soviet Union years ago. I met a tall man with a black beard. His name was Andrus Do you know if he's alive or dead?"

Immediately, conversation stopped. Natasha's eyes brightened. "You know Andrus?"

I learned that contact could be made, but not at the church. Not even here were we safe. Directions were whispered in my ear.

The next day, at exactly eleven A.M., I left the hotel for a "stroll." At the magazine stand on the corner, I glanced over my shoulder. At once, I recognized the big, black-bearded man following at a distance. Turning a corner I found the alley I'd been told about and picked my way between the trash cans to another street—then made a dash for the car that was idling at the curb.

Andrus dashed in behind me.

A half-hour later we were in the middle of a windy soccer field outside Tallinn, where no one could come up behind us. And once again I looked into those dark eyes, like burning coals. Andrus wrapped me in a bear hug and I thought my ribs would crack.

His deep voice was breaking. "Terry Law—every day for ten years I pray that God brings you back to the Soviet Union. Thank you for coming."

For a brief moment I was seized by the magnitude of his words, by the realization again that we all, Andrus, Living Sound, and I were but soldiers, fighters in a war for men's very souls.

Then Andrus gave me news from the underground. I gathered, as he spoke, that he had become a powerful leader in the secret church. He said a revival was sweeping Baptist and Methodist young people. One young man had been specially gifted with a healing ministry. The prayer life was rich, the persecution severe. Many were sick and suffering in prison camps, their families struggling to survive.

Then Andrus pointed at me. "You must bring me printing press and instruments. Our young people can play and sing like Living Sound. We must evangelize here, like you."

I mumbled an objection, seeing before me the hard faces of the border guards. How could we—? Andrus overrode me.

"God brings you here. He will make a way."

The wind blew softly, disturbing Andrus' hair. His eyes never left mine. I prayed silently, faced with this man and this immense, impossible challenge.

Lord, these people are paying a high price because they love You. I don't know if I can do what Andrus is asking. But I want to serve You, no matter what it costs.

I reached out and shook his hand. In a little while we walked back to the car.

There would come a day when I'd wish I had never prayed those words.

15

SHIRLEY:
The Enemy

After Jim's decision to become a stockbroker, I continued to fend off the subtle feeling that something
was not right.

On one hand, there were rushes of joy. On July 7, 1977,
at St. Francis Hospital in Tulsa, I delivered a baby girl. We
named her Shawna Marie, though I later called her just
Marie. She had pale skin, like mine, and a wisp of
strawberry-blond hair. Jim and I could hardly stop strok-
ing her round, pink cheeks or smiling into those mist-blue
eyes. I'd decided to leave MasterCard in order to be home
with Marie, and I cherished each moment with her—each
time her tiny fingers touched my jaw or I felt her sweet
breath on my cheek.

And on the other hand, Jim had been offered a position
with a brokerage firm, and he'd accepted. That, and being
a new daddy, put him on a double-high.

I felt only a foreboding about him.

In mid-August, when Marie was only five weeks old,

Jim's firm sent him to New York City for six weeks of training on Wall Street. I secretly hoped the rat-race world of big money would turn him off.

The day he returned he was all smiles. And then the slow changes began.

That fall, I noticed that Jim was losing interest in social gatherings with Christian friends. He was still reading his Bible and praying, but now, on occasion, I was surprised to hear him make humorous remarks about church, remarks with a slightly cutting edge.

On a Sunday evening early that fall, I got ready to go to the seven o'clock service, which we always attended. I dressed Marie in a pretty yellow outfit. Then, slipping into a skirt and blouse, I curled my hair.

Jim never went to church unless his shoes were polished and his tie was knotted just right. But twenty minutes before we were to leave, he was still lounging around the living room.

"Honey?" I called from the bathroom. "Aren't you going to get dressed? I was hoping you'd have time to pack the diaper bag for me."

I heard the newspaper rustle. "I'm not going tonight."

Cradling Marie in my arms, I walked out to the living room. Jim did not look at me. "Is something wrong?" I asked.

"No." There was silence.

"You never miss a Sunday evening service. So what's wrong?"

More silence. Then Jim folded the paper and stood up. "Let's not talk about it, okay?" He walked past me.

I was mystified. "Where are you going?"

"To get the diaper bag for you."

From then on, Jim would be up and dressed for church on Sunday morning. But on Sunday and Wednesday evenings, when we'd normally be in church, Jim insisted he needed to stay home to study stock reports.

Inexplicably, I felt that the wall that had once stood between us was coming back. I knew Jim was trying hard to establish himself in a tough new line of work, so I tried to support him. And Jim continued to be witty and cheerful—at first. But spiritually, I sensed a cooling off.

What bothered me most were the little evidences that the high pressure of the investment world was subtly invading our personal life.

At first I noticed only little changes. Usually Jim loved playing with Marie and caring for her. Now, however, if he was working on his stock reports and Marie began to cry, he got agitated—I'd never seen that in him before—and had to leave the room. And he had always been so easygoing about schedules. Now meals had to be served right on time, because he had important work to do in the evening. Many nights, he was up until two or three A.M. working. Now sometimes his Bible went untouched for days.

I was perplexed. And the changes got more pronounced as time went by.

One evening in January of 1978, I struggled into the house with several heavy bags of groceries. Jim had been at home with Marie and, as I slipped off my coat, he came into the kitchen and started rummaging through the bags.

I was putting some items into the meat-keeper, when suddenly Jim began rifling things out onto the table. Closing the refrigerator, I stared at him. His face was getting flushed. "Jim, what's the matter?"

"Why don't you remember to pick up the things I ask you to buy?"

I was speechless. Jim paced up and down the kitchen, complaining that I didn't listen to his requests.

"Jim," I broke in, "you never asked me to pick up anything for you. I'm sure of it." Then something crossed my mind.

"Honey," I said, "is the pressure of this business too much for you?"

Jim stopped pacing. A remorseful look came over his face.

"I know you've got to work hard to build up your clientele," I offered. "But please try to relax. You're not yourself."

Now he looked unhappy. "I don't know, Shirley. I'm sorry I snapped at you. Sometimes I feel like I have only half a mind."

The likelihood that Jim was overworking himself did nothing to relieve the persistent feeling that something else was going on. But what? I turned to the Bible and the Holy Spirit for wisdom and guidance. Of all the comforting passages I read, two seemed to come back to me again and again.

Nehemiah 8:10 said, "The joy of the Lord is your strength."

And in John 15:11, I read that Jesus said, "These things have I spoken unto you, that my joy might remain in you, and that your joy might be full."

I read these passages and others many times. It seemed to me that God was telling me that I should learn what true joy was. I couldn't know then how desperately I would need to hang onto these words.

What occurred next was so strange, so frightening that, later, I would replay it in my head a hundred times to be sure I wasn't imagining.

One afternoon in May, I'd just gotten the baby down for a nap. Marie, who was ten months old, had played most of the morning in the living room. The crackers I'd fed her had been scrubbed into the carpet. So when I was sure she was asleep at the far end of the house, I got out the vacuum.

Since I had little time to myself these days, I'd developed a habit of praying while I worked. Immediately, when the vacuum went on, I began in my usual way, praising and thanking God. It helped me, as Paul wrote to the Philippians, to set my mind on "good things." Before I was half done with the carpet I was humming to myself as I thought of my many blessings: Marie, our health, the fact that Jim was beginning to make a good income as a broker, for Christian friends, our home. . . .

Over the whine of the vacuum, I heard a squeak—like hinges opening in the front hall. Then a door slammed. I switched off the machine.

"Jim?" I called. It was too early for him to be home. But who else would walk in uninvited? Unless the cleaner had drowned out their knock.

No answer. I went to the front hall. No one was there; no one on the porch or front walk either. It had been sultry and muggy all day, with not so much as a breeze. I checked the door. If it *had* been ajar, it was definitely shut tight now.

I went back to my vacuuming.

Not two minutes later, I heard the familiar squeak of the front door opening once again. Immediately, I hit the off switch. The door slammed loudly. I heard footsteps.

"Jim? *Jim?*"

The footsteps paused. No answer.

My heart was racing. Someone was in my house—silently poised in the front hall—listening. I could feel a presence. Two more steps. It stopped again. I wanted to run to Marie, but my hand was frozen on the vacuum.

And then—whether audibly or just in my head, I could never tell—I heard a husky male voice: *You may have trusted God for a healthy child and a home. And you may be trusting*

God for your husband's soul. But I'm coming to take him from you.

As instantly as it had come, the fear vanished. I realized I'd been holding my breath and suddenly relaxed. When I walked to the front hall no one was there.

After the strange incident, I felt confused, anxious. I kept checking on Marie, as if she might stop breathing. I ran to the phone and called Mama Goodwin, asking her to come over. She was not free then, but promised to come the next day.

When she came I nervously told her about the voice—or what I thought was a voice. Her kind expression became one of concern. When I finished, her face was grave. "Shirley, I don't know what it is about Jim. . . . Have you noticed that he is changing?"

I leaped at that. "Yes, I sure have. He's trying so hard, but he's irritable most of the time. I can't figure out what I've done wrong. He won't open up, though."

I also told her about the unusual experience at Mr. Barnes' seminar, when I had sensed dark hands clutching at Jim. "What's happening to me?" I pleaded.

"It's not what's happening to you—at least not directly," Mama Goodwin replied. Thoughtfully, and from an outside perspective I, of course, did not have, she pieced together a picture: Jim's decision to leave the ministry, the grip of the success syndrome. As she talked, I saw Jim's slow but definite backing away from spiritual interests.

"I believe something is coming against Jim—a spiritual force," she concluded.

I didn't want to believe that. I believed there were evil spiritual forces. But I resisted looking for a "'demon in every teacup," as did some people I'd met. Jim was a Christian after all, and a good person. "He would never lay himself open to any kind of evil," I countered.

"Of course not," she said, gripping my hand. "But it

may be that he has somehow, unknowingly, stepped into an area where there's evil. Since he's had such a love for God, it's not hard to believe he's just the sort of man who might be in danger of spiritual attack, is it?"

That, at least, I could accept. Besides, I'd prayed for understanding. And it was obvious Jim was battling spiritually, either with an outside influence or simply within himself.

Mama Goodwin encouraged me, just before she left, to continue praying specifically for Jim every day.

I wouldn't be honest if I said the commitment to pray for my husband every day was easy. It was not. After getting breakfast, seeing Jim off to work, bathing and dressing the baby, throwing a load of clothes in the washer, cleaning up the kitchen, rescuing Marie off the back of the sofa, reading books to her—well, then it was lunchtime. Then I'd finally get Marie down for her nap, thinking I had just enough time to phone a friend for a couple of minutes before I had to think about supper. But I would force myself to stop and ask, *Are you committed to Jim or not?* All I could think of were the pressures of Jim's work, and how hard he was trying.

Taking the phone off the hook, I would kneel at the living room sofa and pray. So many days the words felt wooden. Yet I kept at it, believing that, as Paul wrote, *nothing* could separate Jim from the love of God in Christ Jesus. More often than not I relied on the promise in Romans 8:26, trusting that, when I didn't know *how* to pray, the Holy Spirit would pray through me.

In the next six months, however, things did not get better. In fact, I felt that he was turning away more and more.

One evening in October, Jim was sitting at the table balancing the checkbook at the dining room table. I noticed him running his hands through his hair and drumming his fingers. Then he crumpled his notepaper in exasperation and started over.

I'd also noticed recently that, many times when he was figuring his clients' stock accounts, he'd tire easily. Sometimes he had to lie down and nap before finishing.

Not wanting to disturb him, I went to put Marie in bed.

About forty-five minutes later, I returned to the dining room. Jim was in a state of agitation. I knew our checkbook was in pretty good shape, yet crumpled papers were strewn across the table. Silently, I prayed, *Father, something's wrong with Jim. I ask You to love him through me.*

I laid my hand on his shoulder, meaning only to comfort him. "Why don't you let this go now, hon. You've been at it for hours—"

"I *know* it," he shouted. "You don't have to bug me about it. Just leave me alone!"

Immediately, his face fell. He pushed away from the table. "I—I'm sorry," he apologized. "I just get so furious with myself. I can't even balance a crazy checkbook anymore."

He got up and left the table.

Later that night, I felt an unusual calm in the house. I was putting dishes away in the kitchen when Jim came up from behind and put his arms around my waist.

"What's gotten into you, Shirley?"

I wanted to ask the same of him. Instead I replied, "What do you mean?"

"You're different. Stronger. I know it's been tough for you. But things seem to roll right off your back."

"I've been praying. Mostly for you." I saw no reason to hide it. I turned and wrapped my arms around his neck. Softly I said, "When do I get my old Jim back?"

He held me tightly. Then, in a moment, he whispered, "Just don't stop praying. Okay?"

When Jim went off to bed, I had a chance to think about

the evening. I felt encouraged—mainly because I could see that learning to pray diligently did something for *me*. Tonight, when Jim had yelled at me, it had been so easy to overcome the temptation to self-pity. Now I understood what David meant in the Psalms when he so often referred to the Lord as his "shield." I actually sensed the Father's strong arm around me.

In the coming months, even though I felt this strong comfort, Jim's inner fight only intensified.

Just after Marie's first birthday, I took her to Portland to visit my family for a few weeks. Dad was about to take a job working on the Alaskan pipeline and was so happy at the chance to hold Marie before heading north. Roger and David played with her like proud uncles. Mom was just plain glad to see us, all misunderstandings from the time of our wedding long since resolved. It was a wonderful visit.

I felt disturbed, however. I'd had "feelings" before—an occasional "awareness." I'd learned to pray about these feelings. And now, strong, clear thoughts were coming.

As I prayed, I sensed God telling me, *Jim is doing something behind your back. You need to confront him and let him bring it into the light.*

When Marie and I got back to Tulsa, I waited until evening when she was in bed. Then I went out to the living room where Jim was watching a ball game on TV. "I'd like to talk to you," I interrupted.

"Okay," Jim mumbled, reaching for the button. "Is your dad getting cold feet about going to Alaska?"

I chuckled. "Please. This is serious."

Jim settled back in his chair, but I could not sit. "It's silly," I began, "but I felt that—well, that you did something behind my back while I was gone. Something major. What was it?"

His face dropped so quickly there was no hiding the

truth. "Whew. This beats all. Well, I guess you might as well know."

Thinking he could get by for a while without telling me, Jim had taken a good-sized chunk of money out of our savings and invested it, hoping to turn a big profit.

"I don't understand it," he said, shaking his head. "Overnight, it fell apart. I can't believe I'm making such bad judgments."

"So the money's lost?"

"Worse than that," Jim replied glumly.

The investment was a disaster. Not only did he lose our original sum, the deal had cost him $10,000. Trying to pull himself out by the bootstraps, he'd borrowed $10,000 *more* and sunk that into the mess, too.

I felt sick. "You're telling me you not only lost our money, but we owe something like $20,000?"

He nodded miserably.

It was a somber homecoming, to say the least.

Six weeks later, Jim informed me that he had borrowed another $10,000 from a friend—and lost it, too.

Strangely, I felt compassion, not anger. "Please, Jim. Is it the business? Is it so stressful that it's causing you to make bad decisions? Your personality is changing. You're becoming a stranger to me."

That got me nowhere.

All the rest of that year I fought from slipping into inner turmoil. Things were going from bad to worse. It was not at all like Jim to be so hungry for money that he'd risk so outrageously. He'd always been cautious. But, I reminded myself, that was the "old" Jim. Even more, I was bothered by this question: Why wasn't prayer "working" for me? Sure I was stronger inside. But when would the actual situation change?

Yet I knew I *couldn't* allow that line of thinking to drag me into self-pity of the worst kind: The kind that says,

"Well, I've done everything I know how to do, and the Lord just didn't come through." It's a self-pity that exalts its own labors and sacrifices above the eternal wisdom and loving plan of God.

Throughout 1979 and 1980 there were many changes for Jim and me. In February 1980, our second child was born, and Marie played proud "little mother" to our towheaded Jason. That year we also moved to a new brick house in a fine neighborhood in south Tulsa, and Jim accepted a position with another outstanding brokerage. By then, Jim had worked us out of the financial blow of 1978 and was making a substantial living.

I'm sure that, in the eyes of Jim's business associates who enjoyed his never-ending sense of humor, he looked like the man who had everything. But I rarely saw him pray or open his Bible. Work became an obsession. Once Jason was born, Jim began working at the office until late in the evening, complaining that he couldn't get anything done with the kids distracting him. And when he was at home, he'd work until two or three A.M. He spent more time on his accounts and reports, but got less done.

The most hurtful part for me was that Jim had always been a wonderful daddy. Almost overnight he changed.

Before we had moved to the new house Jim and I had done yard work at the old place. One morning he was mowing the lawn and I was on my knees weeding out a flower bed. Marie played contentedly in the dirt at my side. One of my friends, Judy Butler, came by to help with some painting and stopped outside to chat. I brushed off my hands and stood up.

A couple of minutes later, I heard Jim shout over the roar of the mower. I turned and saw him stomping across the lawn toward us. That was when I noticed Marie, looking up at me with smiling blue eyes, a pretty blossom clutched tightly in her fist. She was offering it to me.

Before I could accept it, Jim was upon us. He grabbed Marie's arm and jerked her off the ground. *"Haven't I told you not to pick any more flowers?"* he shouted. Marie screamed in pain as her arm twisted.

"Jim!" I begged. "Stop it! You're hurting her."

As if my voice had wakened him from a bad dream, Jim's expression changed. Quickly, he handed Marie to me. Still screaming with fright, she clutched at my neck and would not look at Jim. Obviously mortified, he tried to touch her, but she only screamed louder. He turned and walked away.

Marie sobbed on my shoulder. And my friend, who had witnessed the whole thing, looked pale. "I've never seen Jim like that before. Shirley, please forgive my saying this—but is there something wrong with him?"

There was. And I felt so helpless.

Later, when I was alone, I prayed, *Lord, I can't go on alone much longer. Give me someone to lean on.*

Inwardly, I was tempted to curl up in a shell and just let someone stronger care for me.

That was why I fended off Buddy Harrison's request when he stopped me after church one Sunday morning: He wanted me to lead an intercessory prayer group that met on Saturday mornings at the church. The Harrisons were certainly aware of our personal circumstances.

The idea of leading a group, however, seemed too much. I had enough to do keeping my own sanity intact. And what did I have to give to anyone else? I told him I didn't think so but agreed to consider it.

No sooner had Jim and I gotten the kids in the car than I heard a small clear voice: *I want you to lead the group.*

The next day, I called Buddy and agreed to "try it."

From the very first week, I understood why I was in there: God knew I needed to be.

Always a private person, I'd felt close to only a few

people in my life—the Maiers, Buddy and Pat, the Goodwins, and the Hagins. It was excruciating for me to let people see my need without feeling I'd betrayed Jim. But in this group of faithful and wise Christians, I found loving and discreet concern.

Gradually, I recognized another gift that came to me through the group: A glimpse of my loving Father in heaven—a Father who provides for us, even before we know we have need. For without the group's support, I don't know how I would have survived the steady deterioration of our home life over the next year or more.

In January of 1982 the lesson of God's loving provision was reinforced in a remarkable way, though I did not recognize it at first.

One morning, we'd just come in from picking up Marie at her preschool. For some reason she was crying. Jason was screaming for a peanut butter sandwich. The phone rang.

On the line was a man who said he was calling on behalf of a large local bank. He explained that I had made a sales call to him seven years before, in 1975. It had taken him a week to track me down, but he had an offer.

"Our bank needs someone who knows the credit card business and can really sell. You impressed me. Are you interested in work?"

I was flattered. At the moment, however, I had a weeping four-year-old pulling on my sleeve and a famished two-year-old climbing up my leg. Besides, Jim and I had decided I would not work again at least until the kids were both in school. I explained that briefly and tried to hang up.

"But every time I talk to someone in the field they tell me that *you* trained them!" he protested. "You're getting pretty high ratings."

Just out of curiosity I asked what the job paid. The figure

he told me was peanuts as far as I was concerned. When he saw that that didn't sway me, he promised to talk to the bank president about a bigger salary.

To get him off the line, I said I'd have to talk to my husband about it.

That evening when I brought it up, Jim's response was immediate: "Out of the question."

That was fine with me.

But the idea somehow took root in my mind, almost against my will. Every day, new and creative ideas surfaced—new sales techniques, training methods that I wanted to try. Several times in the next two weeks, people from the bank contacted me, including the president: First, he rejected the idea of more money; then called to say he'd reversed his decision.

When I brought up the job offer to Jim again, my attitude had changed. We discussed it and Jim was wary. I shrugged. "I can't explain it. But I feel like I need that job."

He grumbled.

Again I let the subject drop.

A few days later, early in February, Jim was getting ready to drive up to Oklahoma City for the day where he was to take a test in order to be licensed as a broker out-of-state.

"They're expecting an answer from me today," I said gingerly. "I just want to be sure. You don't want me to take this job, right?"

Jim was pulling on his overcoat. He picked up his briefcase. "You're always getting those *feelings*. Okay. If you feel strongly that you should take the job I trust you. Take it."

I was dumbfounded. "You're joking."

"No. I'm serious. It'll be good for you." Then he pointed one finger at me. "But I want to make one thing real clear.

If the job comes before me and the kids, you quit." Saying that, he walked out.

I felt almost brazen when I called the president to accept the job. But there was one more shoe to drop. "I need two hundred dollars a month more to pay for a good sitter for my children."

He almost choked. "You want me to pay for your baby-sitter?"

I bit my lip. "Yes. I know it'll be worth it to you not to have my attention divided."

Then I heard him chuckle. "You really are a good sales-woman. Okay. Come in today and sign the employment forms."

Later that afternoon I suffered a little nostalgia. It had been hectic, hauling Jason with me to the bank, then hur-rying to pick up Marie from preschool. Even though they'd gotten into three fights before I could get them down for a nap around two o'clock, I was going to miss being with them during the day. Then there was the challenge of being a working mother.

I wondered why on earth I thought I needed a job.

Around three o'clock, I got a call. It was one of the other brokers from Jim's firm. I made some joke about the li-censing tests. He wasn't laughing.

"Shirley, sit down. Jim's had a seizure. It was real bad. We had to admit him to the hospital."

16

SHIRLEY:
Crossing Over

Jim's attitude after his collapse in Oklahoma City was confusing. When I picked him up his eyes were bloodshot and his face a sickly white. Despite my insistence, he refused to see a doctor and said he'd feel better in the morning. When we got home, he simply went to bed.

At breakfast the next day, I begged him, "Please, Jim, make an appointment with our doctor."

"I'm just tired," he replied. His voice sounded murky. I noticed, when he tried to lift the coffee cup with his left hand, it shook.

"Then take a day off."

"Nope. Too much work."

With that, he dressed and he left for the office.

Though Jim had always been a master at sidestepping big issues, denial did not help him this time. Two months later, at the end of April, he had another seizure.

Early one morning I was scrambling eggs for Jason and

Marie and waiting for the housekeeper to arrive. I heard a noise from our master bathroom, like something falling.

I rushed down the hall, Jason and Marie trailing behind. When I opened the bathroom door, my knees went weak.

Jim was down on the floor, his body stiff and shaking. He'd fallen with his neck against the edge of the tub. Small choking noises came from his throat. Dropping to my knees, I saw that his lips were blue. The weight of his body was pressing his windpipe against the tub. He was strangling.

Terrified, I wrapped my arms around his chest and strained to lift him. "Please, Jim—oh please, God, help me," I cried. His body wouldn't bend, and I couldn't lift his full weight.

Marie and Jason stood in the doorway, wide-eyed with horror. Once again, that unusual inner calm came over me.

"Go get someone—a neighbor," I directed. "Hurry."

Obediently, Marie seized Jason's hand and pulled him with her. I heard a door bang shut.

A raspy sound came from Jim. I tried to hoist him, just an inch. He sucked in air. My muscles were burning. I lowered him again, bracing myself for the strangling sounds. Miserably, I pictured Marie's terrified face as she dragged little Jason from door to door, searching for someone to save their daddy's life. Would they find help?

It seemed like forever—then I heard footsteps pounding across the yard. Fortunately, our backdoor neighbor, Richard Poyner, had not left for work yet. He ran in and maneuvered Jim onto the floor while I called an ambulance.

On the way to the hospital Jim slowly came out of the seizure.

At the emergency room, Jim lay groaning on the stretcher, barely able to speak. The doctor explained it was urgent that Jim be admitted for neurological tests. Jim wouldn't hear of it. The doctor turned to me. "Your husband is not capable of making decisions at this point. But we can't do anything unless you go over his head and admit him."

I felt too shattered to handle this on my own. I called Buddy. He came at once with Pat. Together they convinced Jim that I would have to admit him. Since there was a good neurologist at the City of Faith on the campus of Oral Roberts University, we decided to have him transferred there.

Jim's head cleared enough so that he cooperated with Dr. Richter, the neurologist, during three days of CAT scans and other tests. The bedrest seemed to help, too. The morning he came home, he said blithely—to my frustration—that rest was probably all he'd needed.

For two days we waited for the test results. Jim was relaxed. He insisted on going back to work. I could hardly focus on my new job.

The morning we walked into Dr. Richter's office for the test results, Jim looked fine and I felt awful.

Dr. Richter was gentle and straightforward. He showed us results of the blood tests, then pictures from the CAT scan. There was an irregularity on the right front lobe of Jim's brain, a *glioma*, he called it. "It's as if hundreds of tiny fingers or roots have worked in between the brain cells. Most of the right lobe is slowly being covered."

My mouth was dry. "What are you telling us?"

Dr. Richter looked from Jim to me. "I'm afraid Jim has a primary brain neoplasm—a tumor. It's inoperable."

The next thing I knew, a nurse was standing over me. My head throbbed and the smell of ammonia was gagging. I thought, *I'm waking up in a nightmare.*

When I was able to sit up, Jim helped me back into the chair. I held tightly to his hand as the doctor answered our questions. Jim had probably had the tumor, Dr. Richter explained, for seven to ten years. I made a mental note when he said that a brain tumor could cause personality changes. The tumor wasn't considered cancerous because it was slow-growing, fed by a tiny blood flow. Even heavy radiation would not destroy it, just slow its progress. Yes, there would be side effects from radiation treatment—nausea, hair loss, headaches.

An hour later, as we left Dr. Richter's office, Jim promised to get back to him with a decision about the treatments. As we walked to the parking lot I fought the numbness by planning out loud. "I'll set my appointments around your treatment schedule. I want to be with you."

"There's no need to go through all that," Jim shrugged.

"Jim, you can't go alone."

"I'm not going at all."

I stopped. "Not going? Do you realize what that means?"

He didn't even look at me. "Yes." He got into the car.

Jim went on to work just as if he hadn't heard the news that he was dying.

Later, alone in my office, I closed the door. As I sat there things became clearer, like Jim's personality change. According to the doctor, he may have had the tumor as long as we'd been married. Was that a factor in his growing coldness toward God? Or had he stepped out of God's protection and opened the door to a life-crushing force?

Words echoed back at me from the past—Jim's words. Several times he told me, "I'll never live to be forty." I'd paid no attention. Was this the open door?

I slammed my fist on the desk. Some Christians, I knew, got wrapped up in theologies that can't be proven one way or the other. The only thing on my mind was: How could I influence my husband to choose *life*—to move closer to God even if he chose not to prolong his earthly life?

That afternoon, I saw where we stood spiritually. Jim

213

and I were at the head of a path facing the "valley of the shadow of death." The thought terrified me. Death from a brain tumor must be a hideous ordeal. How would I face it? How could I be of any comfort or help to Jim?

The only thing that came to me later that week was to keep the Scriptures with me at all times—in my purse, in the car, at the office. I read every spare moment, and verses touched me. But constantly my prayer was that of the psalmist: *The Lord is good and His mercy endures forever.*

Still I wondered. Could I hold on to God's Word on this dark path we were traveling?

That spring our nightmare became real.

Since Jim's tumor was so far advanced he was already on a fast downhill slide. Another brokerage might have forced Jim to quit because he was less clearheaded. He had to take fourteen pills three times a day. Some were to reduce the brain's swelling, some to control high blood pressure and suppress seizures. But the secretaries and other brokers were so loyal. Patiently, they helped Jim at the office. And, with instructions from Jim's doctor, I trained some of them in what to do in case of a seizure.

When Jim came in at night, he was spent. He could barely keep his head up during supper. It was an effort for him to listen to Marie's or Jason's not-altogether-clear stories of what happened during the day. Then he would drag himself to the couch and drowse there until bedtime. Our physical relationship rapidly tapered off.

Jim's faltering energy also meant extra work around the house for me. Weekends, there was grass to cut, shrubs to trim. Daily, I thanked God for providing someone who did light housekeeping along with watching the kids. It was a struggle just to roll out of bed most mornings.

On top of that was the emotional toll.

Throughout 1982 and into 1983 Jim would go for a month without a seizure, then suffer two in a week. His face was bloated-looking. His mood swings were wild. He loved taking Jason and Marie to McDonald's nearly every Saturday, while I continued to lead the intercessory prayer meeting. Then, later, he'd lash out at Marie for no reason. She would cry and hide in her room. Jim would just stand there looking hurt. He couldn't help himself and he was aching inside. But how could I explain to a six-year-old that Daddy still loved her, that he was sick and didn't mean to hurt her?

In Marie's innocent, freckled face, I saw the pain and confusion I'd felt as a child. Why was it happening all over again to my child? Was this God's "goodness"? Over and over I refused that inner voice that wanted to blame God. I turned to the Psalms and prayed on behalf of Jim, Marie, Jason and me: *Surely goodness and mercy will follow us . . . .*

In July of 1983 I faced trouble on another front.

First, I had to take over our financial matters entirely because Jim's ability to make sound decisions was failing. I'd known we were on shaky ground but did not know how shaky until now.

We could scrape together our July house payment but August looked doubtful. We were behind in our electric and phone bills, too. Jim didn't have disability insurance, so he was forced to keep working while his income dwindled. I had to cut back on groceries. The empty checking account upset Jim more than the fact that he was slowly dying.

Then one morning, while the toast was burning and I was trying to get the kids dressed, I heard Jim fall in our bedroom. He was having one of the worst seizures I'd witnessed. The pressure in his head must have been excruciating, because he writhed in agony. Gradually it passed. When I helped Jim into bed, I was trembling. I never would get used to seeing my big, strapping husband thrashing helplessly like an infant. He was thirsty and motioned for me to get some water. I tucked a blanket around him and went to the kitchen.

While I was reaching for a glass the phone rang. My mother was crying at the other end of the line: Dad had just suffered a massive heart attack. He was dead.

I held the receiver numbly, half-listening to the details. How could all this be happening? Shutting my eyes tightly, I tried to find strength. To my amazement, calm slowly seeped into me. I hung up the phone after promising to make plane reservations as soon as possible.

Carrying the glass of water back to Jim, I felt hemmed in by shadow. In this darkness, I clung to the knowledge that God was my only hope.

On my trip to Portland, I found a much-needed measure of comfort.

During the funeral I wept, not just because Dad was gone—he was with the Lord—I wept for the family life we *might* have had, for the angry, hurt side of Dad that had controlled so much of his life.

At Mom's house after, Dad's sister and I had a quiet moment, reminiscing. "I wonder what made him change those last few years," she said wistfully. "He was a different man. Happy. Peaceful."

On the plane trip back to Tulsa, I mused over her words. I knew why Dad had changed. And comfort came from the humbling knowledge that one small sacrifice—asking Dad to be in my wedding—was the thing God used eventually to woo Dad to Himself. And it occurred to me that the darkest moment in Dad's life, when all his own strength was gone and he was ready to put a bullet in his head, was really the breaking of dawn for him.

As I stared out the plane window, Jim's face was before me. I recalled a morning before we discovered the tumor. He was walking out the door for work, complaining about our finances. I said I'd tighten my spending.

Jim wheeled about angrily. "If the Lord's such a big stud, why doesn't He get on the stick and work things out?"

Now, looking out at the mountainous clouds beneath the plane's wings, I considered: Jim had turned from God in pursuit of big money. Then he'd flung a challenge in God's face. Was God able to conquer our bleak situation and woo Jim back to Himself?

Perhaps I was just weary. I believed in my heart that God triumphs over our difficulties. But at the moment, I just couldn't see how.

Upon returning to Tulsa, I had to face our need for *real* cash. Eighteen months had passed since Jim's first seizure. In August, September, and October our finances bottomed out.

Late one night in November I slumped over a calculator and stacks of bills. I'd squeezed the grocery money so tight we were all sick of cereal and tuna noodle casserole. If some of the wonderful people in my prayer group hadn't brought me fresh vegetables from their gardens, we'd have lived all summer on peanut butter and jelly—but now those vegetables were gone. Jim needed more medicine. Besides that, the electric and phone companies had both sent cut-off notices for non-payment. And it was uncanny the way things started collapsing: In October the oven went out and the washer broke; then my car stalled out in the middle of traffic. Our biggest single bill was the mortgage, and we were three months behind in that. The bank was calling.

My pencil was worn to a nub from all the figuring. My frustration grew. Nervously, I tore up the scribbled sheet. No matter how I planned, there just wasn't enough to cover all the urgent, red-lettered notices.

Two days later, on a cool Saturday afternoon before Thanksgiving, Marie skipped into the kitchen.

"Mommy," she said, tugging at the sleeve of my blouse, "can we make chocolate chip cookies? Please? *Please?*"

"No, hon," I apologized. "The oven is broken."

Marie's face clouded. "You said God was going to fix our oven. How come it's not fixed?"

Her words stabbed my heart. I'd bought her off with that answer and now I wished I hadn't. In reality, I couldn't afford to buy a bag of chocolate chips. Now, I faced the challenge in her eyes.

Wearily, I knelt and looked at her. "Marie, we are going to bake those cookies—I can't tell you exactly when. But God will see that our oven gets fixed."

Immediately, a negative voice inside countered: *Haven't you pushed God far enough out on a limb? Why not drop all the God-talk and tell her there's no money?*

Marie was still looking at me. Could she, at six, really understand what faith in God meant? And then, in her face, I saw myself standing in our kitchen in North Dakota while my family seemed to be falling apart. God had become my only hope, even as a little girl.

No. I wouldn't give in to the negative voices.

"You know what, Marie?" I said, hugging her. "The Bible says, 'The joy of the Lord is my strength.' That means knowing the Lord is joy itself. We need to enjoy *Him* right now, no matter how hard things look." My voice trailed off.

Marie stared at me, whether satisfied or puzzled, I couldn't tell. Then she kissed me and smiled. "Okay, Mom."

After she'd gone back outside to play in the crisp fall air, I thought about the tremendous task I had as a Christian parent—to plant in my children unbelief, or real hope. The choice was up to me. I prayed for strength always to choose His way.

One evening, just a week later, the phone rang. It was

Buddy. Since we'd kept our financial crunch a secret, I was floored by his offer. "Pat and I feel that you have some needs. We'd like to help out a little. Is there something you need?"

Immediately, I thought of my car, the stacks of dirty clothes waiting for the laundromat—and Marie's wish for homemade cookies. Maybe Jim wouldn't like this, but . . . "Well, as a matter of fact . . ." I ventured.

The next day Buddy sent repairmen around to fix the oven and washer, and arranged to have my car serviced. Jim was grateful, if reserved in his thanks. I splurged on a bag of chocolate chips. Marie, with a brushing of flour on her chin and a wooden spoon in hand, helped to mix the cookie dough. As far as she was concerned, God fixed the oven.

Together we thanked the Lord for this provision.

It was the larger issues that were becoming too heavy to bear.

In more lucid moments, Jim began to talk about his death as casually as he'd discuss a stock option. "When I'm gone, Shirley, you take that wedding band off and start a new life." Then, more wistfully, he added, "It's been a long time since I've been a husband to you."

That was worse for me than the verbal haranguing. It was funny that, in a strange reversal, Jim was facing things honestly for once, while I fought looking at what lay ahead. The tension was ripping me up. Mornings, I'd awaken, sick and vomiting. I refused to let Marie and Jason see that; not only was Daddy dying, but Mommy was trying to keep from falling apart.

Early in December I was driving to a business appointment in Sand Springs, outside Tulsa. It was cold. The grass and trees along the highway were a dismal gray-brown. A radio station was playing carols. Traffic was fairly heavy for midday, and I decided I'd have to get home early to avoid all the holiday shoppers going to the malls to buy for Christmas.

Christmas. I didn't have a single toy for Jason or Marie. I'd wanted to buy a new sweater for Jim because he was always cold. We'd be lucky to have a tree this year. I'd have to face them on Christmas morning and say we just couldn't afford . . . couldn't afford anything. Food. Electricity. The phone. A heavy weight was settling on me. *And no presents.*

It was like the final shovel of dirt thrown on my head. I snapped off the festive music on the radio. The hum of snow tires on pavement sounded empty. I felt buried.

I wiped the tears away with my fingers and started unloading on God. *No one understands how we all hurt. My husband's dying. I've been living like a widow. My kids are losing their daddy. We're going to lose everything. Why, God? Why is this happening?*

As I continued to heap my feelings on God, an unusual thing happened. It felt like the whole universe was tilting, turning upside-down. In my mind's eye, I suddenly saw Him enthroned above the gray trees and cold sky. He'd been buried once—now gloriously risen over all. God was not overwhelmed. And I did not have to be either.

Words came to me, a truth I'd first seen in a little pink Bible as a little girl: *You will know the truth, and the truth will set you free.*

Fresh tears came. Happy tears. I had not known, not as profoundly as I knew at that very moment with the snow tires singing along the pavement, that Truth is a Person. He promised He would never leave us and that, though hell might empty its arsenal against us, we could be of good cheer: "For I have overcome the world."

In that instant, I felt mountains of joy bursting inside. On impulse, I braked and pulled the car off onto the shoulder of the highway. If I didn't do something to release the emotion I was going to split.

Swinging open the car door, I leaped out. With my hands raised I began running around the car, my high heels wobbling in the gravel, and yelling, "Someday I'm going to break through . . . . I can't see Your provision yet, Lord . . . but I praise You that You're the Provider!"

Other cars were whizzing by, the drivers staring. I wondered what they thought about a crazy woman in a business suit running around with her hands in the air. But I didn't care. In a moment, I collapsed in the driver's seat, winded but happy.

After catching my breath I put the car in gear and carefully eased onto the highway. A deep peace filled me. A Scripture, Hebrews 11:1, came to me: *Faith is the substance of things hoped for, the evidence of things not seen.*

I knew we were going to make it.

That evening after work the phone rang. It was my neighbor, Betty Poyner. She sounded awkward. "Shirley, I went to the market to buy meat today. And—well, do you need meat?"

Hastily, almost embarrassed, she said she'd been ready to make her small purchase. Something had told her to buy for us, too. "I hope you have room. I bought you a freezer full."

She couldn't have known our freezer was absolutely empty. I was weeping so hard, I could hardly thank her. When I told Jim, he choked up.

Two weeks before Christmas, we got a bigger surprise.

It was snowing the evening a couple from our church knocked at the front door. When I answered, they swept inside, their arms full of packages. "Merry Christmas!" they chorused.

Jim came out to see what was happening. They were

beaming as they heaped packages in our arms. "These are for you."

We were humbled. These people didn't have much money. Yet they were so excited as they explained. They'd been shopping for Christmas gifts. On the way home, though, they'd thought about us. "We know this is a rough time for you," the man explained. "So we want you to have these."

After fending off Jim's polite refusal, they hugged us and disappeared out the door as quickly as they'd come. Jim's lips trembled as we looked in the packages: There were toys, a man's sweater.

"The Lord really loves us, Jim," I whispered. He hugged me tightly.

So there was a glow in our darkness. It would be tempting to come up with a formula: I praised God in my weakness, and He delivered the goods. In truth, I sensed we were involved in a holy mystery much deeper than words can explain. Christmas was a happy time, strangely enough, because Jim and I sensed instinctively that this would be his last.

Two months later, in February 1984, Jim's seizures had gotten so bad the doctors insisted on more tests. The results showed that the tumor had permeated a huge portion of Jim's brain. Dr. Richter did not venture a duration, but the look that he gave me said, *Not long.*

I'd been watching for signs that my greatest prayer was being answered, that Jim's relationship with God was being healed. Since that incredibly blessed Christmas, I saw a change. Jim was now so weak he'd quit work. We'd hired a new housekeeper, Joan Armistead, to help with the kids while I was at work. Almost every day, she repeated a new joke Jim had come up with. It wasn't just the sense of humor—that had always been a strong suit. As spring came something was stirring in Jim's spirit.

Around the first of April, I was out in the garage on a Saturday morning. Jim wandered out as I was unloading some heavy boxes from the trunk of my car. "Let me do that," he offered.

I almost reminded him how weak he was, but caught myself. I'd been forced to become independent, yet I knew, at this moment, it was important that Jim feel needed. "Great, hon," I said, stepping aside. "I'd appreciate that."

Leaving the garage I was going to busy myself with something in the kitchen. I hadn't gotten two steps inside the door when I heard Jim stumble.

Rushing back into the garage, I saw the box's contents had spilled. Jim was lying on his side behind the car, looking up at me with a silly grin.

My shoulders relaxed. "What are you doing down there?" He didn't miss a beat. "I knew you'd swept the floor this week, and I just wanted to see if it was clean. Lookin' good. You missed all this junk, though."

I smiled as I helped him up. My old Jim was returning.

All that week, I noticed a bouyancy in him that had not been there for a long time. When I commented on it, he replied, with a faint smile, "Things have been too heavy around here. When I die I want you to remember that, no matter how dim everything looks, you can laugh. Laughter preserves you."

I thought of the proverb, "A merry heart doeth good, like a medicine." Jim had quoted it to me, and I knew he was reading his Bible again. Now, too, he was in church almost every time the doors opened.

The weekend after his tumble in the garage, violent headaches kept him in bed all day Saturday. Marie and Jason tiptoed to the door of our darkened bedroom, and would only go in if I nudged them. The air felt close and smelled strange.

Sunday I woke to find Jim in the kitchen fixing breakfast. He looked pale. Somehow I knew I shouldn't leave him, and decided not to go to church.

That morning, while the children watched television, Jim sat me on the sofa and drew me to him in a big hug. For an hour he just held me, saying he knew how hard life had become. "But you've been so strong. Even when I was hard on you, you were steady. You'll never know how much I respect you."

Silently, I thanked God over and over for helping me not give in to bitterness or self-pity.

At lunchtime I was fixing sandwiches for the children, when Jason came into the kitchen. I looked down at him. With a look wise beyond his four years, he said, "Daddy's going to die this time."

It was a statement, not a question. I meant to say, "No he's not." I couldn't find my voice.

Sunday night, Jim slept fitfully. Even with the electric blanket doubled over and turned on high, he shook with chills. Jason's innocent words chimed in my head.

By morning, Jim was drifting in and out of consciousness. My head wasn't clear. We had to get to the hospital, but I didn't want an ambulance to roar up and terrify the children. We needed someone close, not a stranger. I dialed Buddy's number.

Shortly, he pulled up in a van. He wrapped Jim in a blanket and nearly carried him outside. Joannie had come to be with Jason and Marie. As I got in, I said smoothly, "Mommy will be home later."

Gravely, they craned for a last look at Jim, who was unable to manage even a wave.

On our way to the City of Faith, Jim's head lolled with the swaying motion of the van. When we arrived, white-coated orderlies came to lift him onto a stretcher. His eyes flickered. My hand rested on one of his upon the blanket.

The fingers of his other hand feebly sought mine. With thumb and forefinger, he tugged at my wedding ring.

My stomach knotted at his silent message: He was leaving me; I should let him go. Months before, he'd made me vow to take my wedding ring off when he died and remarry.

Now I nodded weakly. But inwardly, I couldn't deal with the thought. Who could I ever find who would understand the pain we'd all been through or the solid faith I'd found in the midst of it all?

Twenty minutes later, after I'd signed the admitting papers, I stood at the door of Jim's room in the Intensive Care Unit. The blond man lying there, wired to so many monitors, seemed a stranger amid the nurses and doctors who worked about him. His face looked pale, even against the sterile whiteness of hospital sheets. His eyes were closed. When a needle pricked a vein in his arm, he did not move.

"Mrs. Arnold," someone said as I stared at his once-full face, "your husband has slipped into a coma."

Suddenly, they all seemed like wax figures. Unreal. Macabre. I could not go in and turned away.

The rest of that day, Monday, was a string of horrible gray snapshots. Waiting. Seeing Jim from the doorway. Buddy and Pat were there, and Kenneth and Oretha Hagin, consoling me with loving words and hugs. It was that *other* touch—that invisible arm I'd felt so often in the past— that I prayed to feel. Nurses brought hourly bulletins: Jim's blood pressure dropped, his pulse grew fainter.

Tuesday, Jim's family came. Buddy talked to them, because I couldn't trust myself to speak. I wanted to go in that room, where the form of my husband lay, but could not.

That evening, Jim's mother, his sister, Corky, Tom, his younger brother, and our niece, Barbara, were with me in the waiting room. My brother Roger had just flown in, too. Buddy was explaining Jim's condition: Any minute. . . .

Pat was next to me. Inside, I heard, *There is no more time.*

I could not make myself stand. But then, as if strong arms were lifting me, I suddenly rose to my feet. "I've got to see Jim," I said to her quietly. "Will you come with me?"

This time, I made it beyond the doorway. Jim was still flat on his back, a still life against the white sheets. Monitors hummed. I touched his hand. His fingers were cold, his jaw slack. *Where are you, Jim?* I longed to be with him, to have him know . . . .

Bending down, I whispered in his ear, "Jim, I guess you can't hear me, but I love you." I rubbed my hand against his hair. Again I told him I loved him. "I don't hold any of our hardships against you. You've given me so much—two beautiful children. Marie and Jason and I are going to miss you."

Inside, I had the unusual sense that I'd completed a crucial task—that Jim was now ready to go on.

Buddy and the others had come in while I was bending down. Roger was at my side. He put his arm around me when I stood up. Jim's family rimmed the foot of the bed. Two nurses came in. It was then I noticed Jim's face.

His eyes were still shut tight—but tears were streaming out at the corners, mingling in the fine hair at his temples. He was grinning.

Buddy stood across the bed from me, next to Pat. I caught his eye. A tear slid off his chin onto Jim's hand. And then he grinned, too.

I smiled.

Buddy chuckled—that musical chuckle that always got to me.

I began to laugh—out loud. The nurses scrambled to

shut the door. Laughter swept me up. I was aware that the others might be horrified, but I couldn't stop. I felt light-headed, as if I were moving quickly up a steep path.

Closing my eyes, I doubled up. Laughter rolled out of me. I had an uncanny sensation: Jim was standing beside me, his hand in mine. He looked virile, and his grip was strong. And at the same moment, I sensed a bright Presence, drawing us. We were rising.

Inwardly, I was caught up in praise as we moved upward in growing light. *Who am I to complain, Lord, when You have become so real to me? Thank You for becoming my Provider, my Shepherd, my Husband.*

My praises went on for some minutes, and we seemed to emerge, the way you come out of fog into sunlight near the top of a mountain. Jim's face was beaming, his eyes alight.

And then, in that place above the darkness, I felt his hand slip from mine. He moved on ahead and away from me, turning just once to smile and wave . . . .

I was aware that I'd fallen silent. Peace surrounded me. No, it carried me. I opened my eyes. Jim's silent form lay before me, the smile, like dawn, on his face.

Stooping, I kissed him and said goodbye.

I felt so drained, but—joyful. Turning, I walked from the room. I had to go home and sleep.

At 5:46 the next morning, Wednesday, April 11, the hospital called. Jim was gone. But I could have told them that.

We had finished the race together. And we'd won.

17

TERRY:
Where Angels Tread

After accepting Andrus' challenge to help him in his work in Russia, I had serious misgivings.

He'd asked for a printing press, musical instruments, sound equipment. The small press I had in mind cost $15,000. As far as taking in a team, food and lodging in the Soviet Union was astronomical. Where would all the money come from?

I'd also been reading about Soviet politics and society. They didn't call it the Iron Curtain for nothing. Those border guards north of Tallin had practically peeled the paint off our bus in their search. How on earth was Living Sound going to get supplies in to the underground church?

And I had misgivings about my own safety—that is, not for myself, but for my family. In 1978 Jan delivered our third child, Rebecca. Gordon Calmeyer, an evangelist with one Living Sound team, and his wife, Stella, helped Jan with the kids while I was away. At five, Scotty was getting interested in soccer and football, and Misty also needed

228

Daddy's attention. What would happen to my family if I didn't come back from one of these missions?

Plus there was a more delicate, personal matter.

Jan had gained weight with the birth of each child. Adding pounds to her once-slim figure hit Jan hard. Her bright optimism occasionally gave way to depression. We prayed and read Scriptures together, but, being away so much, I felt inadequate to help her.

Nonetheless, I'd made a promise to Andrus—and to God. I could only hope He would knock down all the obstacles that stood in the way of my fulfilling that vow.

Almost immediately, it seemed as if the windows of heaven were flung open. Where Living Sound had always been short on cash flow, I was staggered at the money that began to come in. A Canadian businessman, having heard me speak about our mission to Russia, handed over $15,000 for Andrus' printing press. An English businessman surprised our European office with a donation of £18,000—more than $40,000. The British pop singer Cliff Richard, a strong Christian, had just performed in Moscow. He sent a check for £1,000.

This kind of giving astonished me. I saw in it God's tender love for his persecuted people in Russia. Yet it did not help me rest any easier.

Several months into 1979, while I was wrestling with the enormous job before me, I received a phone call from a nationally televised Christian talk show. I'd been interviewed by the program's host several times and his office was calling to ask a special favor.

They were about to interview Pastor Roland Buck about his book on angels, which was causing controversy all over America. Some were calling Pastor Buck a fraud. Since I was the only one they knew who had worked with him, the producers wanted me to be on the show with him.

Though my mind was on Russia, I agreed to appear on the program.

Just before the broadcast, I was in the dressing room backstage with Pastor Buck. I found him plainspoken, humble, just as I had several months before during the crusade in Boise. Out on the set, I heard the floor director say, "Five minutes." Buck and I were alone.

He turned to me suddenly. "Back in Boise, you wanted me to ask the angel about the future of Living Sound. Do you remember that?"

My face got warm, remembering how embarrassed I'd been at Gordon Calmeyer's queston. "Oh—uh, that wasn't me."

"Well, I did ask," he said, then paused. "What does the name Dwight McLaughlin mean to you?"

My mind raced. I'd never told anyone that story. "What are you talking about?" I challenged.

"Remember the camp meeting when you were fourteen?"

Gooseflesh crawled up my arms.

Pastor Buck continued, "The angel told me about another angel who was sent by God to wake up McLaughlin that night. That's when God gave McLaughlin a message for you about your worldwide mission. Isn't that right?"

Before I could respond, he had more. "I'm to tell you that every time you go behind the Iron Curtain, a band of warring angels goes before you to open the way, and a second band follows to protect you."

This was impossible! The awesomeness of what he was saying pummeled me.

I stared at him, speechless as the floor director came in. We were needed on the set.

After the show, we had little time to talk, and on the plane flight later, his words continued to burn in me. What was that last thing he'd said? Something about "even harder times ahead." I couldn't imagine anything harder than what we'd been through.

What was I to think of all this? I'd drawn pictures of angels in Sunday school. But roving bands of them, going into the Soviet Union? Surely God was using Pastor Buck to confirm our mission—granted, in a startling way. *That* was the kind of encouragement I needed right now.

On October 13, when I flew to West Germany to meet Living Sound Team IV, angels were the furthest thing from my mind. During that summer of 1979 we'd purchased $50,000 worth of guitars, amplifiers, electric keyboards, and professional tape recorders. The printing press had already been taken in by others in a way I promised not to disclose. Getting the musical equipment inside was our job. This wasn't just a concert tour—as the Soviet tourist agency expected. It was like a secret assault.

When the jet touched down in West Berlin, the team leader, Randy Innes, met me. He drove me to the hotel where the team was staying. There, he filled me in on the latest details.

In case our run-in at the Finnish border a year ago had been reported, Living Sound had taken on an assumed name, and our European office had scheduled concerts with secular musical groups along our tour route. This was our smokescreen: Underground concerts were planned along the way. Andrus' inside information told him we might be watched. Therefore, utmost secrecy had to shroud every step of the trip.

Then Randy dropped the big one. "Terry," he said, leading me to the room where our musical equipment was stored, "there's something you should know about."

With a screwdriver, he took six bolts off the back of one of our monitor speakers. "Take a look."

I bent down. Taped along the inside of the cabinet were thin metal plates—stacks of them.

"Three hundred printing plates of the Bible," Randy said, gravely. "A mission here has been trying to get them in for three years without success."

I stood up. "And *we're* supposed to get them in? Randy, the music stuff is one thing. We can leave equipment, and they may not notice. But printing plates—"

"Please, Terry," Randy begged. "Before you say no, pray about it."

That night, I prayed, "Please, Father. Not this."

From what I'd read of Russian law, smuggling got you a fast trip to a Siberian prison camp. How could I ask a team to risk that—let alone risk it myself?

Yet, as I prayed, I knew the answer in my gut.

On October 15, the Living Sound team—now using another name—drove into Poland. The three hundred plates were still taped inside the monitor speaker. Randy and I decided not to tell the rest of the team. In the event of questioning, they could answer with perfect innocence.

Our first stop was Kiev in southeastern Russia. On our trip up through Poland, we stopped outside Krakow at Auschwitz, one of the most infamous World War II prison camps.

The long, low huts, where tens of thousands had suffered their final agony, were scrubbed clean and painted. But nothing could whitewash the sense of death that still hovered.

The stop was a big mistake. As we neared the border late that evening, a dark oppression clung to me.

It was around ten-thirty at night when our bus pulled into the station. Two guards with machine guns waved us over to one side. I jumped out and, as expected, an inspector ordered a search. I hoped the man didn't see how nervous I was. Under the glare of floodlights, the team piled off the bus and began to unload everything.

We'd been there about a half-hour and, as things came

off the bus, the guards rummaged about. When one of our young men, Gary Cass, hoisted out the monitor speaker, I got very interested in a stone on the pavement at my feet.

"Good grief," he complained. "What's in this thing?"

I went cold. Silently, I shouted, *Shut up, Gary!*

A guard walked over, looking suspiciously at the speaker box. The bus driver shrugged. "Nothing in there. I'll get a screwdriver and show you."

My knees nearly buckled. Randy went over to the far side of the bus. I could hear him getting sick in the bushes as the driver began to unscrew the back of the monitor.

Yet my eyes were stuck on that case—and the turning screwdriver. Two screws were out. My mind reeled. *We're dead.* The third screw *plinked* on the pavement. I thought about Jan and the kids, so far away. The fourth screw fell. The fifth.

Suddenly the guard motioned with his gun to one of the big main speakers. "Not that one. The one over there."

Gary looked at me and rolled his eyes. "Sure. Whatever you say."

Apparently, Gary had seemed too eager to open the monitor thus diverting suspicion from it. The other, of course, was empty.

Almost six hours later, at four A.M., we were allowed to depart for Kiev. Someone in the back of the bus remarked, "Gee, that wasn't as bad as I expected." Randy swallowed hard. Underneath my jacket, my shirt was soaked.

Lord, I prayed, *I don't know how You pulled us out of that one. But I thank You with all my heart.*

The next morning at our assigned hotel in Kiev, we had our first chance to talk to the official Intourist guide who had met us at the border. He was a disagreeable man with the improbable name of Igor, whose smile did not veil the hatred and suspicion in his eyes. That afternoon, I found a small microphone wired behind a picture frame in my room.

Late in the evening, Randy and I had to slip out for a *rendezvous* with our first underground contact, whose code name was "Viktor." Igor was in the hotel bar with his hands all over a young woman, and we made our break.

We got lost several times, but shortly past eleven P.M., we found what we were looking for: a floodlit square where a dazzling marble statue of a cossack on a stallion reared high in the air. At the base of the statue we met Viktor.

I had only a moment to study him—blond, tall, about twenty-eight years old—before he shoved us into a waiting car.

For an hour we sped around Kiev in crazy circles while Viktor talked. Andrus knew we were going to preach on this tour and that the K.G.B. would be all over us at once. He decided we had to drop the equipment right away, rather than wait two weeks as we had planned.

"Tomorrow afternoon," said Viktor, "you will play a jam session with jazz musicians of the Kiev Philharmonic. There, you unload the plates. Then I take you to a small church outside Kiev. Near there, you unload the equipment."

All we had to do, said Viktor, was get rid of Igor for the day.

The next morning, to our relief, Igor seemed almost indifferent when we first told him about our jam session. We'd seen him corner one of the maids and could guess what he had in mind for later. So it dismayed me when, just after lunch, Igor became agitated.

His voice got husky, mean. "That's all? A jam session? I think I'll come, too. Would you like that?"

I fought to stay cool as his eyes locked on mine. They felt like hands, groping into my soul. Calmly, I replied, "If you like jazz, you'll love this jam. C'mon with us."

He smiled. "No. Jazz is not my 'thing,' as you say."

In the bus on our way to the jam session, Randy looked at me. "There's something about that guy. Like he knows what's going on in our heads."

I nodded. "Yeah. But let's hope not. Or we're sunk."

The concert hall was located on a busy street in downtown Kiev. We got off and Viktor strolled up immediately. He seemed calm, as if he did this sort of thing every day. Already I was warming to him.

I'd let Craig Watson, one of our sound technicians, in on the secret. He made sure the monitor speakers were left in the rear hatch under the bus, while I helped the musicians unload their instruments.

Inside, one of the officials watched us nervously. We were to play from 2:00 till 4:00, after which I was to speak on behalf of the group. By 3:30, the musicians were really cooking. Viktor and all the singers were settled in chairs at the front of the hall. I was pretty sure no one would notice me, and I excused myself, as if I were going to the men's room. Instead, I slipped outside.

We had to work fast. At exactly 3:45 our pickup man was due. And I'd have to get back inside before I was missed.

Fortunately, there weren't many people on the sidewalk. Craig opened the rear hatch. Two people had just walked by. Otherwise, there was no one. I dove inside. Craig jumped in after me, and pulled the lid down.

Quickly, Craig opened the monitor cabinet with a screwdriver as I held the flashlight. He had to steady his hands as he carefully peeled tape off the bundles of printing plates, then laid them inside a large, battered suitcase Viktor had brought. Then he replaced the back of the monitor.

We had to wait several minutes until the sidewalk was clear. Then we crawled out. It was 3:43.

Two minutes later, a young man turned the corner. He paid no attention to us, until he was just ten feet away. Then, looking around quickly, he veered toward us.

"Viktor sent me," he said in a low accent. His eyes looked like those of a frightened animal.

He hardly missed a step as I handed him the suitcase. Just beyond the bus, he charged into the street. Hailing a cab, he jumped in and was gone.

When Craig and I rejoined the group inside, sweat had beaded on my forehead.

Ten minutes later, as planned, one of our musicians gave me the nod. Though I was only supposed to preach at the churches on our tour, I didn't want to miss any opportunity. For twenty minutes, Viktor translated while I talked to these musicians about God's love for them.

When I finished praying, some applauded openly. A few glared at me. The official looked agitated, but he said nothing.

Quickly we reloaded the bus. It would take more than an hour to make our way from downtown Kiev, out to a Baptist church in a rural area beyond the city, where we were to play our first concert in a registered church.

The bus rumbled along in the heavy traffic, and I felt a million pounds lighter. After what we'd just pulled off in broad daylight on a city street, anything else had to be a snap.

The moment we'd pulled away from the concert hall, however, someone had picked up a phone.

It was dusk when we drove through a wooded area and came to the church. About a hundred and fifty young people swarmed around us in the parking lot as we came off the bus. In the crowd I was elated when I recognized several young people we'd met before.

A young girl tapped me on the sleeve. She pulled me

aside. "Andrus is waiting out in the bush. I'll take you to him."

We slipped out of the crowd, around the bus, then dashed across the road to a narrow path that wound through scrubby trees. In the failing light, I caught my feet on roots and branches. It was cool, and the moldering smell of fallen leaves filled my nostrils. We trudged on for about a half mile. A road, which was no more than dirt track, intersected the path. In an overgrown field, Andrus was waiting with several cars.

"Take our equipment out through the back door of the church." Then he gave me detailed instructions on how to find a spot about a mile away from the church. "This way, the pastor knows nothing about it. And we will pick it up late tonight."

We embraced hurriedly, and I rushed back over the path.

I stepped out of the bush and smiled when I saw about a hundred young people gathered around the door outside. The church was filled to overflowing. Then my heart skipped.

A police van was parked in front of the church! Somehow we'd been followed. Policemen with rifles were sitting in the van. I had to get across the road before they saw me.

My temples pulsed as I set foot in the road. From inside the church, I could hear the team warming up. I was halfway across the road, when the two officers in the van looked up. I swallowed hard.

Their eyes never left me as I neared them. Suddenly, the engine started. The driver smirked. Then he stepped on the gas and tore out of the parking lot. I watched the van go down the road, brake, and turn off into the bush!

Closing my eyes, I fired a prayer heavenward. *Father, You've got to warn Andrus. Let him know they're coming.* Squeezing through the crowd, I went inside. We were performing for a harvest festival and the church was full of pumpkins, corn shocks, and vegetables. Quickly I gave the instructions to the three guys who would deliver the equipment. When I finally sat down beside Viktor, he elbowed me. "They're here," he muttered.

"Who's here?"

"The K.G.B."

"How do you know?"

"Just watch when we pray," he said drily. "They won't close their eyes."

I couldn't believe he could keep a sense of humor at a time like this.

He wasn't mistaken.

The moment I stood up to greet the crowd, two men also stood up. One began snapping my picture with a 35 mm camera. The other had a tape recorder. He paraded up to me and thrust the microphone right in my face as I spoke.

The K.G.B. never heard a clearer presentation of the Gospel than the songs and testimonies they taped that night. And the whole time, I prayed silently for Andrus and his men out in the bush and thanked God that the three guys I'd sent with the equipment had returned safely.

When the concert ended, I hurried outside. There was no sign of the police van. Randy and I rounded up the team quickly. Viktor had disappeared. Only the Lord knew what had befallen Andrus and his men. If they *had* escaped, I wanted things to quiet down fast so they could get out into the woods beyond the church later without being seen.

I was counting heads when Roger Friend, our drummer bounded up the steps. His face was blanched. He'd been hauling his trap set out a side door. Out of the darkness, a man had come up behind him, speaking fluent English.

"We know who you are," he'd told Roger, grinning.

"You call yourselves by another name but you're really Living Sound. You've been in the Soviet Union before. This time we're going to stop you dead."

That wasn't our only head-on confrontation that night. Back at the hotel, Igor was furious. From what I gathered, as he shouted in my face, he'd been in bed with the hotel maid when the K.G.B. found him. He'd been cursed and derided for letting us "Christianize" the city while he enjoyed himself. Curling a meaty fist in my face, he cursed me and blasphemed God.

Alone in my room that night I knew we were in more serious trouble than we'd ever been in before. From a secret pocket inside my suitcase, I dug out a small New Testament. This thin little book felt like my only lifeline.

On my knees beside the bed, I prayed, *Lord, I feel so helpless. I'm responsible for the lives of fourteen other people. If I make a wrong step, we all go to jail. I know I've got to do it Your way, Lord.*

As I prayed, a looming, oppressive feeling came over me: Morning was going to be a turning point. I was going to face someone who held our fate in his hands. *Father, please,* I begged. *I need Your wisdom.*

For hours I stayed on my knees, pleading for guidance. Gradually, the heaviness I felt eased. I prayed for Andrus and his team. I prayed for the K.G.B. More time passed. I thanked and praised God—and even prayed for Igor. About four-thirty in the morning, I had an uncanny feeling. It was as if a door had flown open. I hadn't felt anything like it before. A Scripture came into my head. *Acts 4.*

Flipping to it in my New Testament, I skimmed the page: Peter and John had been arrested by the evil priests and Sadducees who ordered them to stop preaching about Jesus. My eyes riveted on their reply: *"Whether it be right in the sight of God to hearken unto you more than unto God, judge ye. For we cannot but speak the things which we have seen and heard.*"

I would rather have turned up the verse that said Elijah went to the back side of the desert for forty days. But with that verse came a luminous *peace.* Whether our cover was blown or not, I had to be bold.

The next morning, on my way downstairs to breakfast, Viktor met me in the hall. How he popped in and out was a mystery. "Look out. You're in for trouble," he whispered. Then he was gone again.

The team was seated at several tables in the dining room, sipping cups of steaming tea. Immediately, Igor grabbed my arm. "Someone wants to talk to you."

As he led me down a hallway, I tried to cling to that peace I'd felt during the night. But my heart was racing again. We'd been seen, heard, taped, and photographed preaching. I had no idea how I could defend myself and the group now. Igor shoved me into a small room.

Inside, the shades were drawn. I was pushed into a chair at a table, with a bright light shining in my face. In the dimness across the desk sat a uniformed officer. I also noticed a man in plain clothes seated in a far corner of the room staring at me.

Immediately, the officer fired his accusation. "You went to a church last night. You did not have permission. It was not on your official schedule."

Quietly, I said that was true.

Furious, the officer began shouting that we had broken the law and must be punished. I closed my eyes, remembering the boldness of Peter and John. But what was I to say now? *Father, give me the words.*

The officer was still shouting.

I held up my hand, and he paused. "You have something to say?"

"Yes," I replied. *What, Lord. What do I say?*

I opened my mouth. The thoughts that came to me in that instant astonished me. I supposed that in my research about Soviet society, I must have read these facts. But where? And how could I be so confident in the details, as I looked at him and said, "According to your new Soviet constitution, ratified in 1977, article 52 declares that you have freedom of religion in the U.S.S.R. Is that correct?"

The officer's face was blank.

I repeated, "Is that correct?"

"Yes, but—"

A burning filled me. "Your constitution protects my religious rights. Then why can't I go to your churches? Your law says I can. So I'm going to go to every church I can and tell about my faith.

"And by the way, sir," I pressed, "has anyone ever told you about Jesus Christ and how He died on the cross for you?"

At that moment, the man in plain clothes in the corner jumped off his seat. "You don't interfere in our domestic affairs!" he shouted.

"This is a religious affair," I said, defying him. "Now I've told you up front what I'm going to do." I stood up. "So, gentlemen, I bid you goodbye."

Out in the hall, I nearly collapsed. The boldness was gone. Where had those facts about Russian law come from? I staggered down the hall and back to the team. Who was going to believe this?

From that day on three men followed me wherever I went. But the tour went on—from Kiev to Rostov on the Black Sea, south to Tblisi, and into Armenia on the Turkish border. Then the team swung north again to Moscow, Leningrad, and into Tallinn.

In each place, we felt the warm fellowship of the believers. Despite the threats that followed us, no one regretted the decision to bring the word of hope to these brothers and sisters in Christ. I often had to run down alleys and dodge K.G.B. men in subways.

By his own secret means, Viktor turned up just before each concert to interpret even though the police were hunting for him everywhere. Concerned for his safety, I practically begged him to leave us and go back home.

Viktor looked at me with eyes I could not fathom. "Eight years ago, I was the head of an atheist club. The day I accepted Jesus I knew that one day I might have to die for my faith.

"I made my choice, Terry. So don't worry about me. Eight years ago, I died. What can they do to me now?"

When Living Sound left Russia, after completing our tour, I would never forget the many brave pastors and Christians we'd met—but none more sterling than Viktor.

Later, I was to learn that Andrus and his men had successfully picked up the equipment. They had been stopped twice on the way back to Leningrad, but, by some quirk, the police hadn't even asked about the instruments. That equipment is now safely stored and being used for God out in the bush.

Back in Tulsa, as I went over all these events with Jan, I was flying high. I couldn't get Roland Buck's message about warring angels out of my head. Even so . . .

"That's pretty far-out, Terry," Jan agreed. Still, we both had to rejoice at the uncanny split-second interventions that had saved Living Sound from disaster. Surely a divine power had been at work on our behalf.

Misty had a different reaction to my homecoming.

The night after I got home, I went into her room to tuck her into bed. She was old enough now to sense adult feelings, and must have become aware that preaching the Gospel in Russia was very dangerous. When I pulled the covers around her, she suddenly wrapped her arms around my neck.

"I was afraid you might not come back," she said tearfully.

I stroked her dark hair. "Don't worry, Misty. There's nothing Satan can do to stop us. God wants His Word to get through. As long as I obey God, we're okay."

Kissing her goodnight, I went to tuck in Scotty. Jan was putting little 'Becca into her crib. The house was so quiet, peaceful. A deep contentment came over me.

Already I was thinking about another trip behind the Iron Curtain. We'd beat the authorities once. I felt certain we could do it again.

I had no inkling of the darkness that was gathering—for we had bearded the lion

18

TERRY:
A Deeper Love

The drone of the jet engines had a lulling effect. We were somewhere over the Atlantic, headed for England, in the early morning hours of Tuesday, September 28, 1982. In the seats beside me, Jim Gilbert and David Weir were dozing. I wasn't looking forward to the major restructuring of our European office, which David was taking over. Though I needed sleep badly, my mind was churning.

Events in the three years since Living Sound's first tour of Russia left me confused. If God had cleared the way for our work there, why had so many near-disasters befallen since then?

Shutting my eyes I could almost plot the curious rise and fall of my ministry on a graph.

For me, 1979 and 1980 had been peak years. Living Sound made more trips into Russia. We'd helped young people in several major cities start contemporary gospel music teams. Besides providing them with equipment, we

244

trained them in the Bible. Now the Iron Curtain mission God had called me to was going on even when I was not physically there and lives were being changed.

The summer of 1980 brought a special honor. In August, Living Sound was invited to give a special performance in Vatican Square for Pope John Paul II, who, as a Cardinal in Poland, had heard us perform at music festivals in Czestochowa. Besides the Pope, some 60,000 looked on.

After those "golden years," however, we'd suddenly plunged into a downhill slide. Undoubtedly, it began with Viktor's arrest.

Actually, he was picked up in Leningrad, moments after parting company with Living Sound in 1979. No sooner had our bus turned a corner than he was swarmed by police. There was no chance of fleeing—and no question he'd be imprisoned for helping us. For two years, Viktor's words stalked me: *"Eight years ago I died. What can they do to me now?"* I knew what Christians suffered in Soviet prisons: beatings, hunger, cold, solitary confinement, torture. Because of mistreatment, Viktor had gone blind temporarily in one eye.

In 1981, he'd been released. Hoping to see him, I'd gone into Russia. But he was under police surveillance. I never got to him—never got to thank him for all he'd endured because of his love for the Lord. I felt personally responsible: I'd known the danger and should have made him leave us.

And on the heels of Viktor's tragedy came this year's near-disaster in the ministry. Six months before, in the spring of '82, we were plunged into a major money crisis.

Living Sound's yearly operating budget had reached nearly $1 million. Then the U.S. fell into an economic recession, causing donations to drop by fifty percent almost overnight. For three or four months, I didn't receive a salary. Close friends had to be let go, reducing our staff to a handful.

And in the midst of that uncertainty, rebellion broke out in one of our teams during a summer trip to Spain. Planning had been poor and when the team was forced to sleep on bare floors, some became justifiably angry. I'd made an emergency trip to Europe to help, but tempers won out. Before my eyes, the team dissolved.

I'd flown home from that blow to find Jan crying.

"There's nothing in the refrigerator, Terry," she said. *"Nothing.* What am I going to feed the kids for supper?"

Only a miracle pulled us through. That evening Scotty's baseball coach unexpectedly drove up to our gate and handed him an envelope. Inside were ten $100 bills. How he knew about our situation was a mystery.

Now, a few weeks later, sitting in the dim-lit cabin of the jetliner headed for England, the truth was that we were still in danger financially. And emotionally, I'd have to go through the pain of letting people go from our European operation as well.

Jan must have heard the weariness in my voice when I'd phoned her from JFK only hours ago to say I wouldn't be gone long.

"Things are going to work out, Terry," she said. I smiled. That was Jan, lifting me up when I'd called to encourage her. "I love you," I replied. "See you soon."

Drowsiness came over me. I couldn't wait until the problems in Europe were solved. We'd be ready for God to use us again. Yet, as I drifted in and out of a fitful sleep, a half-formed question surfaced: Had I done something wrong to bring on all this upheaval?

Hours later, when office staff met us at Heathrow Airport in London, the question was forgotten. A residual uneasiness remained, however, like a dirty film in a glass.

That evening, after several hours of driving, we sat in

the parlor to visit. I was enjoying the hum of the conversation. Strangely, at about nine P.M., something felt so wrong.

Thoughts glanced through my head. *I wonder what Jan and the kids are doing.* Then, *Maybe I shouldn't fire any more of the staff.* My head was jumbled.

In a few minutes, I excused myself. All I wanted to do was go back to the guest room at our office and sleep.

The room was sparsely furnished. Turning off the single bare bulb in the ceiling, I crawled wearily into the bottom bunk bed. Everything felt so heavy—my arms, my eyes, my heart. Pulling the covers up to my chin, I shut my eyes and curled up. Sleep came in a few moments. . . .

Someone was shaking me. I woke groggily, blinking into the light. The clock showed eleven P.M.; I'd been asleep only an hour. David Weir was leaning over me. He'd been crying.

"Terry, wake up. I have a terrible message for you." Then his voice broke. "We've had a call from Tulsa. Jan has been killed in a car accident."

A thickness, like fog, rolled over me. Other men stood near, including Jim Gilbert, crying, but somehow far, far away. Slowly, I sat up on the edge of the bed. For some minutes, I stared at my bare feet. "No. That's not right, David. Just let me go back to sleep."

David shook me. "Hear me, Terry. Jan's been killed."

Why were these tears stinging my eyes? If I could just keep his words away. . . . "That can't happen, David."

A pressure hit my chest, and bolts of pain. I grabbed the springs of the bunk above me and squeezed till the wires dug into my fingers. Truth came thundering in on me.

"*No!*" I shouted. "*God! It can't be!*"

For a long time I wept. I asked, "Is there a chance she's not dead?" No. "When did it happen?" About two hours ago. Nine our time. "Where?" A quarter-mile from the office. None of the children was with her. "Who are they with?" The Calmeyers. "I have to talk to them."

Someone placed the call. Gordon answered. He'd had to tell them already. Then Misty came on. Her voice was flat, shocked-sounding. "Don't worry about us, Daddy. We'll be all right."

So brave for an eleven-year-old. I steeled myself. "Do you realize that Mommy is gone? We won't see her anymore." I heard her sob. "Why did God do this to my mother?"

It hurt to make myself say, "God didn't do it." I had to say that; I wasn't sure it was true.

Scotty was crying when he came on the line. At eight, he was so tenderhearted. Then 'Becca—four years old, having no idea why Scotty and Misty were crying, no concept of death. I had to explain the accident. "Now Mommy's with Jesus."

Hearing their voices, having to say the words made it real. Final. I prayed with each of them. When I hung up, I ached all over.

The rest of that night and the trip home was a blur of anguish. On the plane, pain beat at my ribs and in my temples. Jonah's words came to me. *"I have been banished from your sight . . . the deep surrounds me. . . . But I, with a song of thanksgiving, will sacrifice to you."* I hid my head beneath a pillow. The words were ridiculous. *I'll never be able to praise You again.*

Friends met me at the airport on Wednesday: Gene Eland, Gordon, Joel, Dr. Farah, and others. Their embraces were all but lost on me. Nothing mattered except feeling Misty, Scotty, and 'Becca wrap their arms around me when I dropped to my knees in the Calmeyers' living room. I looked into their lost, wounded faces, wishing all their pain could be heaped into me.

The bitterest part was going home—the absence of Jan's

bright greeting when I opened the door. In the living room, I felt a warmth and smelled—what? The vague scent of Jan's favorite cologne lingering in the air. I carried my suitcase down the hall and stopped at the door of our room. On Jan's dresser were a few of her things: her brush, her Bible, a card I'd sent. I could not go in.

That night, though the house had filled with out-of-town guests, I felt a terrifying loneliness. Only the exhaustion of nearly sixty hours with no sleep drove me into our empty bed.

On Thursday morning, Dad arrived from Canada, with Lorne and Lois, and my old Bible-school friend, Brian Stiller, now head of Youth for Christ in Canada. I had unanswered questions about the accident, and asked Dad and Brian to take a drive with me.

We drove by my office on 101st Street and continued down the long hill, heading west, the way Jan would have been driving on her way to pick up 'Becca from preschool. At the bottom of the hill was a narrow bridge over a stream. The sun would have been directly in her eyes, which was why the police supposed her car drifted to the right until the tires caught on the right shoulder. Someone jogging further down the road reported, however, that a car had swerved into Jan's lane. Trying to get back on the road, Jan had apparently jerked the wheel to the left, sending the car careening back across the road.

Pulling off onto the gravel shoulder, I got out and stumbled down the weedy embankment. Since it was morning, the sun was in the east, behind me. Brian and Dad followed. Wading through the deep grass, still wet with dew, I saw fresh-turned dirt in the roadside ditch, which had acted like a ski jump, rocketing Jan's out-of-control car up into the air. Twenty yards away was a small earth dam, bearing the gouge made by her front bumper.

Cresting the dam, I walked on into the field where the

car had flipped end-over-end. I picked my way along, finding pieces of chrome, shattered glass. My head was throbbing. Something dark in the grass caught my eye.

Stooping, I touched my fingers to it. Sickness and sorrow gripped my throat.

Dad and Brian came up from behind. "What is it?"

Unable to answer, I stared at the dark red stain on my fingers: Jan's blood.

They turned away, while I wept inconsolably. Why hadn't I been here? Jan died of a broken neck, but not immediately. Had she been conscious, her eyes searching the frightened faces working over her, wishing I were with her and not thousands of miles away?

From inside, lines came to me, written by the English poet Thomas Carlyle, whose wife had died suddenly while he was far from home. Ironically, I'd used them in a sermon recently: *Oh, that I had you by my side for one hour! that I might tell you all.*

Remorse was overpowering: Why had I been away from Jan so often? Could I have comforted her more in her depression over the weight-gain? Why hadn't I sent her flowers more often? Had I remembered to say I love you when we last spoke? *Oh, that I had you by my side. . . .*

My face buried in my hands, other questions pressed in, too. What had I done wrong to bring this on my family? How had I let God down? Wouldn't He have protected my family if I were truly doing His will?

Half-blind with grief, I turned away from the stained spot on the earth.

The next morning, Friday, at Jan's memorial service, Oral Roberts gave a warm, uplifting eulogy. He talked about Jan's eyes, their lively expressive quality, and the love for God that shone through her when she sang.

Surely it was superhuman power that allowed me to get up and talk about Jan. Joel Vesanen had handed me a note when I'd stepped off the plane from England, telling me not to forget the dream God had given Jan and me. Standing before that shocked, pain-filled group of family and friends, I talked about that dream of ministering around the world, how Jan and I had shared in it, how she'd struggled to accept the calling before we married, how scared she'd been.

"But she *did* it. And I'm jealous that she's already with Jesus," I said. "She's seen His smile, and heard Him say, 'Well done.' "

There were smiles, tears of sadness and joy mixed. A note of victory sounded in that painful moment.

But later, at home, when all those offering condolences had left and I was alone with Misty, Scotty, 'Becca, and my mom, I went to the bedroom to be alone. All the talk of dreams and serving God could not replace the haunting emptiness. Did I ever have a dream? Or was it just delusion?

Lord, I thought, lying back on the bed. *I wanted to dream big dreams, and do big things for You. But beneath it, Lord, all I've wanted all my life was to hear You say, "Well done, Terry. You gave it all you had."*

Lying there, I saw my life was scattered on the floor in shreds. All the evidence was in: First, Viktor's imprisonment, then the financial disaster. Surely Jan's death was the final proof. The sentence was final: No matter how hard I tried, I was unacceptable to God. My dream was just a fantasy.

In the days following Jan's funeral I existed in some gray zone, not fully alive anymore. What would have happened without Mom there is hard to say. She cooked, got the children up and off to school, and fitted together the pieces of an ordinary routine. When the ministry's music direc tor, Don Moen, hinted about remarriage I bristled. I couldn't *think* about getting married for two years. Don backed off.

I could manage the days, even in an office that seemed almost empty since most of the staff was gone; the ministry was floundering. But nights were agony. After the children were in bed, I'd get in my car and drive the streets of Tulsa, or find an all-night coffee shop just to be near people.

One night, past midnight, I was slouched in a booth alone, next to a window, nursing a cup of coffee. A young couple took the booth opposite me. I looked away, out at the dark, but in the window-glass was their reflection. Their fingers touched across the table. I squeezed my eyes shut.

Prison would be better, or death, I thought. But not this living hell of grief and loneliness.

For a month, I considered quitting the ministry. But something wouldn't allow me. Over the last several years, Oral and Evelyn Roberts had suffered triple-tragedy: first, the deaths of their daughter and son-in-law, then the death of their oldest son. How on earth did Oral find the strength to go on telling people that God is loving and merciful?

Late in October, I knew I needed a lifeline, and fast. Perhaps Oral could help in some way; otherwise I was ready to fold up the ministry. I made an appointment to see him.

The next day, seated in his office, I weighed Oral's every word. He told me first of his own painful wrestlings regarding God's part in the deaths of his children. He concluded, saying, "I know that God did not kill them."

I countered with many questions. Oral kept bringing me back to the Bible. "Jesus said, 'I give life more abundantly.' Satan is the one who steals and kills. Satan is the destroyer—not God. God is *for* us. You've got to keep your head straight on that."

Then he leaned forward, intently looking at me. "I'm going to tell you something that will save your life—if you'll do what I say."

I was ready for anything.

"Go home," said Oral, "get on your knees, and begin to praise the Lord."

My heart sank. That was it? Go home and praise the Lord? For what? That my children were crying themselves to sleep at night without their mother? Praise was the one thing that made no sense at all right now. It was out of the question.

Oral was explaining that we did not have to praise God *for* everything, but that we must praise Him *in* everything, whether in sickness, financial loss, or even the death of someone who means more to us than life.

We talked a while longer. Then, thanking him, I excused myself.

As I drove home, the streets were gray, the buildings flat and lifeless. Pulling into the driveway, I shut off the engine. If praise was my only way out, then it was truly over.

But what if . . . ? Oral's been through it. He knows. What if there's one last chance?

That night, before crawling into bed, it took all my determination to set the alarm for five-thirty A.M.

The next morning, before dawn, I forced myself to get up. In the darkness, I knelt by the bed. What was I supposed to do now?

Mechanically, I said, "Thank You, God. Praise the Lord. Hallelujah."

Immediately, a voice fired at me. *Law, you're a hypocrite. Why are you praising God? Your wife is dead. You can't mean those words. How can you praise God, feeling as bad as you do?*

For some minutes, as the light of dawn grew in the

room, that voice scalded me with accusations. I had to get off my knees. This was ridiculous.

I started to get up, when the words of David came to me, words he'd written in one of the bleakest moments of his life: *I will bless the Lord at all times. His praise shall continually be in my mouth.*

I paused. *You've got to be happy to praise God. You're not good enough for God to use you. You're not good enough to be saved. . . .*

In that moment, I saw the lie—an old one I'd stumbled over so much of my life. Of course, I was not "good enough"; that wasn't the point. Of course I was hurt; that wasn't the point either. God is not the dealer of death, but the bringer of joy. He is joy.

Setting my jaw, I shut my eyes. *I will praise! I will praise You, God, for who You are!*

"Bless Your name, God!"

Nothing happened. "God, You are mighty." Pain and death and evil were laughing in my face. Sunlight grew, brushing the walls. I stayed on my knees for an hour; two hours; the words were wooden. A pressure built inside.

Give it up, Terry. . . .

I fought back. *Thank You, God. You are holy and loving. You are worthy. Worthy!*

All at once the pressure let loose. My hands went up, and I shouted, "You are worthy. Praise You, Lord."

As I praised, joy flooded in. I was taken out of myself. I saw my anger, bitterness, self-pity. I saw the wrong thinking that had crippled me most of my life—the idea that God loved me and used me only when I did good things, but was ready to cast me away when I displeased Him.

"Forgive me for accusing You, Father," I prayed.

For hours, I continued praying, replacing my anger with words of love and adoration. Cleansing came. And healing. When I got off my knees, some time after ten that morning, the terrible ache inside was gone. I couldn't understand it, but a miracle had taken place.

For the next few weeks, I pondered what had happened to me. I began to search the Bible.

The first Scripture I turned to was Jonah chapter 2, which had come to me on the plane. In verse 9, I read, "But I, with a song of thanksgiving, will sacrifice to you."

Then I turned to the Psalms, and read:

> . . . therefore will I offer in his tabernacle sacrifices of joy. . . .   Psalm 27:6

> O give thanks unto the Lord, for he is good: for his mercy endureth for ever. . . . Oh that men would praise the Lord for his goodness. . . . Let them sacrifice the sacrifices of thanksgiving, and declare his works with rejoicing.
>   Psalm 107:1, 21–22

Was David saying that joy and thanksgiving were, themselves, a sacrifice at times? That we could offer thanksgiving to God when we didn't feel like it? All my life I'd thought I could only praise God when I felt good. But that left a huge number of days when I *couldn't* praise Him. The Bible seemed to be saying that, in the worst of times, for the sake of my own soul, I *must* praise God.

Further, in Psalm 116, I read:

> I will offer to thee the sacrifice of thanksgiving, and will call upon the name of the Lord.   Verse 17

I knew, from past studies, that there are several names for God, each revealing an aspect of His character. For instance: *God Who Provides, The Lord my Shepherd, The Lord Who Heals.* In light of this new understanding I began to see praise differently. Rather than focusing on the circumstances, we are to focus on the name of God, that is, His character. We praise God for who He is—Father of the fatherless, Comforter, our Strength.

In late November, I was still following this train of study, when I received new light on a curious event in the life of the apostle Paul. In Acts 16 I read that Paul and Barnabas were imprisoned for preaching about Jesus. They'd been stripped, beaten, and chained in a cold, miserable prison cell. Verse 25 said, "At midnight Paul and Silas prayed, and sang praises unto God. . . ."

I'd always wondered how they could thank God for being whipped and imprisoned. Now my point-of-view was different: They were praising the goodness of the God they served. And as they praised, an earthquake shook the prison, the doors flew open, and their bonds fell off. Praise opened the way for a miracle.

A few days later, I was praying in my room at home again, still trying to get some bearing on a direction for the ministry. Unexpectedly, the words came to me: *You've learned healing through the sacrifice of praise. If you teach this to people, you'll see the salvation of the lost, deliverance of the oppressed, and healing of the sick.*

I nearly came off the floor. Was God really telling me that He would *heal* people as they learned the true nature of praise? And that *I* should teach them? Surely not.

Then I felt a shock of new insight. For so long, I'd fought to overcome "mountains of difficulty," just as the old pastor prayed at my ordination. To me, these "mountains" were things like getting a team into Africa, or preaching behind the Iron Curtain—physical challenges or dangers.

Now I saw another sort of mountain. Inside most people is a voice saying, "Anything bad that's happened to you is God's punishment for the wrong you've done. You don't deserve to have God do anything for you. He may help others, but He won't heal you, save your marriage, set you free from sin." Mountains of legalism and doubt separating people from God's deep, miraculous love for them.

I dug further into the Bible, hunting through concordances and lexicons. Everything I found verified the concept that as we focus our inner being on God, His power is released. Or as Paul said, "Though we walk in the flesh, we do not war after the flesh: (For the weapons of our warfare are not carnal, but mighty through God to the pulling down of strong holds)" (2 Corinthians 10:3–4). Having seen the ministry nosedive for over a year, I began to make new plans.

I called Don Moen, my music director, and asked him to shelve every song in our repertoire that was not specifically praise and worship.

Concerning the ministry, at least, I felt the first stirrings of new purpose, new life.

February 1983 saw our first "Praise and Healing" crusade in a church in Woodward, Oklahoma. It was snowing heavily when I drove into town with a hastily formed team of former Living Sound members. Some seventy brave souls ignored travelers' warnings to come that night.

Yet in that sanctuary, with sleet pelting the windows, we saw several significant healings. I must admit I was as delighted and relieved as anyone else. I would never give up the Iron Curtain ministry, of course, but I had found a new sharpening of my life's work.

For the next year-and-a-half, the ministry hit an upswing. We traveled all over America, Canada, and Europe, and at every new crusade, we saw diseases and sicknesses healed, lives oppressed by sin and spiritual forces set free, and new commitments to Christ. My confidence in the healing power of God's Word continued to grow.

Still . . . there was one area in which my confidence was a little shaky.

At the end of September 1984, Don Moen and I were flying back to Tulsa on a Monday morning after some weekend meetings in Phoenix. We'd gotten aisle seats across from each other so we could talk.

We hadn't been airborne long when Don looked across the narrow aisle and said, "Terry, you told me two years ago this month that you wouldn't consider remarrying for two years. The two years are up. Are you ready to reconsider?"

I leaned my head back against the seat. I'd talked very little about my loneliness, though I supposed Don and others close to me often saw my hangdog look in the long months since Jan's death. Mom, bless her, was still living with us, and many nights when I came in late from haunting a coffee shop, she was still awake, praying. I knew what she was praying for. But I *hadn't* thought much about remarriage, not until recently. And then, my chances didn't look so great.

Who's going to marry a forty-one-year-old widower with three children? Who could understand the trauma that Misty, Scotty, 'Becca, and I have gone through?—or understand what I've learned about God's power in all this?

Don was still watching me from across the aisle. I knew how badly he and the staff missed Jan. But I also knew they were praying for me, wanting me to get on with a new life.

"Yes," I replied, thoughtfully, "I've thought about it." I hoped that would satisfy him.

"Do you know who you want to marry?" Don continued.

"No."

"Do you know what kind of woman?"

"I believe she'd have to be a widow."

"Have you ever met her?"

"No." I didn't know any widows near my age.

"Are you willing to pray?"

I considered. "Yes. Sure."

To my surprise, Don reached across the aisle and grabbed my hand. "Lord," he began, "Terry wants a wife."

Suddenly self-conscious, I looked at the other passengers. Several were looking. I bowed my head, hoping Don would hurry up.

"You know Terry's need, and his children's needs," he prayed. "We believe You have a plan already at work. There's a widow somewhere in Tulsa. Let them meet soon." Then he looked at me. "Agreed?"

"Yes."

"Thank You, Father," Don pronounced, "that it's done."

I had to smile at Don's faith. Not that I didn't know, after all that God had done, that He isn't a wonder-working God. But I'd gone out a little in the last year and knew that, in Tulsa, widows my age didn't grow on trees. And I wasn't about to go looking.

That week was hectic. We now had Living Sound teams in Europe and the U.S. again, not to mention important things going on behind the Iron Curtain. I also had a meeting the following weekend in Portland.

On Saturday morning, around ten o'clock, the kids and I piled into the car. Later that day, I'd be leaving for a week of meetings in Portland and Seattle. So, as I did most Saturdays, I wanted to take the kids out to breakfast.

We were pulling out the driveway when I asked, as usual, "Where do you want to go?"

Misty didn't hesitate. "Denny's."

Scotty and 'Becca voted for Denny's, too.

I glanced at my watch. My suitcase wasn't packed. And

I had some phone calls to make. Maybe we could go to Denny's next time. "I need to get a quick breakfast today. Let's go to McDonald's."

Everyone agreed. Turning the wheel, I pulled out of the driveway.

And with that one small decision, our lives were about to change.

Epilogue: A New Path

SHIRLEY:

The lines inside McDonald's were long, which made it worse. I hadn't planned on coming here in the first place.

It was a little after ten o'clock on a bright, warm Saturday in September. Jason and Marie were outside playing on the slide, while I stood in line to place our order. At the counter the waitress handed someone his tray, and the line advanced. Now there were only three in front of me.

This is really crazy, I mused.

Just forty-five minutes ago, I'd been standing in my kitchen in a bathrobe fixing toast and eggs. The thought had taken me completely by surprise: *Take the kids to breakfast at McDonald's.*

I'd glanced into the living room. Marie and Jason were still in pajamas watching cartoons. Jim had usually taken them to McDonalds on Saturdays. But I'd never eaten breakfast there in my life. Besides, I already had the orange juice poured and the toast buttered.

Stirring the eggs with a spatula, I called, "Kids. Wash your hands and come to the table."

I heard water splashing in the bathroom. *Take the kids to McDonald's.*

261

I'd learned not to ignore these inner nudges. But break-fast at McDonald's?—with a hot meal on the table? That was ridiculous.

Still it persisted.

Marie and Jason scuffled into the kitchen and climbed up into their chairs. Standing beside them with the frying pan in my hand, I thought, *We could go to the drive-through window.*

Not the drive-through. Go inside.

Crazy as it was, I gave in. Twenty minutes later, we were dressed and out the door.

On the way, though, we'd hit one snag. Unexpectedly, Marie burst into tears. "McDonald's makes me think of Daddy," she sobbed.

Stopping the car, I said, "Why don't we pray about it?" We did, and when we finished, Marie had brightened. "God's going to give us a new daddy."

"Someone who loves God," Jason piped up.

I hadn't said a word. But inwardly, I rebelled. Not that I was still mourning Jim, exactly. The mourning happened all during the long, long months of seizures. But I didn't think I was ready for that kind of relationship. Not yet.

Now, the line in front of me cleared and I placed our order. When the food came, I thought of the eggs, hard-ening in a pan on the stove. Jason and Marie had come inside and taken a booth by the window when I joined them.

We'd nearly finished, when a man and three children set their trays on the table opposite us. I recognized him at once. He was Terry Law, director of the music group that had sung in my home church in Portland back in 1969. Funny, I'd wound up living in Tulsa where his ministry was based. Some time ago, I'd heard his wife had been killed.

All at once, mid-bite, I had the unmistakable feeling I

was to introduce myself. *Lord,* I argued silently, *I can't do that. He doesn't even know me. What would I say?*

Then I recalled that a girlfriend from Portland, Paula, had joined Living Sound. She'd eventually married a guy from the group, Bo Melin. I hadn't heard from her in awhile.

Awkwardly, I walked up to the table and said, "Excuse me. I'm Shirley Arnold—a friend of Paula and Bo. I was wondering if you've heard from them recently."

He explained that the Melins were pastoring a church in Alaska—looking at me, I thought, a little oddly. As we chatted, he asked a few questions: When I'd come to Tulsa from Portland, the kids' names. He introduced his children, Misty, Scot, and 'Becca. Then he asked, "What does your husband do?"

Suddenly uncomfortable, I glanced at my left hand. Though I'd kept my promise to Jim and taken off my wedding band, I still wore a ring from time to time. "Jim died last spring," I replied, "I'm a widow."

Terry nearly knocked over his styrofoam coffee cup. He looked disturbed. What on earth was wrong?

He mopped up the splashes with a napkin and said he was sorry about Jim's death. Pursuing his question about work, I explained that I was thinking about starting my own business as an independent sales contractor of credit card services. Terry said he knew an attorney who could help. "Call me, I'll give you his name," he said.

I nodded, but I had no intention of calling him.

Marie and Jason were ready to leave. Just as I turned to go, Misty asked, "Do you like to shop?"

"Well," I stammered. She looked at me with big, pleading eyes. "Yes. I like to shop."

"Will you take me?"

Terry looked as if he wanted to crawl under the table.

"Yes, I guess so." What was I getting into?

263

Gathering Jason and Marie, I gave Misty my phone number, and said goodbye. Once we were out in the car, I breathed a sigh. I sure wanted to help Misty. But . . . I put my key in the ignition. I didn't want things to get complicated.

The very next afternoon, the phone rang. It was Misty. Politely, she asked about our shopping trip. I found myself liking her. I suggested a Saturday afternoon. She said she'd have to check and get back to me. Then we hung up. What with getting Marie's things ready for school the next day, I quickly forgot about the call.

Late that night, I was roused from a sound sleep. My bedside phone was ringing. Rolling over, I switched on the lamp and glanced at the clock: It was after two A.M.

When I answered, the voice was unfamiliar. "Shirley?"

"Who is this?"

"It's Terry Law. I'm calling from Portland."

I rolled my eyes. "It's two in the morning. Why are you calling?"

He fumbled for words. "I'm so sorry. I just got out of a meeting, and I forgot the time difference. Um—I called to say you can take Misty shopping."

"Good. Fine," I said groggily. I was also about to say goodnight.

"Shirley?"

I heard it in his voice—the small note of loneliness. I felt it, too. He'd told me Jan had died two years ago. I knew it must have seemed like an eternity. He wanted to talk. Sitting up in bed, I propped myself on the pillows. As long as I was awake . . .

We talked for a half-hour, about children, about how difficult it can be when your spouse is gone. When I really couldn't keep my eyes open any longer, he surprised me. "I'll be back in town next week. Would you be open to having dinner on Tuesday night?"

I hesitated. We did have something in common, really. "Okay," I replied. When I hung up, I wondered if I'd hear from him.

The following Monday evening, when Terry called to confirm our date, I was bogged down with business paperwork. I happened to mention the problem I was having. He offered to come over and have a look at the problem. I agreed and hung up—then I smiled. I'd just been maneuvered.

When Terry came over, we went into the living room and sat on the sofa. *He* sat on the sofa, that is. I sat across the room in a chair.

What impressed me right away was how natural it felt talking with Terry about the Lord. Not just that he was a man in ministry, but because of all the Lord had taught us through difficult times. When Terry began to talk about healing through praise, I got very interested.

After a time, Terry began to talk about Jan, how much he missed her. I found myself missing Jim, talking about our good times together. Somehow, with Terry, it was easy to share myself. He understood.

After he left that night, I realized something rare had happened. We'd talked for more than two hours on a deep level. We'd shared our grief; we'd shared our joys. There wasn't the hint of sexual overtones. I found myself looking forward to our date the next evening.

When Terry picked me up at seven o'clock on Tuesday, he was smiling. "I have reservations at 'Le Chalet.' I hope you like French cuisine."

At the restaurant the waiter lighted a candle in the middle of the table and left us alone. Immediately, I was impressed at the way our conversation picked up right where it left off. The waiter came back and took our order. And then, quietly Terry asked. "May I hold your hand?"

That impressed me more. He was gentle, so vulnerable, knowing I could turn him down. I could not.

It felt good to hold someone's hand.

After that evening, Terry asked to see me again. Throughout the rest of October and into November, in fact, we saw each other whenever Terry was in town. Our friendship grew stronger. I enjoyed his company.

And then, there was that special day when Terry took me out for a day in the country.

We were shuffling through fallen leaves on a wooded bike-trail. Occasionally a biker would breeze by us, but mostly we were alone with the November wind and the scent of autumn. Terry took my hand, and then asked if he could kiss me.

Something swift and beautiful was happening between us.

And yet . . .

When we were not together I thought more rationally. Especially about the prospect of five children under one roof. I had huge questions.

I'd spent a little time with Terry and his children. But could our five get along together? Could I really love someone else's children? Terry and I knew these were important questions—questions I wasn't sure I was ready to face. I began to pray. *The next move is Yours, Lord. I've got to know this relationship is really in Your will.*

One evening, two weeks later, I was having a holiday get-together with some friends when the doorbell rang. Terry was standing on the front porch—with Misty, Scot, and 'Becca—red-faced. "Sorry," he smiled nervously. "I just thought we'd drop by. I didn't know you had company."

I insisted they stay, and ushered them inside from the cold December air. I was helping 'Becca take off her coat when Marie came up. "Can she play, Mom?"

Terry was introducing himself to someone. "Sure," I said.

"C'mon," said Marie, taking 'Becca's hand.

Off they trooped, with Scot and Jason trotting after them. Before long, even thirteen-year-old Misty had joined the younger children. Shortly, when Terry was ready to leave, the kids all groaned in chorus. "Do they *hafta* go?" Jason begged.

My eyes met Terry's.

He was grinning. . . .

TERRY:

As the kids stepped out onto the porch, I pulled on my overcoat and gave Shirley a peck on the cheek. "Sorry about dropping in like this. I'll call you tomorrow."

We climbed into the car and 'Becca asked, "Why are you smiling?"

"Oh, Daddy's just happy, honey." But inside, as I started the car, my thoughts were going a mile a minute. Never in a million years had I thought I'd find a beautiful Christian woman like Shirley. How amazing that I'd met her just days after Don Moen had prayed I'd find a wife.

Slow down, Terry, I warned myself. *Don't jump into this.*

Driving home, I weighed all the factors. Sure our meeting had been uncanny. And I was able to talk with Shirley about deeply personal things. No—it was more than that. I'd fallen in love with her! *And* I was beginning to love the daylights out of those kids. Certainly, I wasn't taking that added responsibility lightly. But Marie was so sweet. And Jason, what a pistol. All boy. A perfect little brother for Scotty . . .

But there I was—doing it again. I was arranging things, just the way I'd done it when I was married to Jan, like a bull in a china shop. Now, I hoped, I was a little wiser.

You've been alone for two years, I reminded myself, sternly. *Shirley may need more time.*

Then I prayed, *Okay, Lord. For the sake of the kids—for all of us—I need to know this is right. I'm not going to force this one. It's up to You.*

That night at home, I felt a little glum. Shirley wasn't ready to marry. Not only was it a lot to ask her to be the mother of five, but something else troubled me. I'd still be on the road. I'd taken Jan for granted so much of the time. Could I really love Shirley? And how could she ever feel a part of the work? By bedtime, I'd all but convinced myself it would never work out.

And that was why I was so nervous when, on Saturday a week later, Shirley told me she wanted to talk about things that were going on inside her.

Over coffee in a small restaurant, she told me, "I stayed up late every night, praying, asking God to show me His will for us." That made my ears perk up.

"I was up every night this week, praying about my feelings—about the ministry, the children. I read the Bible. Of course, there was nothing specific in Scripture that said, 'This is the right thing to do.' "

What was she leading up to?

"But the most amazing thing happened," she said, taking my hand. "Every morning this week, I woke up thinking about your kids. Things like, 'Did Misty remember to study for her test? Were Scotty and 'Becca dressed warm enough for this cold weather?'

"Terry," she said, her eyes filling, "I don't know how else to explain it except that God must be giving me a supernatural love for Misty, Scot, and 'Becca. I—I feel I want to raise them as my own."

My heart was leaping inside. That was all I needed to hear.

About three weeks later, on New Year's Eve, I invited

Shirley to a Phil Driscoll concert at ORU's MABEE Center. It was snowing so furiously at about ten P.M., just as we were getting ready to leave, that my sister, Lois, and her husband, Lorne, who were visiting, tried to talk me out of it.

But I had to get us there, or my plan would be sunk. At my insistence, everyone donned his coat, and we braved the snow and ice.

About one minute past midnight, just as the concert was coming to a close, I took Shirley's hand. "Come with me."

She eyed me curiously, but followed. I led her out into the lobby and around a corner. "What is it, Terry? Where are you taking me?"

Finally, when we were far from the crowd, I turned to face her. "I just have to ask you an important question. Will you marry me?"

For one heart-splitting instant, Shirley drew back, stunned. Then the tears came. Hers and mine.

"Yes," she said.

We threw our arms around each other.

Just four weeks later, on January 28, 1985, we were married.

After our honeymoon came the more-than-normal challenge of settling in together. Scotty hugged Shirley every chance he got, and in public people thought little blonde 'Becca was Shirley's natural daughter. I loved our family devotion times most, when any one or *all* of the kids would pile onto the sofa next to me. God had really heard my prayers, and was healing not one but two wounded families.

And there was another prayer He was about to answer.

In August, Shirley and I were in a large church where I was to speak. As we sat down beside the pastor together,

Shirley whispered to me, "No surprises this time, Terry
Law."

I grinned sheepishly.

A week or two before, I'd shocked Shirley by introducing her from the pulpit of a thousand-member church.
Then I'd asked her to share her story and what God had
done. After, two couples, both on the verge of divorce,
sought her out. Hearing about the power of God that had
come through her struggles, both couples were in tears,
willing to work at reconciliation.

Through that experience, I'd learned, however, that
Shirley is a private person. She didn't like my "surprise"
one bit, and told me so later.

"No surprises, honey," I whispered in her ear. "I'll *ask*
you this time. The pastor says there's a girl here tonight
who's been abused by her father. He was an elder in a
church. I know it's painful. But I know you could help
her."

The pastor introduced me then. When I stood, Shirley's
head was bowed in prayer. For twenty minutes, I taught
about praise. After, Don Moen led several worship songs.

What followed was a powerful time of prayer and healing. A man whose jaw was misshapen in a huge overbite
felt a snapping, and a release from pain: His jaw and teeth
slid back into place. Broken bones mended. Illnesses were
gone. All across the auditorium, physical healings took
place.

Just as I was finishing praying, Shirley was at my side.
I looked at her quizzically.

"I think there's more than one here, Terry," she whispered.

"More than one what?"

"More than one person who's been abused."

I glanced at the hundreds of faces. Yes. I knew that even
among Christians child abuse took place, burying men,

women, and children beneath emotional devastation and guilt. But I also knew there was a way to overcome.

Shirley prepared to speak, and I sat down. And then a prayer came back to me, one I'd uttered in 1969 in Shirley's church in Portland: I'd wanted to share Christ with people in the presence of my wife and not feel guilty. Then, I was so busy trying to *prove* I was good. Now, I'd learned the most freeing secret: Only by setting our hearts on God's grace and His Word can we overcome our own shortcomings and whatever life throws at us.

Shirley's voice distracted my thoughts. She began to read from John chapter 8: "You will know the truth and the truth will set you free. . . . " Then she began to tell how God had been with her even as a child.

I was beginning to see the power that comes when a husband and wife, together, yield their woundedness to God. Across the huge sanctuary, I knew that hearts were about to be set free.

Other powerful books by Terry Law:

The Power of Praise and Worship
Praise Releases Faith

To receive a full listing of books and teaching materials by Terry Law, or to receive more information about Terry Law Ministries, contact·

Terry Law Ministries
P.O. Box 92
Tulsa, OK 74101
(918) 299-4461